RUDOLF STAMM

The Shaping Powers at Work

Fifteen Essays on Poetic Transmutation

HEIDELBERG 1967

CARL WINTER · UNIVERSITÄTSVERLAG

To

Dame Peggy Ashcroft, D.B.E.

TABLE OF CONTENTS

PREFATORY NOTE

THE SHAPING POWERS invoked in the title of this book are the imagination and the critical faculty of the creative writers whose ways of transforming a given material, or form, or tradition is studied in the following essays. Both powers were active in all the transmutations investigated, but in some of them the imagination was the predominant element, and the critical faculty in others. A conflict between the two powers is observed in several of our examples. These examples are clearly very different in kind. It is a far cry from Shakespeare's methods of transmuting the physical data of his stage, or his source materials, so that they became part of the dramas enacted before his mind's eye to the slow transformation which some of the Puritan literary forms underwent at the hands of Daniel Defoe or to the attempts of modern playwrights to overcome dramatic and theatrical conventions which appeared sterile or dead to them. Even within the more restricted field of the adaptation of existing works to a new taste the variety of situations and solutions is extraordinary. The same could be said of the art of translation, had we admitted more than a single essay on this subject to our pages. It is the author's hope that the unity in the diversity of this volume will be found in his conviction that transmutation in all of its many forms is a peculiarly rewarding subject for the literary student because it concentrates his attention on the texts and can yield a subtle and precise kind of evidence leading to an intimate knowledge of a writer's artistic purpose and achievement and, in many cases, to valid conclusions concerning the taste of his audience or readers.

As the following pages show, the present writer was frequently attracted by studies of this nature at different moments of his working life. Most of the essays in this collection are reprinted in their original form. A number of omissions were necessary, however, in order to prevent repetition and overlapping.

The essay "*The Spanish Tragedy* and *Hamlet*" is an expanded version of a paper read at the Sixth Conference of the International Association of University Professors of English held at Venice in

August 1965. It will be published in the *Acta* of the Conference. "The Glass of Pandar's Praise" appeared in *Essays and Studies 1964*, New Series, vol. XVII, published for the English Association by John Murray, "Word-Scenery in *Macbeth* and Some Other Plays" under the title *Shakespeare's Word-Scenery* as Heft 10, Reihe B der Veröffentlichungen der Handels-Hochschule St. Gallen (1954), "The Transmutation of Source Material" in vol. XII of *Shakespeare Survey* (1959), "Sir William Davenant and Shakespeare's Imagery" in vol. XXIV of *English Studies* (1942), "George Bernard Shaw and Shakespeare's *Cymbeline*" in *Studies in Honor of T. W. Baldwin* (1958), "*Hamlet* in Richard Flatter's Translation" in vol. XXXVI of *English Studies* (1955), "Daniel Defoe: An Artist in the Puritan Tradition" in vol. XV of *Philological Quarterly* (1936), "*The Sorrow of Love:* A Poem by William Butler Yeats Revised by Himself" in vol. XXIX of *English Studies* (1948), a German version of "William Butler Yeats and *The Ballad of Reading Gaol* by Oscar Wilde" in *Studies in English Language and Literature* presented to Professor Dr. Karl Brunner, *Wiener Beiträge zur englischen Philologie* Bd. LXV (1957), "The Orestes Theme in Three Plays by Eugene O'Neill, T. S. Eliot and Jean-Paul Sartre" in vol. XXX of *English Studies* (1949), "The Dramatic Experiments of Eugene O'Neill" in vol. XXVIII of *English Studies* (1947), "*The Iceman Cometh*" under the title "A New Play by Eugene O'Neill" in vol. XXIX of *English Studies* (1948), "'Faithful Realism': Eugene O'Neill and the Problem of Style" in vol. XL of *English Studies* (1959) and "Christopher Fry and the Revolt against Realism in Modern English Drama" in vol. LXXII of *Anglia* (1954).

The author expresses his gratitude for the permission to reprint these essays to Professor Benvenuto Cellini (†), who planned the *Acta* of the Sixth Conference of the International Association of University Professors of English, to the English Association and Professor W. A. Armstrong, editor of *Essays and Studies 1964*, to Professor Georg Thürer, editor of Reihe B der Veröffentlichungen der Handels-Hochschule St. Gallen, to the Cambridge University Press and Professor Allardyce Nicoll, editor of *Shakespeare Survey*, to Professor R. W. Zandvoort, editor of *English Studies*, to the Trustees of the University of Illinois Press and Professor

D. C. Allen, editor of *Studies in Honor of T. W. Baldwin*, to Mr. John E. Simmons, director of the Department of Publications, University of Iowa, and the editors of *Philological Quarterly*, to the director of the Verlag Braumüller, Vienna, and Professor Siegfried Korninger, editor of *Studies in English Language and Literature* presented to Professor Dr. Karl Brunner, and to Professor Walter Schirmer, editor of *Anglia*.

This volume is dedicated to one of the great actresses of the modern English theatre, whose impersonations excite our admiration for her exquisite charm, her professional skill, her power of empathy, and also, especially in the Shakespearian plays, for the intellectual curiosity and the creative energy with which she absorbs and transforms the findings of criticism and research.

R. St.

Basle, December 1966

I.

The Theatrical Physiognomy of Shakespeare's Plays

1. *The Spanish Tragedy* and *Hamlet*

FOR WHAT reason has the term "theatrical physiognomy" been smuggled into the discussion of Elizabethan drama in recent years? The interest in the subject covered by this new and hard term springs from our dissatisfaction with the purely verbal interpretation of drama which flourished under the auspices of the New Critics and also with the corresponding attitude of the theatres, which, believing what the New Critics preached, took the text of a play for words, poetry, in any case a raw material to be given theatrical form and life by actors, producers and scene-designers. It is, of course, no accident that there are also contemporary translators proclaiming the intention of producing theatrical, instead of poetical, translations of Shakespeare. The endeavours of these critics, theatrical artists and translators have resulted in strange distortions of the plays permitting the suspicion that they start from an imperfect understanding of dramatic art.

They seem to have forgotten that the dramatist, when he tries to create an imaginative experience in his spectators, does not restrict himself to the use of words, and possibly music, as his means of expression but relies perhaps even more on gesture, movement, stage business, properties and scenery. They seem to forget, too, that, if, according to T. S. Eliot, a rhythm may be the germ of a poem, a gesture may be the germ of a play. Out of the gesture a situation and a plot may develop and out of the rhythm inherent in and coexistent with the gesture the words and the poetry of the play may spring. It is important for us to remember this common origin, the brotherhood, of gesture and word in drama.

Unlike other artists, the playwright cannot keep the end product of his art, i. e. the play-in-performance, entirely under his control. He makes a contribution to a communal creation, to which his collaborators — the actors and, possibly, the producers and scene-designers — make theirs. It is one of his most difficult tasks to know where to give scope and freedom to the individual talents of his collaborators and where to keep them under control if the play-in-performance is to correspond to his vision of the play.

Our inquiry is directed towards the methods by which he can organize and control the gestic, mimic and scenic form of the play-in-performance. In pursuing it we are not primarily interested in the stage directions because, as a method of control, they are far less essential than the gestic impulses, implied gestures, mirror passages, reported scenes and the word-scenery integrated in the speeches themselves. The term "theatrical physiognomy" tries to cover the ensemble of these aspects of a dramatic text. Like everything else in a play the theatrical physiognomy is influenced by the stage conditions for which the play is written. It seems important to realize that it is only *influenced* by them; it is by no means identical with the way in which a play was originally staged. An inquiry into the theatrical physiognomy is an aesthetic, not a historical one. Historical considerations may be necessary sometimes, but they are subservient to it.

Such an inquiry leads, among other points, to the discovery of an important kind of perspective in drama. The playwright cannot only change from pantomimic to almost entirely rhetorical passages, but, between these extremes he can combine speech and action in many different ways. Besides, the gestic and scenic elements can appear with many different degrees of distinctness in the speeches. Gestures may e. g. be implied in certain kinds of words, grammatical forms or syntactical structures. The conduct of the metre, especially metrical irregularities, may provide gestic impulses; a metrical gap may leave room for business. A gesture may be named and it may be very precisely characterized in speech: in this case we use the term mirror passage. When an actor has to interpret an implied gesture or to respond to a gestic impulse he relies upon the acting convention in which he finds himself as well as upon his own conception of his part. When he has to execute a gesture mirrored in speech his task is different. There is a third, very important element to be reckoned with: the will and vision of the playwright. And what about the scholarly interpreter of drama? He finds himself faced by many highly fascinating questions: What is the effect of the mirror passage compared to that of the implied gesture or the gestic impulse? What sort of gesture, whose gestures tend to appear mirrored in speech? What is the function of the reported scenes, which happen entirely before the eyes of the mind and in which gestic events are described in detail and some of them even re-enacted? And, in the related sphere of word-scenery: When is a place and time definition dispensed with? When are place and time indications given in an incidental and matter-of-fact way, and when are they developed so as to be essential parts of the complete meaning? In answering such questions the scholar will be careful to see every passage in its context of situation, of character and of the meaning of the play as a whole.

Today I wish to illustrate some of the possibilities of this kind of study in a comparison of two famous examples of the Eliza-bethan revenge play: of *The Spanish Tragedy*, whose author knew more about the integration of the theatrical physiognomy in the speeches than any other early playwright, and *Hamlet*.

I begin with a glance at the functions of the demonstrative pronouns, the simplest links of speech and gesture. Some of them are strikingly illustrated in the following speech, addressed by Hieronimo to the old man Bazulto:[1]

> HIER. O my son, my son, O my son Horatio!
> But mine, or thine, Bazulto, be content.
> Here, take my handkercher and wipe thine eyes,
> Whiles wretched I in thy mishaps may see
> The lively portrait of my dying self.
> > *He draweth out a bloody napkin.*
> O no, not this: Horatio, this was thine,
> And when I dy'd it in thy dearest blood,
> This was a token 'twixt thy soul and me
> That of thy death revenged I should be.
> But here, take this, and this — what, my purse? —
> Ay this and that, and all of them are thine,
> For all as one are our extremities.   (III. xiii. 81—92)

[1] Quotations are from *The Spanish Tragedy*, edited by Philip Edwards for *The Revels Plays*, London 1959.

Like many others of Hieronimo's speeches these lines abound in gestic elements. He begins with an invocation of his murdered son Horatio, requiring an intonation and gesticulation which differ considerably from those accompanying his frequent addresses to persons alive and present. One of these occurs in the line "But mine, or thine, Bazulto, be content". The two possessives in it exemplify another type of gestic impulse: the one contained in adversative constructions. "Here", in the line: "Here, take my handkercher and wipe thine eyes" is a mere impulse word connected with the gesture of giving. The following imperative names the offered object, and renders the stage direction inserted after line 85 almost superfluous. Two lines later, when Hieronimo remembers how he dyed the handkerchief in Horatio's blood, the stage direction becomes entirely superfluous. His "O no, not this" implies the withdrawal of the intended gift, explained in the second invocation of Horatio. The repeated "this was" and the corresponding demonstration turn the blood-red napkin into a more and more conspicuous symbol of revenge. Now Hieronimo, struck by the similarity of his own and Bazulto's plight, regrets the withdrawal of the intended gift and, following a half-crazed impulse of generosity, showers the whole contents of his pockets on the stunned old man. All this is concentrated in the strikingly effective staccato lines:

> But here, take this, and this — what, my purse? —
> Ay this and that, and all of them are thine,

with their demonstratives repeated in quick succession and with the interpolated rapid question "what, my purse?" which breaks the metre and produces a rhythmical shock full of gestic force. The whole passage is a powerful piece of speech-action and a rich and detailed characterization of Old Hieronimo as he is after the murder of his son and before he sees a way to his revenge: passionate, impulsive, imaginative, hasty, seeking activity for the sake of activity because, for the time being, he finds himself debarred from the act that will give him peace.

Shakespeare's young revenger inherited Hieronimo's restlessness but, in him, it is mental rather than physical. In the closet scene, however, when Hamlet shows the portraits of the two kings to his mother, he comes very close to Hieronimo's passionate demonstration of the blood-stained napkin. Here, his speech is also full of demonstrative gestures[2]:

> Look here upon this picture and on this,
> . . .
> See what a grace was seated on this brow;
> . . .
> This was your husband. Look you now what follows:
> Here is your husband, . . .
> . . .
> Could you on this fair mountain leave to feed,
> And batten on this moor?
> . . .
>   and what judgement
> Would step from this to this?   (III. iv. 53 ff.)

Together with the accusing exclamations we have not quoted, the repeated demonstratives again demand rapid passionate gestures. These remain more controlled than those of Hieronimo. This is not the only difference between Kyd's and Shakespeare's scenes. Kyd's is incidental: just one of Hieronimo's fits of passionate but aimless activity; Shakespeare's is climactic: the comparison that finds its scenic and gestic consummation here has agitated Hamlet's mind since the beginning of the play. Besides, Kyd's scene suffers from the fact that Bazulto, Hieronimo's interlocutor, has absolutely no function in the play except that of duplicating the bereaved father's own situation. Shakespeare's queen, on the other hand, is much more than merely a foil for Hamlet's rage. The closet scene is solidly integrated in the structure of the play whereas Hieronimo's outbreak remains a splendidly realized single effect in a series of similar ones.

Another interesting use of the demonstrative occurs in the following passage when the deluded viceroy of Portugal indulges in a symbolic fall to the ground:

---

[2] Where no other source is indicated the Shakespearian quotations in this book are from William Shakespeare, *The Complete Works*, edited by Peter Alexander, London and Glasgow 1951.

VICE. Then rest we here awhile in our unrest,
        And feed our sorrows with some inward sighs,
        For deepest cares break never into tears.
        But wherefore sit I in a regal throne?
        This better fits a wretch's endless moan.
                                        Falls to the ground.
        Yet this is higher than my fortunes reach,
        And therefore better than my state deserves.
        Ay, ay, this earth, image of melancholy,
        Seeks him whom fates adjudge to misery:
        Here let me lie, now am I at the lowest.   (I. iii. 5—14)

The first "this" in this speech may be taken to refer to his fall, the
second certainly refers to his new position on the ground. The
stage direction after line 9, though by no means indispensable, is a
help towards the correct apprehension of the intended action. The
passage shows an important tendency in Kyd's thoroughly dramatic and theatrical art: he endeavours to develop his imagery and
symbolism out of his stage events. Hence the handling of significant properties is a frequent feature in his play. His talent for the
invention of interaction of speech and gesture is remarkable
although his effects of this kind strike us sometimes as rather arranged and obvious.

    Shakespeare knew how to avoid this fault. Right at the begin-
ning of his play, when he is creating the appropriate atmosphere for
the apparition of the ghost, he makes a very subtle use of the
demonstrative "this" in the question of Marcellus:

            What, has this thing appear'd again to-night?   (I. i. 21)

His first allusion to the terrifying experience of the two preceding
nights is vague. "This thing" implies that his interlocutors know
what he is talking about. The demonstrative is purely abstract in
so far as it refers to a piece of common knowledge. But there is
also a slight gestic impulse in it, demanding a quick glance or
gesture in the direction where the ghost has appeared before and
where it will appear again presently. The combination of the
definite pronoun with the indefinite noun "thing" helps to produce
that sense of uncertainty, doubt and fear which pervades the whole
scene. The demonstrative is repeated three times with a similar

effect before the first apparition of the ghost: "this dreaded sight", "this apparition" and "let us hear Bernardo speak of this".

How pliable our demonstrative became in Shakespeare's hands appears in Hamlet's first soliloquy, too. It finds a place in the famous line:

> O, that this too too solid (or sullied) flesh would melt,
>
> (I. ii. 129)

where its object hovers between the concrete sense of "body" and the more abstract one of "life", and where the corresponding gesture cannot be either quite specific, i. e. directed to some part of Hamlet's body, or quite vague and general. Here it is an actor's grasp of Hamlet's character and predicament which must give him the appropriate gesture. There is a striking contrast between the two following occurrences of "this": In

> How weary, stale, flat, and unprofitable,
> Seem to me all the uses of this world!

it is inspired by that youthful and immature tendency to generalize his own misfortune and unhappiness which is so characteristic of Hamlet in the early parts of the play. In

> That it should come to this!

the speaker comes to the point, to the cause of his pessimistic generalization. There is more precision in this use of the demonstrative than in the preceding one, and this must appear in the tonal and gestic rendering. The next "this" in the soliloquy is still more specific. In

> So excellent a king that was to this
> Hyperion to a satyr;

the demonstrative has all the sharpness of overpowering contempt and disgust. It calls for the violent gesture of throwing a repulsive object into the gutter where it belongs.

Our examples have shown that the interpretation of the implied gestures is comparatively simple in Kyd's text because they are clear-cut and straightforward, and that, in *Hamlet*, the adequate execution of many of them presupposes a sensitive reaction to unique and complicated situations of scene and character. Our understanding of the implied gestures is sharpened by the study of the gestures appearing in mirror passages. Hieronimo, in his first violent outbreak in front of the king, cries:

> Hier. Away! I'll rip the bowels of the earth,
>> *He diggeth with his dagger.*
>> And ferry over to th'Elysian plains,
>> And bring my son to show his deadly wounds.
>> Stand from about me!
>> I'll make a pickaxe of my poniard,
>> And here surrender up my marshalship:
>> For I'll go marshal up the fiends in hell,
>> To be avenged on you all for this.   (III. xii. 71–78)

Again, we see the old man in one of his fits of crazy activity. After the line

> Away! I'll rip the bowels of the earth,

the stage direction "He diggeth with his dagger" is inserted. A metaphorical speech gives a rather puzzling piece of business its ominous, murderous meaning. The reference to Horatio's "deadly wounds" is a simple retrospective mirror passage, recalling a sight seen by the audience in the murder scene. The command "Stand from about me!" holds a midway position between words with a gestic implication and a mirror passage: an attitude of command is implied, and the action expected of the interlocutor is named. The line is a broken one, leaving room for Hieronimo's digging business.

The scene we have considered has a parallel later in the play when Isabella, completely out of her mind, is cutting down the fateful arbour and accompanying her actions by mirror speeches replete with metrical gestic impulses:

> Down with these branches and these loathsome boughs
> Of this unfortunate and fatal pine:
> Down with them Isabella, rent them up ...   (IV. ii. 6–8)

Beside such reflexive mirror passages there are many transitive ones in Kyd's play. At the opening of its second scene the king at once creates its happy and victorious atmosphere when he welcomes his general in the following words:

> But what portends thy cheerful countenance,
> And posting to our presence thus in haste?   (I. ii. 4 f.)

This is Hieronimo's reaction when he sees the old man Bazulto for the first time:

> But wherefore stands yon silly man so mute,
> With mournful eyes and hands to heaven uprear'd?
>
> (III. xiii. 67 f.)

In both cases the behaviour of a stage figure is precisely mirrored and thus raised to a degree and kind of impressiveness unattainable by either speech or action in isolation.

Another characteristic use of the mirror method occurs in the course of the défilé of the victorious army before the king. The king asks:

> Was that the warlike prince of Portingale,
> That by our nephew was in triumph led?

Having received an affirmative answer, he continues:

> But what was he that on the other side
> Held him by th'arm as partner of the prize?

And Hieronimo replies proudly:

> That was my son, my gracious sovereign, . . .
>
> (I. ii. 111—116)

This is not merely an introduction of three of the main characters in the play; it is also a mirror of its first conflict situation. Both Lorenzo and Horatio have a share in the victory over Balthazar. Kyd is not satisfied with a detailed report on their fight. He creates a stage situation symbolizing the conflict, and gives it the additional emphasis of a mirror passage. The device is effective enough but it shows again that excess of explicitness on which we have commented before.

There is also a touch of pedantry in the extraordinary use to which the mirror technique is put in the highly stylized love-scene between Bel-imperia and Horatio which precedes the nocturnal murder in Hieronimo's garden. Their love-making is expressed by the imagery of war. It begins with the encounter of their hands and feet. A closer engagement is opened by the twining of their arms. Dying will be the end of their warfare — the verb is used with its special sexual sense; but before they can reach this consummation Horatio dies quite another death under the hands of his murderers. The scene is planned and executed with great skill. The gestures of the lovers are mirrored one by one in the passionate rhymed lines they speak; they are arranged in a balanced pattern of give and take and suggest the rhythm of a measured dance:

HOR. What means my love?
BEL.   I know not what myself:
       And yet my heart foretells me some mischance.
HOR. Sweet say not so, fair fortune is our friend,
       And heavens have shut up day to pleasure us.
       The stars, thou seest, hold back their twinkling shine,
       And Luna hides herself to pleasure us.
BEL. Thou hast prevail'd, I'll conquer my misdoubt,
       And in thy love and counsel drown my fear:
       I fear no more, love now is all my thoughts.
       Why sit we not? for pleasure asketh ease.
HOR. The more thou sit'st within these leavy bowers,
       The more will Flora deck it with her flowers.
BEL. Ay, but if Flora spy Horatio here,
       Her jealous eye will think I sit too near.
HOR. Hark, madam, how the birds record by night,
       For joy that Bel-imperia sits in sight.
BEL. No, Cupid counterfeits the nightingale,
       To frame sweet music to Horatio's tale.
HOR. If Cupid sing, then Venus is not far:
       Ay, thou art Venus or some fairer star.
BEL. If I be Venus thou must needs be Mars,
       And where Mars reigneth there must needs be wars.
HOR. Then thus begin our wars: put forth thy hand,
       That it may combat with my ruder hand.
BEL. Set forth thy foot to try the push of mine.
HOR. But first my looks shall combat against thine.
BEL. Then ward thyself, I dart this kiss at thee.
HOR. Thus I retort the dart thou threw'st at me.

BEL. Nay then, to gain the glory of the field,
        My twining arms shall yoke and make thee yield.
HOR. Nay then, my arms are large and strong withal:
        Thus elms by vines are compass'd till they fall.
BEL. O let me go, for in my troubled eyes
        Now may'st thou read that life in passion dies.
HOR. O stay awhile and I will die with thee,
        So shalt thou yield and yet have conquer'd me.

                                    (II. iv. 14–49)

With all its artificiality this is an impressive representation of
physical passion and a carefully calculated preparation of the
following catastrophe. In his less calculated and more imaginative
style Shakespeare attempted a similar feat when he gave the first
meeting of Romeo and Juliet the form of a sonnet.

In *Hamlet* we cannot find anything like it. The mirror technique
in this play is far more rapid, allusive and organic than in *The
Spanish Tragedy*. It is used extensively where the playwright
creates the impression of the ghost in the first scene, and it helps
him to keep "this thing", "this dreaded sight", "this apparition"
in a twilight between the unknown and the known.

        Look where it comes again   (I. i. 40)

Marcello whispers. And Bernardo continues:

        In the same figure, like the King that's dead.

And he insists, turning to Horatio:

        Looks 'a not like the King? Mark it, Horatio.

For the audience, who have not seen the old king, this is a definition
and no definition. Gradually a few concrete features of the appearance and behaviour of the neutral "it" perceived by the watchers
become visible in the mirror of speech: It has the "fair and warlike
form In which the majesty of buried Denmark Did sometimes
march". It wears the very armour in which the king "the ambitious
Norway combated". Horatio is struck by its frown, identical with
one he observed on the old king's face, when "He smot the sleaded
pollax on the ice" (Q2), a line which does not fit into its context
unless it refers to an impressive and characteristic gesture of Old
Hamlet, his throwing a heavy weapon down on the ice in anger.

There are the two allusions to the spectre's gait: It stalks away; it goes with martial stalk by the watch. Two further mirror passages help to preserve the balance between definiteness and vagueness that is so effective in this scene: Bernardo observes: "It would be spoke to" and Marcello: "It is offended", but they leave the ghost's gestures, on which their conclusions are based, in the dark. Two other mirror passages are quite clear and direct; they show the effect of the apparition on the sceptical Horatio. One of them is reflexive ("It harrows me with fear and wonder."), the other transitive ("You tremble and look pale."). When the ghost appears a second and later, in the presence of the prince, a third time, the mirror technique is used in a similar way. The experience of the first scene is particularized and sharpened and the events of the fourth and the fifth scene prepared in Horatio's report to Hamlet. It opens with an account of the first apparition of the ghost witnessed by Marcello and Bernardo only:

> A figure like your father,
> Armed at point exactly, cap-a-pe,
> Appears before them, and with solemn march
> Goes slow and stately by them; thrice he walk'd
> By their oppress'd and fear-surprised eyes,
> Within his truncheon's length; whilst they, distill'd
> Almost to jelly with the act of fear,
> Stand dumb and speak not to him.   (I. ii. 199—206)

The fact that this speech is partly report and partly reported scene appears in the extraordinary way how the past and the present tense jostle each other in it. The report then passes into a retrospective mirror passage, in which Horatio tells what he has seen himself. In the following interrogatory Hamlet draws further details concerning the ghost's behaviour from his friend, some of them new to the audience:

> once methought
> It lifted up it head and did address
> Itself to motion, like as it would speak;

The following description of the ghost's expression is an adjustment of Horatio's first impression:

> A countenance more in sorrow than in anger.

The slight inconsistency between the direct and the retrospective mirror passages adds to the mystery of the apparition and sharpens the audience's interest in Hamlet's own encounter with the ghost.

We pass on to some remarks on the part played by mirror passages in the characterization of the prince himself. They help to create his image in the council scene, in which he makes his first entry. Whereas the king attempts to strike a precarious balance between joy and woe, using slightly grotesque mimic imagery ("our whole kingdom To be contracted in one brow of woe"; "With an auspicious and a dropping eye"), Hamlet's attitude is unambiguous. The king refers to the clouds that still hang on him and, later, to "these mourning duties", to "This unprevailing woe". The queen alludes to his costume when she invites him "cast thy nighted colour off", but her concern for the prince, which is very different from her new husband's, of course, also enables her to describe a more personal attitude of his:

> Do not for ever with thy vailed lids
> Seek for thy noble father in the dust.

This harping of the royal couple on his show of grief annoys Hamlet, and his remonstration takes the form of a reflexive mirror passage, beginning:

> 'Tis not alone my inky cloak, good mother,
> Nor customary suits of solemn black, . . .

and culminating in the couplet:

> But I have that within which passes show —
> These but the trappings and the suits of woe.

In it, he not only expresses his radical distrust of appearances, but also hints that what is happening around him has done more to him than just throw him into a period of filial sorrow. He does not understand himself what it has done to him and will struggle with it in his soliloquies and in all his attempts to adjust himself to an intolerable situation. Our conception of his career partly rests on mirror passages and also on the extraordinary account given by Ophelia of Hamlet's visit to her:

> My lord, as I was sewing in my closet,
> Lord Hamlet, with his doublet all unbrac'd,

No hat upon his head, his stockings fouled,
Ungart'red and down-gyved to his ankle;
Pale as his shirt, his knees knocking each other,
And with a look so piteous in purport
As if he had been loosed out of hell
To speak of horrors — he comes before me.
. . .

He took me by the wrist, and held me hard;
Then goes he to the length of all his arm,
And, with his other hand thus o'er his brow,
He falls to such perusal of my face
As 'a would draw it. Long stay'd he so.
At last, a little shaking of mine arm,
And thrice his head thus waving up and down,
He rais'd a sigh so piteous and profound
As it did seem to shatter all his bulk
And end his being. That done, he lets me go,
And, with his head over his shoulder turn'd,
He seem'd to find his way without his eyes;
For out adoors he went without their helps
And to the last bended their light on me.   (II. i. 77—100)

This speech is characterized as a reported scene by the inclusion of a great number of precise details of costume, gesture and behaviour, by the use of the present tense and, in two places, of the impulse word "thus", inviting the teller to imitate the described action:

And, with his other hand thus o'er his brow,
And thrice his head thus waving up and down.

For a short time we, i. e. all of us — actor, producer, spectator, and reader — are in the presence of the Hamlet of Shakespeare's vision. We are looking at him as through a magnifying glass. The famous disarray of his clothes, the unsteady gait, the piteous look show how intensely he suffers because he has that within which passes show. Ophelia summarizes the impression he makes: he looks as if he had come before her to speak of horrors. But he does not speak. Instead, there follows the intense, protracted scrutiny of her face at arm's length, the light shaking of her arm, the three nods of his head, his profound and piteous sigh, and then the exit with his eyes riveted upon Ophelia as long as possible. It were unwise to try to translate the allusive, symbolic gestures of this scene, evidently expressive of a tempest of conflicting thoughts and emotions and also of a final decision of the will, into the language of clear-cut abstract meanings. It would be still more foolish to pass lightly over this scene and dismiss it as a piece of evidence that the prince, on one occasion at least, went nearly mad. The scene shows the moment when the prince decides to cut loose from Ophelia. He is driven to her by the impulse to share with her the weight that is on him and the disastrous destiny that he sees before him. But there is also the knowledge in him that this cannot be done. During his protracted perusal of her face — a beautiful, gentle, but frail face — he finds his expectation confirmed: it cannot be done; the weight of his fate would break her. In his shaking of her arm and in his profound sigh there are the impatience and despair caused by this recognition, in his three nods his acceptance of the fact. The manner of his exit implies that, in spite of his decision, he is still in love with her. This is an attempt to define the leading, decisive thoughts and emotions symbolized by Hamlet's gestures. But it is not for nothing that we spoke of a tempest of conflicting thoughts and emotions in him. He is also tortured by his impulse to generalize his experience. He also discovers in Ophelia the woman, who, like his mother, is frail, easily tempted and seduced, no reliable and strong ally in the fight that he sees before him. Moreover, he realizes, with bitterness, how deeply involved the girl is in the disastrous situation of the court and country of Denmark without the additional complication of being bound to him by love. Perhaps he is even touched for a moment by the insight that their relationship is inescapably tragic: that Ophelia is doomed no matter whether he draws her nearer to him or tries to repel her. In any case he decides for the second way and acts accordingly in the nunnery scene. The kind of gesture appearing in this reported scene was quite beyond the reach of Kyd's art. As we have seen it is not related to one specific thought or emotion, but to many conflicting thoughts and emotions because it remains quite close to immediate experience and anterior to abstraction and explicitness.

Leaving a subject that deserves to be pursued we glance at a very special type of mirror passage, which shows the creation of the speaker's imagination, intuition or obsession, and either distorts the figures and objects visible on the stage or remains unrelated to any objective reality. It occurs frequently in the scenes of Ophelia's madness, but very rarely only in Hamlet's own speeches. This is so although it is easy for his excited imagination to turn Polonius into a fishmonger or "a great baby not yet out of his swaddling clouts", to suggest the form of a camel, a weasel or a whale in a cloud, to see himself as John-a-dreams, a coward, a whore, a very drab, a scullion, although he can picture for himself the most excruciating penitential scenes:

> Who calls me villain, breaks my pate across,
> Plucks off my beard and blows it in my face,
> Tweaks me by the nose, gives me the lie i' th' throat
> As deep as to the lungs?   (II. ii. 566—569)

On one occasion he startles us by referring to a kind of hallucination. In his first interview with Horatio he says all of a sudden:

> My father — methinks I see my father.   (I. ii. 184)

A most unexpected remark for Horatio, who is just on the point of breaking the news of the apparition of the ghost. The famous answer to his amazed "Where, my lord?" is

> In my mind's eye, Horatio.

Hamlet's basic strength and sanity prevent him all through his career from confounding the visions of his mind's eye with the sights of his physical eyes. Nevertheless, the passage we have quoted amounts to a premonition of what is going to happen. This intuitive faculty is always with Hamlet, and frequently it cooperates in a characteristic way with his quick intelligence and his common sense. It makes him distrust his uncle long before the apparition of the ghost; it permits him to look through the purpose of Rosencrantz 's and Guildenstern's arrival; it impels him to rise at night on the boat during the voyage to England and to open Claudius' letter to the English king. It appears for the last time in his premonitions of the final catastrophe. In my opinion, it is this intuitive faculty again which suggests Hamlet's sudden question "Where's your father?" in the nunnery scene. The explanation that he asks this question because he has accidentally overheard the King's and Polonius' plan of hiding behind the arras does serious harm to our understanding of this scene and of Hamlet's character, and is therefore one of the very few conceptions of our great colleague John Dover Wilson at which I think it necessary to demur.

Returning to *The Spanish Tragedy* now, we find that Kyd, in depicting Hieronimo's fits of delusion, made an extensive use of the kind of mirror passage we are studying. In one of these fits Hieronimo takes the old man Bazulto for his son Horatio come back from the shades:

> HIER. But let me look on my Horatio:
> Sweet boy, how art thou chang'd in death's black shade!
> Had Proserpine no pity on thy youth?
> But suffer'd thy fair crimson-colour'd spring
> With wither'd winter to be blasted thus?
> Horatio, thou art older than thy father:
> Ah ruthless fate, that favour thus transforms!
> (III. xiii. 145—151)

When Bazulto denies his identity with Horatio, Hieronimo's wandering mind transforms him into a fury. A moment later, Bazulto having reminded him that he is merely a "grieved man ... That came for justice for my murdered son", he comes to his senses, and speaks these moving lines to what is really a mirror of his own self and situation:

> Thou art the lively image of my grief:
> Within thy face, my sorrows I may see.
> Thy eyes are gumm'd with tears, thy cheeks are wan,
> Thy forehead troubled, and thy mutt'ring lips
> Murmur sad words abruptly broken off,
> By force of windy sighs thy spirit breathes,
> And all this sorrow riseth for thy son: (III. xiii. 162—68)

This sequence of Hieronimo's two delusions and the projection of his own grief on the old man is one of Kyd's most carefully calculated and beautifully executed effects.

He had not only the direct but also the prospective and the retrospective mirror passage at his command. The first is illustrated in the scene of the prying page, who, having opened the box that should contain Pedringano's pardon and found it empty, foresees and describes with gusto what will happen at the poor dupe's execution:

PAGE . . .   I cannot choose but
smile to think how the villain will flout the gallows, scorn the audience, and descant on the hangman, and all presuming of his pardon from hence. Will't not be an odd jest, for me to stand and grace every jest he makes, pointing my finger at this box, as who would say, 'Mock on, here's thy warrant.' Is't not a scurvy jest, that a man should jest himself to death? Alas, poor Pedringano, I am in a sort sorry for thee, but if I should be hanged with thee, I cannot weep.   *Exit.* (III. v. 10–19)

The function of this mirror passage is entirely practical. It makes sure that the audience will respond quickly and correctly to the somewhat complicated events of the sensational hanging scene. A very peculiar retrospective mirror scene occurs in the so-called fourth addition to the tragedy, printed in the quarto of 1602. Here Hieronimo gives the painter an extraordinary task. He wants him to reproduce a ghastly vision of what he himself experienced in the night of Horatio's murder, telescoping successive events on his canvas and expressing sounds of horror through visual symbols:

HIER. Well sir, then bring me forth, bring me through alley and alley, still with a distracted countenance going along, and let my hair heave up my night-cap. Let the clouds scowl, make the moon dark, the stars extinct, the winds blowing, the bells tolling, the owl shrieking, the toads croaking, the minutes jarring, and the clock striking twelve. And then at last, sir, starting, behold a man hanging, and tottering and tottering, as you know the wind will weave a man, and I with a trice to cut him down.

(Fourth Addition, 145–153)

This amounts to a recreation of the frightful scene in the style of Pieter Brueghel or of a modern surrealist artist. It is, doubtless, a more refined and recherché way of depicting Hieronimo's madness than that found in Kyd's original Bazulto scenes.

Another new feature in the fourth addition, absent from the original text, is the reported scene. Here is a transitive one, followed by a reflexive one:

PED. Sometimes, as he doth at his table sit,
He speaks as if Horatio stood by him,
Then starting in a rage, falls on the earth,
Cries out, 'Horatio! Where is my Horatio?'

HIER. I pry through every crevice of each wall,
Look on each tree, and search through every brake,
Beat at the bushes, stamp our grandam earth,
Dive in the water, and stare up to heaven,
Yet cannot I behold my son Horatio.
(Fourth Addition, 10—13 and 17—21)

Both these examples from the fourth addition remain within the stylistic framework of the old play. The mirrored gestures are emphatic, excessive even, and they express the impulses that overwhelm Hieronimo's reason simply and directly. Like the rest of the gestic elements of the play they exploit conventional associations between emotion and behaviour. Shakespeare, in *Hamlet,* relied upon the same associations but he knew how to particularize and adapt them so that they could express the subtler emotions and mixed impulses of his hero and some of his secondary characters.

By way of conclusion we add a few remarks on the function of word-scenery in our two plays. In neither of them is it a very conspicuous feature. In both of them action and gesture are so important that place and time indications are often neglected. There is also a strong interest in inner, mental developments, but only occasionally are these projected upon the surrounding world in the manner characteristic of *King Lear* and *Macbeth*. Lyrical moments, calling for the atmospheric development of word-scenery, are rare.

The one lyrical moment in *The Spanish Tragedy* is the love meeting of Bel-imperia and Horatio which ends so badly. Its setting is prepared in advance when the lovers decide to meet in Hieronimo's garden. Here are Bel-imperia's idyllic expectations:

> Then be thy father's pleasant bower the field,
> Where first we vow'd a mutual amity:
>
> . . .
>
> There none shall hear us but the harmless birds:
> Happily the gentle nightingale
> Shall carol us asleep ere we be ware, etc.
>
> (II. ii. 42 f. and 47 ff.)

Two scenes later the couple are in the garden on their way to the bower, as appears in Horatio's opening words:

> Now that the night begins with sable wings
> To overcloud the brightness of the sun,
>
> . . .
>
> Come Bel-imperia, let us to the bower.
>
> (II. iv. 1 f. and 4)

About ten lines later, after the treacherous Pedringano has received his charge and after Horatio has overcome Bel-imperia's well-founded forebodings, night has come. Horatio says:

> fair fortune is our friend,
> And heavens have shut up day to pleasure us.
> The stars, thou seest, hold back their twinkling shine,
> And Luna hides herself to pleasure us.

Foreshortened dramatic time is created by the simplest of means, and an atmosphere is prepared for the coming love-scene. But there is no lyrical touch without a dramatic function. The night without moon and stars is an ambiguous symbol. It is favourable for secret love, but also for secret murder. Also the allusions to "these leavy bowers", to Flora and to "the birds that record by night" are given definite functions in the progress of Horatio's and Bel-imperia's love-making. It is remarkable how completely all the elements making up this eminently practical and physical love scene are integrated in the progress of the action.

After the murder the trees and the garden, the moonless and starless night become symbols of evil, appearing frequently in the ravings of Hieronimo and Isabella. Here is Hieronimo, seeing nature disfigured by his woes:

> HIER. Where shall I run to breathe abroad my woes,

My woes, whose weight hath wearied the earth?
Or mine exclaims, that have surcharg'd the air
With ceaseless plaints for my deceased son?
The blust'ring winds, conspiring with my words,
At my lament have mov'd the leaveless trees,
Disrob'd the meadows of their flower'd green,
Made mountains marsh with spring-tides of my tears,
And broken through the brazen gates of hell.

(III. vii. 1—9)

And here his vituperation against night, executed in the more sophisticated style of the fourth addition:

HIER.   ...night is a murderous slut
That would not have her treasons to be seen,
And yonder pale-fac'd Hecate there, the moon,
Doth give consent to that is done in darkness,
And all those stars that gaze upon her face
Are aglets on her sleeve, pins on her train:
And those that should be powerful and divine,
Do sleep in darkness when they most should shine.

(Fourth Addition, 31—38)

The only scenes in *Hamlet* in which word-scenery is used at all extensively are the three early ghost scenes. The most elaborate use of it is made in the first of them. Here it contributes much to the atmosphere of mystery surrounding the apparition of the ghost, and it helps to make it a detailed and intensely real experience whose impact on the imagination is irresistible. Basically, Shakespeare employs the technique with which Kyd experimented in his bower scene. Just as Kyd takes his audience in about a dozen lines from dusk to dark night, Shakespeare takes his in about 60 lines from the moment when Bernardo says "'Tis now struck twelve" and Francisco "For this relief much thanks. 'Tis bitter cold, And I am sick at heart" and "Not a mouse stirring" to the hour when "the morn, in russet mantle clad, Walks o'er the dew of yon high eastward hill". The feat is more ambitious, and it is executed with far greater resourcefulness and subtlety. Especially remarkable is the way how the feeling of the approaching dawn is generated after the ghost has vanished at the first cock crow.

To sum up: Our comparison of the theatrical physiognomy of *The Spanish Tragedy* and of *Hamlet* has shown Kyd in almost full possession of the technique employed by Shakespeare, but it has also demonstrated how the younger and greater playwright, with a lighter hand and a finer artistic tact, found new and subtler functions for it in his endeavour to preserve in the figures and scenes of his play the full and individual gestic life of his dramatic vision.   (1965)

2. The Glass of Pandar's Praise: The Word-Scenery, Mirror Passages, and Reported Scenes in *Troilus and Cressida*

THIS PAPER illustrates a kind of study in which the present writer has become intensely interested as the result of a long series of theatrical disappointments. In the period in which Alexander Tairov's "Entfesseltes Theater" flourished he saw a Hamlet, who, acting his father's part in addition to his own, fell into a trance and turned ventriloquist whenever the ghost spoke, a Hamlet who climbed a specially constructed high tower in order to speak the "To be or not to be" soliloquy, a Lady Macbeth gliding along the wall with trembling hands while she said:

That which hath made them drunk hath made me bold;

(II. ii. 1)

a Bassanio belonging to a ruffianly gang of brown-shirts which hunted down an entirely noble Shylock. These and a great number of similar experiences have convinced him that our modern Shakespearian scholarship and criticism have failed to define clearly and irrefutably the line where the modern theatrical interpreter's sphere of freedom and originality begins and where it ends, if a play is to be produced without serious loss and distortion. In order to work towards this definition it seems necessary to take quite seriously the truism that the playwright's material is different from that of the poet and the novelist. His means of expression are not words alone, but words together with the movements and gestures of living actors and with all the resources of the stage. No

32

true dramatist is without the desire to control and manipulate not only the speeches of his characters, but his other means of expression as well. In modern plays we find ample stage directions describing the setting and the appearance, the movements, the gestures, the facial expression, perhaps even the intonation of the characters. In Shakespeare the scarcity and the casual treatment of such directions is surprising. This could lead a superficial observer to the belief that he was primarily the poet who took care of his characters' speeches and left the rest to his actor-friends and to the producers of later ages. The careful reader, however, discovers a great number of explicit and implicit references to place and time, sometimes developed into evocations of atmosphere, as well as to appearance, gestures and business in the speeches themselves. Shakespeare's word-scenery was naïvely misinterpreted by believers in the nineteenth-century picture-stage as the makeshift of a playwright whose misfortune it was to write for a stage with very limited scenic resources. It would be foolish to ignore the makeshift basis of his practice, but even more foolish to overlook how necessity became an important stimulus for his art. It pointed the way towards that entirely functional and organic use of place, time, and gesture which is a distinguishing mark of his mature plays.

Many scenes contain no indications of time or place; definitions of place and time, as well as atmospheric and symbolic settings, are only introduced when they are essential to the meaning. Similarly, innumerable details of appearance, gesture and business are taken for granted or barely hinted at. The playwright could rely on a solid acting tradition, which had evolved effective stage equivalents for the details of behaviour in the common situations of social life. In many rhetorical passages, too, there was no need for him to assume direct control of the mimetic interpretation, because his actor-friends knew how to respond in movement and gesture to the demands of the rhythm and the rhetorical figures.[1] There were other situations, however, where the playwright desired to control the gestic as well as the vocal expression of his meaning.

[1] Cf. on this problem B. L. Joseph, *Elizabethan Acting*, Oxford University Press 1951.

He did this by introducing mirror passages and reported scenes. With the help of these devices he was not only able to influence the acting of particular passages; they enabled him to communicate to his actors and spectators glimpses of his complete creation, which consisted of speech and action; of emotions, impulses, and conflicts expressing themselves through the action of the speech organs as well as through their reflexes in the movements of the whole body of the actor. These glimpses can have and should have a stimulating and regulating influence on our imaginative experience of the whole play, not only of the situation or character directly concerned.

The study of the references to gestures and business, together with the place-time indications, makes visible the inner form of the play-in-performance. This inner form is not identical with any individual performance, historical or modern. It is part of the ideal existence of the play. Without its knowledge an adequate theatrical, or critical, interpretation of it would seem impossible in any period. Its investigation is by no means a new enterprise. Contributions to it have come from many different critics. Otto Ludwig, Bernard Shaw, Harley Granville-Barker and Richard Flatter are eminent among them. The incidental remarks of Ludwig, Shaw and many others, as well as the detailed books by Granville-Barker[2] and Flatter[3], render a more methodical approach to our subject desirable. The lines it could follow are illustrated here by a study of the theatrical physiognomy of *Troilus and Cressida*.

We cannot undertake it without inquiring what the stage directions of the Q- and the F-text of the play contribute towards the definition of place, time, gesture and business. Those in Q "are generally meagre",[4] those in F only a very little less so. They are mainly, but by no means consistently, concerned with entrances and exits and with stage sounds. Characteristically, they rarely add anything of importance to what is deducible from the speeches themselves.

[2] *Prefaces to Shakespeare,* London 1927–47.
[3] *Shakespeare's Producing Hand. A Study of His Marks of Expression to be Found in the First Folio,* London 1948.
[4] W. W. Greg, *The Shakespeare First Folio,* Oxford 1955, 341.

There is very little precise place and time definition in the play. The first line of the Prologue tells us:

> In Troy, there lies the scene.

The Prologue then offers a brief description of the earlier phases of the siege of "Priam's six-gated city", and adds:

> that our play
> Leaps o'er the vaunt and firstlings of those broils,
> Beginning in the middle; starting thence away
> To what may be digested in a play.

Scene i. is "placed" by Troilus' lines:

> Why should I war without the walls of Troy
> That find such cruel battle here within? (I. i. 2 f.)

It is their main function to express Troilus' inner situation; incidentally, however, they also "place" the scene as a whole. Scene ii is vaguely characterized as a street scene in Troy by the coming and going of Trojan people. A topographical detail is added by Alexander's remark that Queen Hecuba and Helena are going

> Up to the eastern tower,
> Whose height commands as subject all the vale,
> To see the battle. (I. ii. 2 f.)

The hints concerning the elevated position from which Pandarus points out the returning war-lords to Cressida are left quite indefinite:

> Shall we stand up here and see them as they pass toward Ilium? (I. ii. 172)

> Here, here, here's an excellent place; here we may see most bravely. (I. ii. 175)

These words from Pandarus are all we hear about it.

Instances of more definite "placing" are rare in the play. Pandarus' "Walk here i' th' orchard..." (III. ii. 16) and Ulysses' "Achilles stands i' th' entrance of his tent" (III. iii. 38) should be mentioned here. The method of "placing" a scene by a remark spoken in the preceding one is employed in V. i. when Ulysses tells Troilus:

> Follow his torch; he goes to Calchas' tent; (V. i. 82)

Having heard it, we know where we are when Diomedes calls at
the beginning of the next scene:

> What, are you up here, ho? Speak. (V. ii. 1.)

Thus the place indications in our play are strictly, even severely,
functional. The city of Troy and the Greek camp are the scene of
the conflicts of love and war which are the theme of the play, but
the poet withholds from them his power of giving atmospheric
reality to a place. There are only a few picturesque touches. We
have quoted the allusion to "the eastern tower", and may add here
the picture of the town called up by Ulysses when he reminds
Hector of its doom:

> For yonder walls, that pertly front your town,
> Yond towers, whose wanton tops do buss the clouds,
> Must kiss their own feet. (IV. v. 219 f.)

Walls and towers, as seen by Ulysses, are alive with the pride of
the Trojans. Similarly, the Greek tents are addressed as symbols
of pride by Troilus at the end of the play. (V. x. 23 f.) Both these
pieces of word-scenery create a certain sense of place, and contribute at the same time to our experience of the human passion
which is the root of the War of Troy.

Shakespeare's allusions to time in *Troilus and Cressida* are functional, too. The fact that it is evening when the lovers are brought
together by Pandarus is suggested by the situation itself and by
remarks on the end of another day's fighting in the preceding scene.
In the following scenes time indications are surprisingly scarce.
At the beginning of Act IV the stage direction mentions torches to
suggest a night scene. When Troilus is about to take leave of his
mistress there are a few speeches to make us feel the early hour:

TRO. Dear, trouble not yourself; the morn is cold. (IV. ii. 1)

TRO. O Cressida! but that the busy day,
  Wak'd by the lark, hath rous'd the ribald crows,
  And dreaming night will hide our joys no longer,
  I would not from thee.
CRES.   Night hath been too brief. (IV. ii. 8 ff.)

At the opening of Scene iii the coming of the day and of the lovers'
separation is succinctly mentioned:

PAR. It is great morning; and the hour prefix'd
       For her delivery to this valiant Greek
       Comes fast upon. (IV. iii. 1 ff.)

The atmosphere and mood of the early morning count for comparatively little here. More important is the lovers' experience of time moving rapidly and rapaciously. It is communicated by the pressure of the events themselves and accentuated by the imagined bustling figures of "injury of chance" and "injurious time", coming alive in Troilus' complaint. (IV. iv. 32 ff.)

Also the second great night scene of the play, in which Cressida breaks her vows under Troilus' eyes, is left with a minimum of atmosphere. We are prepared for the nocturnal meeting in the preceding scene by the good-night wishes of the heroes. Ulysses' reference to a torch in V. i. 82 is repeated in his first speech in the new scene:

       Stand where the torch may not discover us. (V. ii. 5)

The stars and the moon appear just once in Cressida's asseveration:

       By all Diana's waiting women yond,
       And by herself, I will not tell you whose. (V. ii. 90 f.)

The one major use of word-scenery in the play appears near its close. Its atmospheric function is incidental to a symbolic one. It occurs in Achilles' speech immediately before the murder of Hector. There has not been anything in the series of battle scenes before the murder to make us conscious of the time of day, except Troilus' somewhat indefinite exclamation:

       No, by the flame of yonder glorious heaven, (V. vi. 23)

and Hector's declaration: "Now is my day's work done" (V. viii. 3), which clearly points to an evening hour. In spite of this preparation there remains a certain incongruous purple patch quality about the grandiloquent speech in which Achilles acquaints Hector with his impending murder:

       Look, Hector, how the sun begins to set;
       How ugly night comes breathing at his heels;
       Even with the vail and dark'ning of the sun,
       To close the day up, Hector's life is done. (V. viii. 5 ff.)

37

> The dragon wing of night o'erspreads the earth
> And, stickler-like, the armies separates. (V. viii. 17 f.)

The whole passage, evoking the image of the setting sun and the coming of night to accompany and render glorious the end of Hector, is appropriate to the nobility and importance of this hero, but it is hardly in keeping with the miserable circumstances of his death, and it sounds strange coming from the mouth of the trickster Achilles. It is a *tour de force* by which the playwright tried to save Hector's end from being too shocking an anti-climax.

Troilus and Cressida is definitely not an atmospheric play. Its author's attention was concentrated upon his figures, especially upon the influence of their characters on their actions and sufferings. Besides Troilus and Cressida themselves an unusual number of secondary figures are carefully drawn in sharp outline, and each of them is given his full life and individuality. Whereas word-scenery is scarce in the text, direct and indirect references to appearance, behaviour and business abound in it.

To begin with, we consider a number of mirror passages. The simplest kind is before us when a speaker accompanies a gesture of his own by its name. Agamemnon describes a ceremony of friendship, saying:

> Fair Lord Aeneas, let me touch your hand;
> To our pavilion shall I lead you, first. (I. iii. 304 f.)

Preparing the climax of the scene in which the lovers plight their troth, Pandarus arranges an impressive group with the words: "Here I hold your hand; here my cousin's." (III. ii. 193) The following speech of Cressida's mirrors the action by which, in her anxious curiosity, she emphasizes her appeal to Pandarus: "Good uncle, I beseech you, on my knees I beseech you, what's the matter?" (IV. ii. 87 f.) Pandarus' exclamation: "Let me embrace too" (IV. iv. 14) names an action of his own, but tells us at the same time that Cressida embraced Troilus when she cried: "O Troilus! Troilus!" (IV. iv. 12). And Troilus, too, throws light on the action of the farewell scene where he complains that "injurious time"

scants us with a single famish'd kiss,
Distasted with the salt of broken tears. (IV. iv. 46 f.)

During his visit to the Greek camp Hector's fine talent for friendship and generosity expresses itself in gestures as well as words.
"Let me embrace thee, Ajax" (IV. v. 135), he cries, instead of
making his opponent feel his superior fighting power and skill,
and: "The issue is embracement" (IV. v. 148). He offers him his
hand with the words: "Give me thy hand, my cousin" (IV. v. 157),
and also the meeting with Nestor is accompanied by hearty
embracements. To Nestor's: "O, let an old man embrace thee" he
responds with an enthusiastic: "Let me embrace thee, good old
chronicle" (IV. v. 202), and he repeats a moment later: "Most
reverend Nestor, I am glad to clasp thee." We may note here in
passing how constantly and in how many different ways the age of
Nestor is mirrored in the speeches.

Direct naming can be replaced by a metaphorical reference to a
gesture, endowing it with fuller significance. This happens where
Hector lays down his sword with the words:

Rest, sword; thou hast thy fill of blood and death! (V. viii. 4)

and where Achilles describes the sheathing of his sword:

My half-supp'd sword, that frankly would have fed,
Pleas'd with this dainty bait, thus goes to bed. (V. viii. 19 f.)

There are two impulse words in this speech. "This" demands a
demonstrative look or gesture towards Hector's corpse, and "thus"
indicates the moment at which his sword must go into its place,
suggesting at the same time the energy and precision of Achilles'
action.

A rather interesting question is raised by a line addressed by
Aeneas to himself as a warning against the vulgar and — in Shakespeare's play — typically Greek vice of self-praise:

Peace, Troyan; lay thy finger on thy lips. (I. iii. 240)

It would be a mistake to consider this as a genuine mirror passage.
The well-known gesture for demanding silence is introduced to
give emphasis to Aeneas' warning to himself. It has the function
of a metaphor; to realize it in action would most probably render
it silly and ineffective.

Much more frequent than the self-descriptions with which we have dealt so far are references in one character's speech to the behaviour of another character. Before accosting Ulysses, Achilles says in front of his tent: "Here is Ulysses. I'll interrupt his reading." (III. iii. 92 f.) The kissing-game in which the Greek leaders indulge after Cressida's arrival in their camp is consistently mirrored in speech. When Agamemnon begins it, his action is given importance and weight by Nestor's stately line:

Our general doth salute you with a kiss. (IV. v. 19)

There is more subtlety in references to facial expression as we find one in Cressida's words to her lover when she does not want the early callers to find him in her house:

My lord, come you again into my chamber.
You smile and mock me, as if I meant naughtily. (IV. ii. 36 f.)

The quality of Troilus' smile is thus precisely defined. The playwright indicates, besides, that this mocking, and slightly salacious, smile develops into laughter by giving the young man's reaction as "Ha! Ha!" What is evidently a rather bovine stare in Achilles makes Hector say:

Why dost thou so oppress me with thine eye? (IV. v. 241)

Manners of speaking are further important subjects of mirror passages. When Pandarus begins with his comments on the returning warriors and his incessant allusions to the virtues of Troilus, Cressida finds it necessary to warn him: "Speak not so loud." (I. ii. 178) A little later, as Troilus marches by at last, Pandarus' enthusiasm grows so loud that his niece hisses at him: "Peace, for shame, peace!" (I. ii. 222) Early in her decisive meeting with Troilus, Cressida interrupts her first loving words to him before the wish that their happiness may last is formulated. Her courtly lover describes as "pretty" what is really ominous: "What makes this pretty abruption?" (III. ii. 62 f.) Pandarus' manner of opening his most painful interview with his niece is emphasized by her words: "Why sigh you so profoundly?" (IV. ii. 79) The off-stage exclamation which announces Cassandra's first entrance is echoed by Priam: "What noise, what shriek is this?" (II. ii. 97)

Silences, too, are rendered eloquent by spoken interpretation.

Here Diomedes' aside on the reaction of Ajax to Ulysses' purposeful praise should be remembered:

> And how his silence drinks up this applause! (II. iii. 196)

Also Cressida's complaint to her lover:

> See, see, your silence,
> Cunning in dumbness, from my weakness draws
> My very soul of counsel. (III. ii. 128 ff.)

We may mention here that spoken references to sounds produced by instruments are also frequent in our play. Troilus' exclamation:

> Peace, you ungracious clamours! Peace, rude sounds! (I. i. 88)

which corresponds to the Q and F stage direction "Sound alarum", is an instance of this; another occurs in I. iii. 256 f., where Aeneas' order:

> Trumpet, blow loud,
> Send thy brass voice through all these lazy tents;

is followed, at line 259, by "Sound trumpet" in Q and by "The trumpets sound" in F. After IV. v. 275, where Agamemnon commands:

> Beat loud the tabourines, let the trumpets blow,

there is no stage direction in either Q or F. This is certainly not a sign that the order was not executed; it is merely an example of the casual treatment of the stage directions in our texts. The lines we have quoted do service as spoken stage directions, but there is more to them, of course. Like many other mirror passages, they assist the imagination in its transmutation of stage effects into perfect elements of the dramatic world created by Shakespeare in and for the theatre of the mind. To say that the actual theatre with its human and material imperfections is subservient to the theatre of the mind is not to denigrate it. Its glory lies in the fact that, without it, the theatre of he mind cannot reach and hold Shakespeare's creation in its completeness and full vitality. The words in our last quotations give the possibly meagre and routine stage sounds their precise imaginative function, and they achieve this by their rhythm and their onomatopoeic qualities rather than by their plain meaning. A striking example of the transmutation of a trumpet call by a mirror passage occurs at the beginning of IV. v. Agamemnon, having referred to the "appointment fresh and fair" in which Ajax hopes to overcome Hector, asks him to call the tardy Trojan to the lists:

> Give with thy trumpet a loud note to Troy,
> Thou dreadful Ajax, that the appalled air
> May pierce the head of the great combatant,
> And hale him hither. (IV. v. 3 ff.)

The invitation itself seems ironically attuned to the excessive and dull fortissimo which is the characteristic mode of Ajax and which appears presently with unsurpassable vehemence in his order to his trumpeter. Ajax's order transforms this good man into a grotesque caricature of his employment:

> Thou, trumpet, there's my purse.
> Now crack thy lungs and split thy brazen pipe;
> Blow, villain, till thy sphered bias cheek
> Out-swell the colic of puff'd Aquilon.
> Come, stretch thy chest, and let thy eyes spout blood:
> Thou blowest for Hector. (IV. v. 6 ff.)

By this extraordinary piece of rant the trumpet call which follows (again not mentioned in a stage direction) becomes the voice of Ajax's vainglorious pride.

No sounds have a more important function in the play than the knocks at the door that bring Troilus' and Cressida's first and only night of love to its disastrous close. There are three references to them in the text, suggesting that the impatient visitors knock more energetically each time they make themselves heard after their first attempt. Cressida is the first to react. She says:

> Who's that at door? Good uncle, go and see. (IV. ii. 35)

And a little later:

> How earnestly they knock! (IV. ii. 40)

The third mirror passage comes from Pandarus:

> Will you beat down the door? (IV. ii. 43)

The contrast between the hollow sounds, the meaning of which is known to the audience, and the frivolous conversation of Pandarus and the unsuspecting couple is a poignant dramatic effect. It makes this scene a worthy pendant to the knocking at the gate in *Macbeth*.

Returning to mirror passages that remain within the visual sphere, we wish to study a particularly interesting one, showing a habitual trick of behaviour. Ulysses recognizes Diomedes at a distance by his gait:

> 'Tis he, I ken the manner of his gait:
> He rises on the toe. That spirit of his
> In aspiration lifts him from the earth. (IV. v. 14 ff.)

The description of Diomedes' peculiarity is followed by an interpretation in terms of character. Other references to appearance are less decisive, but they all contribute something to our image of one of the dramatis personae. Hector hopes to recognize Achilles "by his large and portly size" (IV. v. 162). Troilus' tribute to Cressida's fascinating eyes: "Sleep kill those pretty eyes" (IV. ii. 4), is improved upon by Diomedes:

> The lustre in your eye, heaven in your cheek,
> Pleads your fair usage; (IV. iv. 117 f.)

From Ulysses, however, who is not among her lovers, comes the famous uncomplimentary interpretation of her charms:

> There's language in her eye, her cheek, her lip,
> Nay, her foot speaks; her wanton spirits look out
> At every joint and motive of her body. (IV. v. 55 ff.)

Moods and emotions, too, have their physical equivalents in appearance and gesture, and these appear in a number of mirror passages. Before the eagerly expected meeting with Cressida Troilus exclaims:

> I am giddy; expectation whirls me round. (III. ii. 17)

The corresponding condition in Cressida is mirrored by Pandarus before her entrance: "She does so blush, and fetches her wind so short, as if she were fray'd with a sprite." (III. ii. 30) The depression of the two lovers after their separation is written on their faces. Achilles promises Cressida:

I'll take that winter from your lips, fair lady, (IV. v. 24)

and Agamemnon inquires concerning Troilus:

What Troyan is that same that looks so heavy? (IV. v. 95)

Besides its numerous short mirror passages our play contains a few complete mirror scenes, in which a whole series of stage events is described and interpreted. The first is the passing of the Trojan heroes before Pandarus and Cressida. Pandarus has his say concerning each of them, but his gabble does not mention many characteristic features. Hector's and Troilus' hacked helmets and Troilus' bloodied sword are noticed. Otherwise he offers no more than a lively general introduction of the Trojan lords, his talk being strictly subservient to his intention of whetting Cressida's interest in Troilus. In her subsequent soliloquy we find the lines:

But more in Troilus thousand-fold I see
Than in the glass of Pandar's praise may be, (I. ii. 276 f.)

Although mainly an avowal of secret passion, they are also a criticism of Pandarus' superficial talk, and they contain a beautiful phrase foreshadowing our own more prosaic and technical terms "mirror passage" and "mirror scene".

Another mirror scene, the fight between Hector and Ajax, was evidently executed according to well-known conventions. The mirror words (IV. v. 113 ff.) throw light on a few incidents of the fight only. A more intimate and individualized scene like the bringing together of the lovers by Pandarus is mirrored in much greater detail. The following speech is replete with mirror elements as well as with gestic impulses for the speaker himself:

Come, come, what need you blush? Shame's a baby. — Here she is now; swear the oaths now to her that you have sworn to me. — What, are you gone again? You must be watch'd ere you be made tame, must you? Come your ways, come your ways; and you draw backward, we'll put you i' th' fills. — Why do you not speak to her? — Come, draw this curtain and let's see your picture. Alas the day, how loath you are to offend daylight! An 'twere dark, you'd close sooner. So, so; rub on, and kiss the mistress. . . . (III. ii. 39 ff.)

The amusing scene in which the Greek princes pass by Achilles without showing the customary signs of respect is first described by Ulysses when he arranges it:

> Achilles stands i' th' entrance of his tent.
> Please it our general pass strangely by him,
> As if he were forgot; and, Princes all,
> Lay negligent and loose regard upon him. (III. iii. 38 ff.)

Presently, the plan is executed before our eyes, and Patroclus describes what is happening in the very words of Ulysses: "They pass by strangely." (III. iii. 71) And Achilles, looking back on the scene, complains to Ulysses:

> they pass'd by me
> As misers do by beggars — neither gave to me
> Good word nor look. (III. iii. 142 ff.)

Thus, by repetition, the significance of the scene as a whole is emphasized; and the behaviour of the princes is precisely defined by the allusions to their way of looking and speaking and by Achilles' striking simile.

The most complex use of the mirror technique is found in V. ii. It has its functions in the would-be-secret conversation between Cressida and Diomedes. His reactions appear in some of Cressida's speeches:

> Nay, but you part in anger. (V. ii. 44)

> You look upon that sleeve; behold it well. (V. ii. 68)

> Nay, do not snatch it from me; (V. ii. 80)

> One cannot speak a word
> But it straight starts you. (V. ii. 99 f.)

The speeches of Troilus, the tormented watcher, are another mirror of what is going on before Calchas' tent. Two of them are quite simple. The statement "Cressid comes forth to him" (V. ii. 6) is uttered with the accent of one refusing to believe what his eyes are seeing. The four words "She strokes his cheek" (V. ii. 51), mirroring the fact so dryly and objectively, are probably the most concentrated and intense expression of passion and suffering in the whole play. These two bare mirror speeches are more heart-rending than any of Troilus' later violent outbreaks with all their powerful rhetoric. There are further mirror effects in Troilus' reactions upon the disastrous scene: the whispering which follows upon Cressida's "Hark, a word with you." (V. ii. 7) provokes Troilus' "Yea, so familiar!" (V. iii. 8). Her: "Hark! a word in your ear." (V. ii. 34) is followed by his outcry: "O plague and madness!" We may add here that Troilus' is not the only viewpoint from which the events before the tent are seen. Thersites, too, is lurking in the dark and snarling forth the lowest possible interpretations of Cressida's behaviour. When she says:

I prithee, Diomed, visit me no more,

he fears that this could be mistaken for the voice of her better nature and comments:

Now she sharpens. Well said, whetstone. (V. ii. 74)

The third great mirror effect of this amazing multiple scene is found in Ulysses' remarks on the reactions of Troilus. His first speech (V. ii. 5) places the watchers. He has then his own not too kindly remark on Cressida ("She will sing any man at first sight." V. ii. 9), but, before long, he realizes the folly of adding fuel to Troilus' passion, the growth of which is reflected in what he says in order to keep the young man reasonably quiet:

You are moved, Prince; let us depart, I pray, (V. ii. 36)

You flow to great distraction; (V. ii. 41)

You shake, my lord, at something; will you go? (V. ii. 50)

The complex system of mirror effects, together with the numerous gestic impulses contained in the speeches, gives the scene before us its three-dimensional reality and its intense dramatic power. Any adequate performance of it must be based on this system and these hints. They cannot be slurred over or ignored for the sake of an "original" conception of the play by a producer who has grasped our great author-producer's method of expressing his total vision in dramatic speech. There is a legitimate sphere for the new producer's originality. Shakespeare's theatrical notation is anything but pedantic. It is precise and definite in certain crucial situations; far more often it is allusive and suggestive. Once they have been caught and understood, there are many different ways of realizing the author's suggestions on the stage. In their realization the talents of new producers and actors and the spirit of a new age should manifest themselves.

We cannot include in this paper a study of the numerous gestic impulses in our text, although, without it, our account of the theatrical physiognomy of *Troilus and Cressida* remains a fragment. But we must devote the rest of the space at our disposal to the reported scenes. In these the characters seen on the real stage appear in additional scenes on the stage of the mind, their behaviour entirely controlled by the author himself. As our first example hesitates between a simple report and a reported scene it is advisable to define the difference between the two forms. In a report we obtain information on facts and events as causes or consequences of other facts and events, on the results of what people think, say, and do; the reported scene on the other hand is concerned with action in progress, with the behaviour, the very words of people in a particular situation. It has a tendency to change from the past to the present tense, and it definitely prefers direct to indirect speech. Here is Alexander's report on Hector's anger:

> Hector, whose patience
> Is as a virtue fix'd, to-day was mov'd.
> He chid Andromache, and struck his armourer;
> And, like as there were husbandry in war,
> Before the sun rose he was harness'd light,
> And to the field goes he; ... (I. ii. 4 ff.)

Only the last line achieves the immediacy of the reported scene. Our next example shows much more of this quality. It is Pandarus' account of the frivolous conversation at the Trojan court, in the course of which Helena tries to make fun of Troilus because there are so few hairs on his chin as yet, and finds his wit rather more than a match for her own. This account is itself the subject of a frivolous, conversation, in which Pandarus cleverly stimulates Cressida's love for Troilus by making her a little jealous. He paints a charming scene of the easy-going life of the Trojan princes when they forget about the war. His reported scene supports the effect of a later acted scene (III. i.) where Pandarus and Helena converse in the same tone. Besides, it adds important touches to our experience of Troilus, whom we never see in a similar situation on the stage.

The most striking reported scene of the play, however, shows how Achilles wastes his time while he is withholding his strength from the Greek cause. It has its place in Ulysses' great speech before the Greek council of war. By way of contrast and relief it introduces gesture, movement, and action into a speech and a scene predominantly rhetorical. In the corresponding situation in the Trojan council of war the irruption of Cassandra has a similar function. The scene presented by Ulysses (I. iii. 142 ff.) has a setting (the tent with "a lazy bed"), a protagonist ("great Achilles", "large Achilles", "god Achilles", "Sir Valour") and a second actor, Patroclus. He amuses his friend by a parodistic imitation of Agamemnon's gait and speech and of Nestor's way of getting ready for a public oration and of responding to a night alarm. Patroclus' imitation is mostly gestic. When he "pageants" Agamemnon he walks in the silly, self-important way of a ham-actor – Ulysses makes this clear by his detailed theatrical simile. His impersonation of Nestor includes hemming and beard-stroking, coughing, spitting and "palsy-fumbling on his gorget". Achilles, though "on his press'd bed lolling", is no passive spectator of the fun. His applause and laughter are loud, and he keeps giving new promising tasks to his talented entertainer. Some of the finest points of the whole wonderful passage spring from the fact that both Agamemnon and Nestor are among Ulysses' audience. Thus we can compare Patroclus' imitations to their originals, and are certainly not expected to find them as weak as Ulysses makes them appear in his suspiciously over-emphatic disclaimers.

Our image of Ajax, too, is derived from many sources besides his own actions and speeches on the stage. Alexander describes his character to Cressida (I. ii. 18 ff.); in the council scene Nestor tells of his behaviour under the influence of Achilles' bad example (I. iii. 188 ff.). There are references to "blockish Ajax", "dull brainless Ajax" when Ulysses and Nestor are hatching their plot of rousing Achilles from his inactivity by pretending that Ajax is the proper match for Hector. Thus his first entrance on the stage does not find us unprepared. In II. iii, where Ulysses and his friends gleefully feed his illusion that he is Achilles' better, we get further characterizing strokes in the contemptuous asides of the watchers. The results of Ulysses' and Nestor's cajolery are the subject of an amusing reported scene coming from Thersites in III. iii: "Ajax goes up and down the field asking for himself." "... he raves in saying nothing." "Why, 'a stalks up and down like a peacock — a stride and a stand; ruminates like an hostess that hath no arithmetic but her brain to set down her reckoning, bites his lip with a politic regard. ..." (III. iii. 245 ff.) Gestures and behaviour are given life and precision by a series of telling similes. When the image of the stalking *miles gloriosus* is fully alive before our imagination, Thersites is struck by the idea of supplementing his reported scene by an acted one, in which he takes the part of Ajax. Through an astonishingly resourceful combination of mirror effects Ajax is shown from many different angles, and becomes a character expressing itself in behaviour as well as speech.

Similarly, our experience of Hector receives a number of important modifications in reported scenes. In IV. v., his qualities as an invincible fighter and generous victor are appreciated by Nestor in a speech that is particularly impressive because it is the tribute of an enemy. His clemency towards a vanquished opponent appears a second time in Troilus' lines:

> When many times the captive Grecian falls,
> Even in the fan and wind of your fair sword,
> You bid them rise and live. (V. iii. 40 ff.)

Like Nestor's tribute, this speech represents a type of reported scene removed from actuality by the fact that it describes habitual action. Nestor's report on Hector's activity in his last battle is different. It has all the force of a spectator's reaction upon what he sees:

> There is a thousand Hectors in the field;
> Now here he fights on Galathe his horse,
> And there lacks work; anon he's there afoot,
> And there they fly or die, like scaled sculls
> Before the belching whale; ... (V. v. 19 ff.)

A reported scene may also introduce the dimension of the future into a play. Cressida, in IV. ii, having vented her grief before our eyes, speaks of the more violent demonstrations that are to follow in her room:

> I'll go in and weep —
> ... Tear my bright hair, and scratch my praised cheeks,
> Crack my clear voice with sobs and break my heart,
> With sounding 'Troilus'. (IV. ii. 104 ff.)

A different future scene, which takes us beyond the time limits of the play, is reported by Cassandra when she adds her prophecy of doom to her family's endeavours to prevent Hector from joining the battle on the fateful day:

> O, farewell, dear Hector!
> Look how thou diest. Look how thy eye turns pale.
> Look how thy wounds do bleed at many vents.
> Hark how Troy roars; how Hecuba cries out. (V. iii. 80 ff.)

Her mantic gift shows her the coming scenes as present and real. By her prophecy the spectator is attuned to the horror and the historic importance of Hector's death, so that the actual death scene can be passed over rather rapidly. After the event the effect of the unhappy news on the Trojans appears in Troilus' words:

> There is a word will Priam turn to stone;
> Make wells and Niobes of the maids and wives,
> Cold statues of the youth; and, in a word,
> Scare Troy out of itself. (V. x. 18 ff.)

Here, no realistic scene is described. The extreme despair of the Trojans is expressed by a series of hyperbolical images. The cessation of movement in Priam and the youth of Troy becomes a powerful symbol. This passage is a good example to show how gesture, so essential a direct means of expression in our play, also pervades its imagery. In this sphere innumerable playlets are enacted before our inner eye by personifications and metamorphosed abstractions. They occur frequently within the speeches, which interrupt the course of events and form a fascinating contrast to the many gestic and bustling scenes. The gestic imagery, again, keeps the highly rhetorical and sententious speeches within the stylistic framework of the rest of the play. "Time", in Ulysses' exhortation to Achilles,

hath, my lord, a wallet at his back,
Wherein he puts alms for oblivion,
A great-siz'd monster of ingratitudes. (III. iii. 145 ff.)

It assumes another part in the same speech:

For time is like a fashionable host,
That slightly shakes his parting guest by th' hand;
And with his arms outstretch'd, as he would fly,
Grasps in the comer. (III. iii. 165 ff.)

For Troilus, at the parting,

Injurious time now with a robber's haste
Crams his rich thievery up, he knows not how.
As many farewells as be stars in heaven,
With distinct breath and consign'd kisses to them,
He fumbles up into a loose adieu. (IV. iv. 41 ff.)

These examples suffice to show how indispensable the gestic mode
of apprehension and expression was for the author of *Troilus and
Cressida*. It is this mode which made him the supreme dramatist.
The desire to learn as much as possible about its manifestations in
the texts should animate the critics as well as the producers and
actors of Shakespeare. It can take them to a common ground
where the line of demarcation mentioned in the opening paragraph of this paper may be profitably discussed.   (1964)

3. Word-Scenery in *Macbeth* and Some Other Plays

MANY OBSERVERS have been struck by Shakespeare's lack of interest in the place and time of many of his scenes as well as by his
marvellous ability of creating in other ones the atmosphere of different lands, seasons, and hours of day and night by his poetic
language.[1] Speaking of *Cymbeline*, James Boaden remarked in

---

[1] Some special studies bearing on the subject are: Edmund Voigt,
Shakespeares Naturschilderungen, Anglistische Forschungen, XXVIII,
1909; C. Meinck, *Über das örtliche und zeitliche Colorit in Shakespeares Römerdramen und Ben Jonsons "Catiline", Studien zur englischen Philologie*, XXXVIII, 1910; Brinus Köhler, *Die Schilderung des*

1825: "Here a problem arises of difficult solution as to Shakespeare. If we did not *know* the contrary, we should be apt to conclude that, dramatically, he lived upon *anticipation*. His fancy for
ever prompted him with scenery, that *his* Globe could never even
affect to exhibit; . . ."[2] It is beside our point that Gerald Eades
Bentley would probably answer that *Cymbeline* may not have
been written for the Globe at all, but for the Blackfriars Theatre.[3]
But we have certainly given up Boaden's poor idea of the Globe
as well as his conception of a Shakespeare hankering after a
theatre that would permit greater scenic display than his own. We
are aware of the unique opportunities offered by its stage in spite
of its solid and immobile structure. We have a fairly clear conception of its main parts, which could be combined in many different ways and changed into many different localities through the
lines spoken by the actors. We know that its physical resources
were by no means so contemptible as Boaden suspected. The
dramatist's words could count upon the support of a bell, a piece
of ordnance, of machinery for producing thunder and lightning,
of music and of trap-doors, simple set pieces, properties, modifications of costume, tricks with fire and smoke, etc.. With all that,
Shakespeare's theatre was incapable of doing very much for a performance if it had to rely on its own resources alone; it was
certainly incapable of covering up the weaknesses of the playwright, on the other hand it was full of opportunities, suggestions
and stimuli for his imagination.

The modern studies of this theatre direct our attention towards
Shakespeare's word-scenery, but our interest in that subject has yet
another source: the successful work devoted in recent years to the
investigation of his imagery. It is true, some, though by no means
the best, of that work has entirely lost sight of the theatrical func-

*Milieus in Shakespeares Hamlet, Macbeth und King Lear, Studien zur
englischen Philologie, XXXXVI, 1912; David W. Rannie, Scenery in
Shakespeare's Plays and Other Studies, Oxford 1926; Arthur Sewell,
"Place and Time in Shakespeare's Plays", Studies in Philology,
XXXXII, 1945, 205—224.*

[2] *Memoirs of the Life of John Philip Kemble, Esq.,* London 1825,
vol. II, 293.

[3] See: "Shakespeare and the Blackfriars Theatre", *Shakespeare Survey,*
I, 1948, 38—50.

tions of imagery. The most outstanding results of it are concerned with iterative imagery, with image clusters, with various types of metaphor and simile, with their functions in the context of individual passages, scenes and plays and with their development in the course of the dramatist's creative life. There are further types of imagery to be investigated, as has been ably pointed out by R. A. Foakes.[4] Our special concern is with those images and pictures in Shakespeare's plays which were, so to speak, projected on his stage or on an imaginary extension of it, in order to define the locality and time of a scene or event and, in many instances, to create its atmosphere, as well as with the interaction between them and the objects visible on the stage. Our problem, seen in terms of the play-in-performance, is a single one, but it has two different aspects: it is related to the function and mood of the imaginary scene, created with the help of those images and pictures, but also to the physical things and events on the stage.

A detailed study of where the dramatist used word-scenery and where he dispensed with it, of his various ways of using it in the individual plays promises to reveal new facets of his dramatic art. It is impossible to undertake it in the present paper, as it involves the examination of all the plays, a consideration of Shakespeare's manner in the several types of plays he cultivated and a comparison with the methods of other dramatists. All we can attempt is to give some illustrations of its possibilities. We are going to do this in the course of an analysis of the opening scenes of *Macbeth*.[5] It will be followed by a sketch of the main types of word-scenery.

It goes without saying that we have to disregard in a study of this type all the stage directions introduced by the later editors, and that, by stressing the function of a passage as word-scenery, we do not in any way deny the further important connexions it may have with the meaning, the symbolism, the characters or with other aspects of the artistic organism of which it is a part.

---

[4] See: "Suggestions for a New Approach to Shakespeare's Imagery", *Shakespeare Survey*, V, 1952, 81–92.
[5] We have used *Macbeth* as a particularly suitable text for our approach in spite of the fact that it shows signs of a certain amount of interference by another author. Our survey of the links between the scenes makes it clear that it is very solidly knit.

At the opening of *Macbeth* we find the short colloquy of the three Weird Sisters, ending with the incantation:

> Fair is foul, and foul is fair:
> Hover through the fog and filthy air.

We do not know where the three meet. The stage direction of the Folio runs: *Thunder and Lightning. Enter three Witches.* This indicates that the available machinery for producing thunder and lightning was used when the witches came in. But Shakespeare did not entirely rely on the machines for his effect. The nature phenomena, accompanying the present as well as the future entries of the demonic creatures, are expressly named in the first question of the first witch:

> When shall we three meet again?
> In thunder, lightning, or in rain?

The answers of her two fellows define the time of the third scene:

2 WITCH. When the hurlyburly's done,
          When the battle's lost and won.
3 WITCH. That will be ere the set of sun.

The following exchange tells the audience what kind of place to expect in the third scene:

1 WITCH. Where the place?
2 WITCH. Upon the heath.
3 WITCH. There to meet with Macbeth.

The last remark even hints at what is going to happen there. Thus the first scene as a whole does not only introduce the motif of the witches; it also prepares the third with respect to time and place. We shall find in what follows that anticipation — in many different ways an important aspect of the dramatist's technique, as Wolfgang Clemen has shown[6] — plays an important role in his word-scenery as well. It is probable that all the entrances and the exits of the witches were made through a trap-door, surrounded by stage-smoke, although the stage directions of the Folio have *Enter* and

---

[6] "Anticipation and Foreboding in Shakespeare's Early Histories", *Shakespeare Survey*, VI, 1953, 25—35.

Exeunt only, except in I. iii and IV. i, where the disappearance of these uncanny creatures is announced by the verb *vanish*. This is perhaps without significance, but it might suggest that their magical exits were reserved for the eyes of their victim Macbeth: a spectacular way of stressing their tricky ways and evil intentions.

The stage direction for the second scene is *Alarum within. Enter King Malcome, Donalbaine, Lenox, with attendants, meeting a bleeding Captaine.* The king and his retinue enter the front-stage through one of the stage-doors, and the bleeding captain appears on the opposite side. His report on the military prowess of Macbeth is received by the King and supplemented by Ross and Angus, who arrive later. The audience is told nothing whatever about the place and time of the meeting.

Now the three witches enter again. We know about the place and time of this event from the earlier hints. There is hardly any amplification of those hints in the great scene itself, in which Macbeth lends ear to the evil suggestions for the first time. There is something of its atmosphere in the single word "heath", which we have heard before and which is once repeated by Macbeth, in combination with the striking adjective "blasted":

> or why
> Upon this blasted heath you stop our way
> With such prophetic greeting?

There is more of it in the strange aspect and behaviour of the witches. Here it is interesting to note that the dramatist did not leave the task of producing the required effects entirely to the tireman and the actor. Banquo describes the strange shapes of the witches at the moment of the meeting:

> What are these,
> So wither'd, and so wild in their attire,
> That look not like th'inhabitants o' th' earth,
> And yet are on't? Live you, or are you aught
> That man may question? You seem to understand me,
> By each at once her choppy finger laying
> Upon her skinny lips. You should be women,
> And yet your beards forbid me to interpret
> That you are so.

These lines make sure that the audience's visual impressions, which may have bordered on the ridiculous, were raised to the proper imaginative pitch: an example of how Shakespeare can use the physical data of his stage as a starting-point of an imaginative flight. He was by no means afraid of this kind of duplication, whereas, in the case before us, most modern producers try to avoid it by having the scene very dark and the figures of the witches as indistinct as possible.

The strange and wild atmosphere of the heath is further suggested by certain images in the speeches of Macbeth and Banquo: an indirect way of attuning the spectators' sense of place and time to the terrible moral event that is the heart and meaning of the scene:

BANQUO: The earth hath bubbles, as the water has,
            And these are of them. Whither are they vanish'd?
MACBETH: Into the air; and what seem'd corporal melted
            As breath into the wind. Would they had stay'd!
BANQUO: Were such things here as we do speak about?
            Or have we eaten on the insane root
            That takes the reason prisoner?

There are a number of expressions here giving colour to the imagined landscape and making it a fit place for Macbeth's first meeting with his doom: the names of the elements "earth", "water", "air"; Banquo's daring attempt to define the nature of the witches: "The earth hath bubbles, as the water has", besides: "what seemed corporal melted, as breath into the wind", and especially "the insane root", which belongs to the heath out of which the witches rise. We note that Shakespeare does not only create atmosphere through direct description; he knows the indirect way of basing some of his metaphors and similes on the properties of the imagined place.

The scene we are considering contains again allusions to the next. Macbeth and Banquo are on their way to Forres; Rosse and Angus meet them in order to conduct them to the king. The spectator will assume that the meeting of the generals with the king takes place at Forres. The dramatist does not offer any further definition of its locality; the stage direction of the Folio is:

Flourish. Enter King, Lenox Malcolme, Donalbaine, and Attendants. There is a remark on the place of the fifth scene; Duncan says: "From hence to Inverness, And bind us further to you." Macbeth's reaction to these words makes it clear that Inverness is his castle:

> I'll be myself the harbinger, and make joyful
> The hearing of my wife with your approach;
> So, humbly take my leave.

Thus the spectator knows what it means when, after the exit of the group around the king, Lady Macbeth appears on the stage, reading her husband's letter. We find the first allusion to the nature of the place in this scene in the lady's second soliloquy:

> The raven himself is hoarse
> That croaks the fatal entrance of Duncan
> Under my battlements.[7]

The impression "Macbeth's castle" is supported by the mention of battlements; at the same time the lines point forward to the scene of Duncan's arrival, which the spectator expects to be accompanied by such ominous signs as the hoarse croaking of a raven. Here a false clue is given, rendering the peace and harmony of the arrival the more striking. The lady's soliloquy contains other less deceptive allusions to the future. Macbeth's first crime is a deed of night, and it is presented in a series of nocturnal scenes. The following invocation prepares the spectator for this:

> Come, thick night,
> And pall thee in the dunnest smoke of hell,
> That my keen knife see not the wound it makes,
> Nor heaven peep through the blanket of the dark
> To cry 'Hold, hold'.

This is not even the earliest hint that there is going to be night,

---

[7] We do not think that these lines refer to the messenger, nor can we find the suggestion in them that I. v. takes place before the castle gates. If there were such a suggestion, it would be totally ineffective in the theatre. The lines strike us as an imaginary anticipation of Duncan's arrival. For a different view see *Macbeth*, edited by John Dover Wilson, Cambridge 1947, 107 and 109.

not only in the souls of the protagonist and his wife, but also in the sphere of the imagined scenes. Already at the court of the king Macbeth, in the clutches of his destructive plans, murmurs:

> Stars, hide your fires;
> Let not light see my black and deep desires.

Thus the association of night and murder, latent in the spectators' minds in any case, is made active well before the beginning of the night of the murder. When the master of the castle joins his wife, time and place of the following sixth scene are defined by his remark: "Duncan comes here to-night."

Thus nobody can miss the meaning of the entry of King Duncan and his retinue. The Folio stage direction mentions *Hoboyes, and Torches* at the beginning of this scene. Dover Wilson rejects the torches as a scribal error, since they seem inappropriate in what he calls, with Bradley, one of the few sunlit scenes of the play.[8] The term "sunlit" is perhaps used here somewhat metaphorically as there is no clear allusion to sunshine in Shakespeare's lines, which also, rather astonishingly, avoid to create the impression that it is evening. This may result from the fact that the famous description of the castle must not mirror anything else except the inner condition of Duncan and Banquo, enjoying the prospect of peace after the happy conclusion of a dangerous campaign, of a joyful feast among friends and an undisturbed night. There is no hint of coming disaster and death in these lines; they seem an unruffled sheet of water, reflecting a peaceful landscape and the sky, on the brink of a wild torrent of destruction. It is just conceivable that Shakespeare avoided the allusions to the evening, which we expect here, because the imagery of evening was too closely linked in his mind with ideas of the end of things, with the images of autumn, age and death, to permit him to strike the evening note without adding a touch of melancholy or even foreboding. On this supposition the scene shows how completely the creation of the outward atmosphere in *Macbeth* is governed by the necessities of the inner drama, in the case before us by the dramatic rhythm, demanding a moment of ab-

[8] *op. cit.*, 110.

solute rest and relaxation before the furies rush in. With or without Shakespeare's approval the book-keeper or some other theatrical authority may have added the missing evening touch by making some of the attendants carry torches. We cannot omit the well-known passage, in which the magic of language changed the solid structure of the stage-wall at the Globe into a very accurate and detailed imaginative picture.

DUNCAN: This castle hath a pleasant seat; the air
               Nimbly and sweetly recommends itself
               Unto our gentle senses.

BANQUO: This guest of summer,
               The temple-haunting martlet, does approve
               By his lov'd mansionry that the heaven's breath
               Smells wooingly here; no jutty, frieze,
               Buttress, nor coign of vantage, but this bird
               Hath made his pendent bed and procreant cradle.
               Where they most breed and haunt, I have observ'd
               The air is delicate.

The next scenes, preceding and following the murder, pass without much definition of localities. In the last scene of Act I the stage direction of the Folio runs: *Ho-boyes, Torches. Enter a Sewer, and diuers Seruants with Dishes and Seruice ouer the Stage.* The butler and the servants with their dishes indicate that the scene is within the castle and that King Duncan and his hosts are at their feast. These impressions are stressed by Lady Macbeth's remark: "He has almost supp'd." Otherwise the scene is neutral as to time and place. Dover Wilson puts an interesting direction at its head, which tries to cover the following three scenes as well:

> *A court in Macbeth's castle, open to the sky, with doors to the rear, one on the left the main gate or south entry, one on the right leading to rooms within, and between them a covered recess running back, beneath a gallery, to a third door, through the which when ajar may be seen a flight of stairs to an upper chamber.*

And he adds in explanation of it: "My locality-direction covers all four scenes, 1.7 to 2.3 (which are continuous), in the context of the Globe playhouse."[9] This procedure would seem to be rather dangerous as it might suggest a solidity of the imaginative functions of the various parts of the stage that they certainly did not possess here or anywhere else in the play, and as it could make us forget that the rapidity and the fascination of the events are such that the author and the spectators have no eyes for the details of their locality. The above-mentioned last scene of Act I takes place within the castle, otherwise it is unlocalized. There is nothing said in it to make us think that we are in the court. In the following scene only (II. i), the short dialogue of Banquo and Fleance creates that impression. Nobody could think of connecting one of the stage doors with the "main gate or south entry", before Lady Macbeth mentions that gate at the end of II. ii.

The place in the castle with which the spectators became best acquainted is one that was never presented to their physical eyes: the bedroom of King Duncan. The scene of the murder is suggested to the imagination as early as I. vii, when the lady says:

> When Duncan is asleep —
> Whereto the rather shall his day's hard journey
> Soundly invite him — his two chamberlains
> Will I with wine and wassail so convince
> That memory, the warder of the brain,
> Shall be a fume, and the receipt of reason
> A limbec only. When in swinish sleep
> Their drenched natures lie as in a death,
> What cannot you and I perform upon
> Th'unguarded Duncan? what not put upon
> His spongy officers, who shall bear the guilt
> Of our great quell?

The locality implied by this situations becomes overwhelmingly real for the imagination in the following scenes, especially for the spectators at the Globe. For them the transition from a locality projected by words on the unchanging stage-structure to an entirely imaginary one was easier and more natural than, for a 19th century spectator, the transition from a realistic setting to an imaginary scene.

[9] *op. cit.,* 112.

Whereas the localities presented in the theatre thus remain fairly indistinct, the atmosphere of night becomes more and more real and charged with horror. We have noticed how some of its shadows fall already on the early parts of the play. The resources of the theatre on which Shakespeare can rely in creating it are modest indeed: mainly a few torch-bearers, notably the one that precedes Banquo and Fleance when they go to their night's rest. Their dialogue suggests that they are in the court of the castle or in one of its galleries, where they are able to observe the sky:

BANQUO: How goes the night, boy?
FLEANCE: The moon is down; I have not heard the clock.
BANQUO: And she goes down at twelve.
FLEANCE: I take't, 'tis later, sir.
BANQUO: Hold, take my sword. There's husbandry in heaven:
            Their candles are all out.

The night is pitch dark; the moon and the stars have all disappeared, and the hour is past midnight. These hints affect us together with Banquo's fatigue, which is accompanied by a strange fear of sleep and dreams. The blacker the night the more stifling becomes the atmosphere of murder enclosing the castle. But the darkness is not dead and neutral; it is alive with the symbols of evil:

                    Now o'er the one half-world
            Nature seems dead, and wicked dreams abuse
            The curtain'd sleep; now witchcraft celebrates
            Pale Hecate's off'rings; and wither'd murder,
            Alarum'd by his sentinel, the wolf,
            Whose howl's his watch, thus with his stealthy pace,
            With Tarquin's ravishing strides, towards his design
            Moves like a ghost.

The tension of the spectators increases steadily during this monologue, Macbeth having sent away a servant at its beginning with the words:

            Go bid thy mistress, when my drink is ready,
            She strike upon the bell. Get thee to bed.

Everybody knows that the bell will be struck for Duncan, not merely for a drink. When the expected sign is sounded, Macbeth goes to his deed:

> I go, and it is done; the bell invites me.
> Hear it not, Duncan, for it is a knell
> That summons thee to heaven or to hell.

We note here that Shakespeare does not only create the impression of the darkness of the night, but that of its stillness as well. The spectator becomes conscious of it while he is waiting for the expected signal as well as when Macbeth speaks of the stealthy pace of murder. In the fearful scene in which he returns from the murder, the reactions of the guilty couple to the stillness of the night and to the very few sounds that break it are of the utmost importance. Through these reactions the strain on their nerves is caught by the audience. Right at the beginning of the scene the lady is disturbed by a night sound:

> Hark! Peace!
> It was the owl that shriek'd, the fatal bellman,
> Which gives the stern'st good-night.

And on the murderer's return they break the sheltering quiet of the night only reluctantly, breathlessly, abruptly:

MACBETH: I have done the deed. Didst thou not hear a noise?
LADY: I heard the owl scream and the crickets cry.
    Did not you speak?
MACBETH: When?
LADY: Now.
MACBETH: As I descended?
LADY: Ay.
MACBETH: Hark!
    Who lies i' th' second chamber?
LADY: Donalbain.

The interaction between the excitement of the two characters and the imagined scenery is as close as possible here. When their and the audience's sensitiveness to sounds has reached the highest pitch, the knocking at the gate is heard:

MACBETH: Whence is that knocking?
    How is't with me, when every noise appals me?

It is the lady who reacts to the second knocking:

> I hear a knocking
> At the south entry;

As well as to the third:

> Hark! more knocking.
> Get on your nightgown, lest occasion call us
> And show us to be watchers.

Macbeth himself says after the fourth knocking:

> Wake Duncan with thy knocking! I would thou
> couldst!

In the following scene of the drunken porter the knocking is repeated another six times. The same simple stage sounds that have impinged first on the proud minds of the lord and the lady, excited by crime, and that have had there the effect of flashes of lightning, are producing now entirely different, ludicrous effects in the humble imagination of the porter, stimulated by alcohol. Thomas de Quincey had excellent reasons for making the knocking at the gate the starting-point of his interpretation of the tragedy.

The treatment of the night sounds in the scenes before us forms a close parallel to that of visual elements in other scenes and therefore belongs among the problems of Shakespeare's word-scenery. The dramatist's concentration on sounds intensifies and particularizes the audience's impression that it is night; the fact that, in the case of the sounds heard by Macbeth before the knocking at the gate, we are not certain whether they have a basis of fact or are entirely fanciful, is among Shakespeare's master-strokes.

I am obliged to break off my investigation of *Macbeth* here and to turn to a short summary of the various types of word-scenery we have encountered, a summary that will be amplified from some other plays. We have noticed the scenes in which word-scenery plays no part at all, scenes dispensing entirely with a place or time definition. They are fairly numerous in Shakespeare's work, and they often contain simple direct action or intellectual discussion. More numerous are the scenes, whose place and time are simply named. The first naming often occurs in a preceding scene, as when Charles tells the audience of the whereabouts of the old duke at the beginning of *As You Like It:*

> They say he is already in the Forest of Arden, and a many
> merry men with him; and there they live like the old
> Robin Hood of England. (I. i. 105—108)

Here, of course, the mention of Robin Hood is a great help for the imagination of the audience. When Rosalind eventually arrives in the forest, she can simply say: "Well, this is the Forest of Arden", and Touchstone confirms the fact: "Ay, now am I in Arden; the more fool I." This primitive way of naming a place, a time, an object, or even an event occurring on the stage was inherited from the mystery plays. The demonstrative "this" is frequently used in it. It throws the audience's imagination entirely on its own resources. In Shakespeare the simple naming is often provisional only, an initial explanation of the properties on the stage perhaps, to be supplemented later by word-scenery. This is true of the Queen's opening remark in the garden scene (III. iv) of *Richard II:*

> What sport shall we devise here in this garden
> To drive away the heavy thought of care?

A remark of this kind applied to the whole of the stage; there are others, giving an imaginary meaning to a certain part of it only. In II. vi of *The Merchant of Venice* Lorenzo states:

> Here dwells my father Jew. Ho! who's within?

This defines the front-stage as a street or square and the stage-door, in front of which Lorenzo is speaking, as the door of Shylock's house. No less frequent is the naming of the objects used by the characters, as e. g. of torches and candles, of table implements and weapons, and even events happening on the stage may be expressly mentioned in order to emphasize them or to facilitate comprehension. In the shipwreck at the beginning of *The Tempest* Gonzalo calls:

> We split, we split! Farewell, my wife and children!
> Farewell, brother! We split, we split, we split!

Direct time indications, referring to the present, past or future, are used in a similar way. They form part of a system of imaginary dramatic time, which, as has often been remarked, moves much faster than actual clock-time. The approach of the night in which

Juliet is going to swallow her sleeping-draught is announced by Lady Capulet in IV. ii of *Romeo and Juliet:*

> We shall be short in our provision;
> 'Tis now near night.

When Juliet sends away the nurse in the following scene, the audience learns that night has come now:

> Ay, those attires are best; but, gentle nurse,
> I pray thee, leave me to myself to-night, . . .

The time of IV. iv is precisely stated by Capulet:

> Come, stir, stir stir! the second cock hath crow'd,
> The curfew bell hath rung, 'tis three o'clock.

The feeling of the early morning hour is evoked by the references to the second cock and the curfew bell. A few moments later the same character exclaims in his eagerness:

> Good faith, 'tis day;
> The county will be here with music straight, . . .

In this way the audience are taken through a whole night in a few minutes, and they are induced to share Juliet's and Capulet's sense of being hard pressed by the fast moving hours.

We turn now to those interesting cases where the dramatist gives much more to his audience than a simple name, where he helps them to visualize a scene, to feel its atmosphere or, even, where he irresistibly forces them into its predominating mood with the help of word-scenery. Here we can observe many different relations between the imagined scenery and the events of the drama. One extreme is the use of a colourful and decorative picture in illustration or as an extension of the outward action of a play. We get an example of simple illustrating word-scenery in Northumberland's answer, in *Richard II* (II. iii), to Bolingbroke's question:

> How far is it, my lord, to Berkeley now?
> NORTHUMBERLAND: Believe me, noble lord,
>   I am a stranger here in Gloucestershire.
>   These high wild hills and rough uneven ways
>   Draws out our miles, and makes them wearisome;

> And yet your fair discourse hath been as sugar,
> Making the hard way sweet and delectable.

This local description is not without its dramatic function, as it offers Northumberland an opportunity for one of his fulsome compliments to Bolingbroke. The most striking examples of large-scale description are the prologues in *Henry V*, where the dramatist employs his technique of word-scenery quite openly and consciously in order to amplify the events on the stage by great historic spectacles. Here he belittles the physical resources of his theatre, and exhorts the audience to be alert and active in imagination so as to rise to the height of his great argument:

> Can this cockpit hold
> The vasty fields of France? Or may we cram
> Within this wooden O the very casques
> That did affright the air at Agincourt?
> O, pardon! since a crooked figure may
> Attest in little place a million;
> And let us, ciphers to this great accompt,
> On your imaginary forces work.
> Suppose within the girdle of these walls
> Are now confin'd two mighty monarchies,
> Whose high upreared and abutting fronts
> The perilous narrow ocean parts asunder.
> Piece out our imperfections with your thoughts:
> Into a thousand parts divide one man,
> And make imaginary puissance;
> Think, when we talk of horses, that you see them
> Printing their proud hoofs i'th'receiving earth;
> For 'tis your thoughts that now must deck our kings,
> Carry them here and there, jumping o'er times,
> Turning th'accomplishment of many years
> Into an hour-glass;

And this is how the Chorus, in his third prologue, evokes an imaginary picture of the king's fleet:

> Suppose that you have seen
> The well-appointed King at Hampton pier
> Embark his royalty; and his brave fleet

With silken streamers the young Phoebus fanning.
Play with your fancies; and in them behold
Upon the hempen tackle ship-boys climbing;
Hear the shrill whistle which doth order give
To sounds confus'd; behold the threaden sails,
Borne with t'invisible and creeping wind,
Draw the huge bottoms through the furrowed sea,
Breasting the lofty surge.

These prologues are invaluable for our purpose. The extensions of the scene they contain do not present static landscapes, but dramatic events with their physical background and their atmosphere. They let the audience into the secret of what the playwright and his actors are doing; they do not try to close the gap between the imaginary pictures and the realities of the stage.

The other extreme, very far indeed from this decorative use of word-scenery, has been before us in the relation between the night and the deed of the protagonist in *Macbeth*. The night and the deed become identified here; we might call the former an emanation, a physical manifestation of the latter. The gap we have mentioned above is forgotten; the audience are not invited to "suppose" something or to "piece out imperfections" with their thoughts; the night is announced to them in Lady Macbeth's fierce apostrophe: "Come, thick night", and later on it overwhelms them together with the horror of the deed.

Equally unique is the relation between King Lear and the thunderstorm on the heath. The fury of the storm is the fury of his passions, which turn the whole creation into their sounding-board. Full of an intense craving for destruction, even self-destruction, the tormented old man glories in the destructive power of the elements. Gloucester, at the end of II. iv, points forward to the storm-scenes, mentioning the two elements that are going to be united in them:

The King is in high rage.
. . .
Alack, the night comes on, and the bleak winds
Do sorely ruffle; for many miles about
There's scarce a bush.

Before the king himself appears on the stage, he is described for us as he tries to out-rage wind and rain: again a careful attuning of the audience's imagination to the spectacle that is to follow.In III. i a Gentleman tells Kent what Lear is doing:

> Contending with the fretful elements;
> Bids the wind blow the earth into the sea,
> Or swell the curled waters 'bove the main,
> That things might change or cease; tears his white hair,
> Which the impetuous blasts, with eyeless rage,
> Catch in their fury, and make nothing of;
> Strives in his little world of man to out-scorn
> The to-and-fro-conflicting wind and rain.

In the king's own storm scenes his changing reactions to the tumult around him express the inmost working of his breaking mind: there is delight in the savage onslaught of the elements, no matter, whether they are experienced as blind annihilating powers, as servile agents of his evil daughters or acclaimed as ministers of justice. Thus the word-scenery is so perfectly harmonized here with the inner life of the play that the possibilities of physical scenery, even if they are supported by our modern lighting technique, seem clumsy and inadequate in comparison. It is in such scenes that the producers of the centuries since Shakespeare have committed their worst outrages.

However, already in Shakespeare's own theatre the problem of coordinating stage-effects and word-scenery must have been a real one in the storm-scenes. A realistic imitation of the storm by a powerful machine would have blotted out the effect of the word-scenery in the original performance as completely as it is reported to have done in many a later production. Shakespeare's chance of making his magnificently tumultuous word-scenery fully effective here should, in my opinion, be sought in the possibility that the raging of the storm, like much of the acting and many of the set pieces, properties and costumes on the Elizabethan stage, was conventionalized and allusive rather than realistic, so that Burbage, in raising his voice in order to express Lear's fury, could success-fully compete with the noises around him. It is certainly not per-missible to use these scenes in justification of a return to the romantic idea that *King Lear* must be viewed as a "dramatic poem" and not as a play-in-performance.

Between the extreme forms we have been considering there are many intermediary ones, in which there is a loose or a close connexion between the word-scenery and the inner life of a scene, but not identification. As an instance I refer to the last act of *The Merchant of Venice*, bringing to a harmonious close a rather problematic comedy. The night and the park, as they appear in the words of Lorenzo and Jessica, are filled with moonlight and the sounds of music and with the happiness of this couple, approaching, after many difficulties, the fulfilment of their love. After the opening words "The moon shines bright", we listen to their tender and playful dialogue with its eight variations of the theme:

> In such a night as this,
> When the sweet wind did gently kiss the trees,
> And they did make no noise — in such a night, ...

The names of Cressida, Thisbe, Dido and Medea call up all the sweet and bitter associations of love. Soon after that music begins to sound:

> How sweet the moonlight sleeps upon this bank!
> Here will we sit and let the sounds of music
> Creep in our ears;

The mood created by the word-scenery and the music, its frequent and powerful ally, is intense, and yet there is a certain distance between the lovers and the park before them. They enjoy it, they indulge in appropriate contemplations, and this is also their attitude to the sounds they hear. Therefore Lorenzo can teach his love so learnedly about the music of the spheres and the wonderful effects of music on all creatures.

In creating moods of this kind Shakespeare does not only use instrumental music in support of his word-scenery, but also songs, in which allusions to the imagined scene are frequent. "Under the greenwood tree" and "What shall he have that killed the deer?" belong to the forest of Arden and Ariel's song "Come unto these yellow sands" to Prospero's island.

A similar connexion between word-scenery and mood is found in numerous descriptions, expanding the imaginary scene beyond the limits of the stage. A striking instance is Oberon's description of Titania's resting-place in *A Midsummer-Night's Dream* (II. i), a play that is naturally rich in passages evoking the mysterious impression of trees, shrubs and flowers in the light of the moon:

> I know a bank where the wild thyme blows,
> Where oxlips and the nodding violet grows,
> Quite over-canopied with luscious woodbine,
> With sweet musk-roses, and with eglantine;
> There sleeps Titania sometime of the night,
> Lull'd in these flowers with dances and delight;

It is doubtful, at least, if lines like these can have their full effect in the open-air performances that are so popular nowadays, as they may be weakened rather than strengthened by the sight of natural plants and trees. In his nature scenery the dramatist instinctively avoids mere static description; it is usually full of life and movement. When Titania (III. i) wants Peaseblossom, Cobweb, Moth and Mustardseed to take care of Bottom after his transformation, she says:

> Be kind and courteous to this gentleman;
> Hop in his walks and gambol in his eyes;
> Feed him with apricocks and dewberries,
> With purple grapes, green figs, and mulberries;
> The honey-bags steal from the humble-bees,
> And for night-tapers crop their waxen thighs, ...

This way of depicting nature was developed by Shakespeare's mythmaking faculty, until Prospero, in the great farewell-speech to his magic art (*The Tempest*, V. i), was able to endow all the natural phenomena on his island with the life of spirits:

> Ye elves of hills, brooks, standing lakes, and groves;
> And ye that on the sands with printless foot
> Do chase the ebbing Neptune, and do fly him
> When he comes back; you demi-puppets that
> By moonshine do the green sour ringlets make,
> Whereof the ewe not bites;

The imaginary island obtains the most intense life here as Prospero does not describe the things of nature directly, but gives a body to their essences, distilled by the popular imagination in the course of the centuries and by Shakespeare's own poetic mind, and presents them in the dance of their ceaseless activity.

Besides such nature descriptions or evocations there are many related passages replete with human drama. We can only allude here to the melancholy account of Ophelia's death and to Enobarbus' description of Cheopatra's voyage on her barge, where every line is aglow with the dangerous fascination of the queen.

A close connexion between word-scenery and mood exists in passages inspired by the "pathetic fallacy". This is part of Orlando's address to the strangers he meets in the forest of Arden (*As You Like It*, II. vii):

> But whate'er you are
> That in this desert inaccessible,
> Under the shade of melancholy boughs,
> Lose and neglect the creeping hours of time;

The speaker's mood is mirrored in "desert inaccessible" and "melancholy boughs"; to some of the other visitors the forest seems hospitable and pleasant. A rather too pointed use of the same device occurs in *Titus Andronicus* (II. iii). The same forest glade that appears lovely to Tamora while she hopes to turn it into the place of an unchaste encounter with Aaron, becomes "a barren detested vale" when she has failed, and begins to slander Bassianus. The artifice is found again, used beautifully and convincingly, in the alba, terminating Romeo's and Juliet's first night of love (III. v). Juliet's desire to prolong the night suggests a pleasing but erroneous interpretation of the bird's song and the streaks of light in the east to her, until she is undeceived by Romeo's reluctant realism.

A different relation between event and word-scenery is present in *Antony and Cleopatra* (IV. xv), where the sight of Antony, prostrate with his deathwound, forces the following passionate outcry from Cleopatra:

> O sun,
> Burn the great sphere thou mov'st in! Darkling stand
> The varying shore o'th' world.

This command to the sun affects the imaginary scene not less strongly than a remark by Ross in *Macbeth* (II. iv):

> By th' clock 'tis day,
> And yet dark night strangles the travelling lamp.

In surveying the examples before us, as well as others that we cannot mention now, we get the impression that Shakespeare, as he advanced in his career as a dramatist, perfected his technique by getting closer to the word-scenery that is identified with the mood and meaning of a scene. He did not drop the simpler and the decorative kinds therefore, but continued to use them in appropriate places. Only unusual scenes required the identification type: scenes, filled with a mood, with emotions or passions of such intensity as could not find expression, unless they were embodied in all the details of the imaginary world surrounding the heroes. Word-scenery of this type corresponds to that kind of inevitable and unique imagery, which, according to Wolfgang Clemen, is characteristic of the playwright's tragic period.[10]

In conclusion, it is well to remember again how conscious Shakespeare was of the shaping and changing power of the imagination, how he experimented with it in all the periods of his creative life, and even used it as a dramatic motif sometimes. There are the passages where he shows how imagination can toy and play with the clouds — a telling symbol of his own relation to the stage in his theatre. In one of his playful and yet not quite harmless encounters with Polonius Hamlet rattles out a number of different imaginative interpretations of one and the same cloud, and Polonius obediently and ridiculously follows his lead. It is a more serious and complicated use of the motif if Antony, overwhelmed by his disasters, speaks of the everchanging clouds, seeing in them his own condition under the influence of Cleopatra (IV. xiv):

> Sometime we see a cloud that's dragonish;
> A vapour sometime like a bear or lion,
> A tower'd citadel, a pendent rock,
> A forked mountain, a blue promontory
> With trees upon't that nod unto the world

[10] See: *The Development of Shakespeare's Imagery*, London 1951.

>   And mock our eyes with air. Thou hast seen these signs;
>   They are black vesper's pageants.

I want to allude at least to that pathetic use of the power of words in *King Lear* (IV. vi), where Gloucester, after the cruel loss of his eyes, tries to commit suicide by a fall from the cliffs of Dover, and where Edgar's description of the fall makes him believe that he has actually jumped and fallen and remained unharmed, whereas in reality his son has only pushed him to the ground. Are we quite wrong if we discover in some of these instances the consciousness of power in one of the lords of the imagination and perhaps a touch of amusement at the thought of the plastic and obedient minds of his audience?

We know from *A Midsummer-Night's Dream* that he saw the humorous side of what he was doing. It is a parody of the playwright's own traffic with word-scenery, when Quince declares (III. i):

>   This green plot shall be our stage, this hawthorn brake
>   our tiring-house;

How often had Shakespeare made his actors say: "This stage shall be a green plot and this tiring-house a hawthorn brake!" Pyramus' strenuous attempts to call down night upon his stage are in the same vein (V. i):

>   *O grim-look'd night! O night with hue so black!*
>   *O night, which ever art when day is not!*
>   *O night! O night, alack, alack, alack, . . .*

But, of course, this scene contains also the conciliatory key-passage:

>   The best in this kind are but shadows; and the worst are
>   no worse, if imagination amend them.

Shakespeare's imagination certainly knew how to amend the resources of his stage. The more mature he grew as an artist the more masterfully did he use the opportunities it offered, did he expand it or change it or unite it intimately with his dramatic conceptions, and the less resistance did it oppose to his sway. His very success in this is the main reason why many readers and critics, to their loss, tend to forget the stage for which he wrote and the performances which crowned his achievement.   (1954)

4. The Transmutation of Source Material

WE TURN now to a subsidiary question: Is there a possibility of giving the study of sources a place in the inquiries we have outlined? Kenneth Muir's greatly needed book on *Shakespeare's Sources* (vol. I 1957), drawing together and correlating hundreds of facts, has effectively stimulated our curiosity concerning the uses of source study. Are the changes undergone by source material in the hands of a playwright significant for those scholars only who want to understand an author's ideas, allusions, characters, and meanings? Most of us are prepared to include plot-arrangement and what we vaguely call "dramatic technique" in the list. This is enough if we agree that, in the case of Elizabethan plays at any rate, "dramatic technique" does not simply mean "way of constructing a drama", but, at the same time, "re-creating a story in terms of theatre". Because the playwright has the play-in-performance before his mind's eye while he is transmuting source material, the comparison of a text with its sources can help the student of a play's theatrical physiognomy.

As an example of this we shall compare the opening scenes of *Antony and Cleopatra* with the corresponding account in Thomas North's version of Plutarch's *Lives*. The relation between the historical account and the play is so close and clear that it forms an unusually good basis for a comparison. Let us call to mind how Plutarch marshals his facts. Before coming to the first encounter of the predestined lovers, he offers a thorough discussion of Antony's character, followed by a striking description of his luxurious and rather wild life at Athens. Then he recounts the exchange of civilities and invitations between him and the queen of Egypt, and draws a glowing picture of Cleopatra's splendour, never more remarkable than during her arrival on her barge and the subsequent festivities and entertainments. He endeavours to explain the overwhelming fascination she had for Antony, mentioning her not quite perfect beauty, her numerous abilities and unrivalled charm. A number of anecdotes illustrate the lavish and extravagant life of the couple at Alexandria: eight wild boars roasted for a single dinner, even Antony's son a reckless spend-thrift, Cleopatra always with Antony, taking part in all his activities, sometimes walking the streets with him at night in a "chamber-maid's array", full of resources in planning entertainments and pranks. One of these, her fooling him by having a salt-fish put upon his hook when he was fishing, is reported in some detail. After this leisurely account Plutarch's story begins to move. Bad news concerning the disasters of his wife and his brother in Italy and the successes of Labienus in Asia rouse Antony. He prepares to fight the Parthians, but is recalled to Italy by Fulvia. Before he can meet her, he hears of her death. His reconciliation with Octavius Caesar, the new political arrangements of the triumvirs, and the new marriage with Octavia are summarized rapidly. Then the conflict and patched-up peace with Sextus Pompejus are given in greater detail.

We shall now observe how this circumstantial account of the growth and nature of the famous love situation, followed by a rapid sketch of Antony's activities after his temporary awakening, is turned into a stage-worthy text by Shakespeare. In this most dynamic of all his plays he has no room for a leisurely exposition. In search for the right beginning he pounces, with his experienced eye, on the point where Plutarch's account begins to move. Antony is in the coils of Cleopatra, but being Antony nevertheless, he is, right from the outset, torn between the two forces whose conflict is the play's leading theme: between Orient and Occident, East and West, Egypt and Rome, Cleopatra and Octavius Caesar, imagination and will-power, the senses and the intellect, to mention only some of its manifestations and significances. There is hardly time, at the beginning of the play, for characterizing the situation before the call of Rome makes itself heard. The opening is made by Philo, who, acting as a kind of prologue or presenter, expresses the Roman view of the situation and, in doing so, confronts Antony's present with his former self. His short speech is replete with theatrical impulses:

> Nay, but this dotage of our Generals
> Ore-flowes the measure:[1] (I. i. 1—2)

---

[1] Quotations are from the facsimile edition of the First Folio prepared by Helge Kökeritz (1955), but the line references are given according to Peter Alexander's edition.

"Nay" implies an angry gesture of revulsion. The third little word "this" presents an interesting problem. As we have pointed out above, demonstratives of this kind, as well as the deictic gestures required by them, are of considerable importance for our purposes. They usually point to parts of the stage, to figures or properties on the stage, or to objects, places or events to be imagined beyond its limits. The "this" before us, however, is of a different, more abstract quality. It points to Antony's condition; it summarizes the entire situation in which the play begins. Its implications are the only initial place-indication for the spectator, and also the only time-indication. The time quality is felt when the "this" sentence is followed by

> those his goodly eyes
> That o're the Files and Musters of the Warre,
> Haue glow'd like plated Mars:

"This" implies the present, "those" the past. They can hardly have been entirely non-gestic. "This" seems to call for a vague, generalizing gesture, probably in the direction where Antony and the queen will presently appear. "Those", on the other hand, would draw Philo's look in another, possibly the opposite, direction, a look beyond the present into the past, accompanied by a gesture of disappointment and loss. The passage on Antony's eyes is remarkable in another respect. It continues:

> Now bend, now turne
> The Office and Deuotion of their view
> Vpon a Tawny Front.

Antony's former and his present self, the proud warrior and the compliant lover, are presented in terms of facial expression. Before the spectator catches a glimpse of the protagonist, he visualizes imaginatively two conflicting expressions on his face, which contain, as it were, everything that is going to happen in the play. Before Demetrius can give any answer, Antony and Cleopatra make their formal entry. Theatrical convention prevents them from hearing and being disturbed by the speaker's devastating remarks about "(The triple Pillar of the world) transform'd Into a Strumpets Foole". His disgusted commentary is accompanied by no less than four invitations to concentrate attention on

the approaching couple, invitations addressed to Demetrius as well
as to the audience:

> Looke where they come.
> Take but good note, and you shall see in him
> . . .
> . . . Behold and see. (I. i. 10–13)

These imperatives were certainly accompanied by appropriate
gestures. It is probable that the conventions permitted fairly unrestrained pointing to the queen and her lover, even when they
were already present on the front-stage; this does not exclude the
possibility, however, that the manner of pointing was influenced
in one way or another by their presence. In any case the fourfold
invitation to look may be compared to the function of the spot-
lights in a modern theatre, which concentrate their rays on the
couple once they have stopped after their entry.

The first exchange of words between Antony and Cleopatra,
devoted to the expression of the immensity of their love, is in
complete contrast to what precedes and what follows it. Four end-
stopped lines, three of them of a very regular metrical structure,
still breathe the rhythm of the formal entry, and invite statuesque
declamation rather than speech-action. For a moment Shakespeare
interrupts the lively flow of the speech-action in order to reveal
one of Antony's basic attitudes directly, before it is broken by the
news from Rome. Only in these four lines and the preceding entry
do we hear and see the couple in that initial situation which is so
carefully and lengthily described by Plutarch. Perhaps it is not
fanciful to discover in their declamatory quality a faint echo of
the historian's epical manner. The fact that the playwright cut
down Plutarch's introduction so drastically does not mean that he
had no use for the many characteristic and picturesque details contained in it. They were either summarized in Philo's biassed
opening speech, resolved into the speech-action of many a following scene or, as we shall see, digested into reports, and inserted
between the speech-action at suitable places. What we have said
concerning the static quality of the four lines on the immensity
of Antony's love requires some qualification. Cleopatra's first
speech:

> If it be Loue indeed, tell me how much.

is the most irregular of the four if we study its metrical silhouette, and it is not far above the normal colloquial level. It is Antony's

> There's beggery in the loue than can be reckon'd

which raises Cleopatra to the pitch of

> Ile set a bourne how farre to be belou'd.

The static seconds, the seconds of declamation, are succeeded by something new and different as soon as the messenger announces:

> Newes (my good Lord) from Rome.

From Antony there comes only a contemptuous "Grates me, the summe": the first two words an exclamation, connected with a movement of revulsion; the second a curt command, accompanied by a new gestic impulse. Before the messenger can answer, he is interrupted by Cleopatra, who is stung at once into a most vehement speech, revealing her temperament, jealousy, possessiveness, wit, and powers of impersonation. This speech abounds in acting impulses. She is seen moving between the messenger and Antony, reflecting Fulvia's supposed anger on her own face, imitating the voice and manner, especially the domineering gestures, of the "scarce-bearded *Caesar*":

> Do this, or this;
> Take in that Kingdome, and Infranchise that:
> Perform't, or else we damne thee.

Thus Cleopatra begins to reveal her dangerous and fascinating self through speech-action, and she continues to do so in the following scenes, where we see her struggling in vain against the Roman thought that has struck Antony and, later on, sending and receiving messages to and from Rome. And in defining herself she gives reality, life, and power to our conception of Egypt, just as, in later scenes, Caesar and Octavia give reality, life, and power to our idea of Rome. But our conception of Egypt is fed and enriched by much else beside the speaking and acting of Cleopatra. There are the scenes of her women and courtiers with their loose talk and manners. And, thirdly, there are the reported events and inset descriptions that offer considerable help to the spectator's imagination. It is remarkable how very little of what appears in speech-action in these early Cleopatra scenes is based on Plutarch. Not one of the lively anecdotes concerning the Alexandrian revels is staged; they are all reserved for occasional reporting.

We shall now study briefly Shakespeare's methods of using those anecdotes. Plutarch's remark that Antony and Cleopatra used to mix with the common people at night is the basis of the following direct proposal:

> No Messenger but thine, and all alone, to night
> Wee'l wander through the streets, and note
> The qualities of people. Come my Queene,
> Last night you did desire it. Speake not to vs. (I. i. 52–55)

The first sentence, an only moderately successful attempt to divert the queen from her jealous doubts, requires the tones and gestures of not entirely convincing encouragement. The second begins with an invitation to the queen to move and leave the disagreeable presence of the messenger without having heard his news, and it ends with a second attempt to overcome the reluctance visible in her behaviour. The final negative imperative is addressed to the messenger, as the departing couple passes by him, and it implies that he tries once more to obtain Antony's permission to speak, expressing his wish by his movements and gestures. The whole passage is thoroughly integrated in the uneasy controversy of the first scene. Through it, the audience, as it were, set foot in Alexandria for the first time. There are streets and people around what has so far remained a neutral place: the place where certain people meet, act, and speak, where the dominating conflicts of the play make themselves felt. The hints that give a certain concreteness to the place of the scene before us are accompanied by corresponding time indications: the words "to night" and "last night" introduce new and concrete time relations, very different from the general and abstract ones implied by the "this" and "those" in Philo's opening speech. A comparison of the two kinds of time indication shows that Shakespeare changes the spectator's perspective in the course of the scene; he begins with a comprehensive, a bird's-eye view of the situation, then he moves closer to his figures and introduces particular place and time relations.

The next use of Plutarch's anecdotes is made in Caesar's speech at the beginning of the first Roman scene of the play (I. iv): a forensic speech, a Roman indictment, which adds vivid details to what we know of the goings-on in Alexandria:

> From Alexandria
> This is the newes: He fishes, drinkes, and wastes
> The Lampes of night in reuell: Is not more manlike
> Then *Cleopatra:* nor the Queene of *Ptolomy*
> More Womanly then he. Hardly gaue audience
> Or vouchsafe to thinke he had Partners. (I. iv. 3—8)

A particular virtue of this enumeration consists in the inclusion, among the vivid new details concerning Antony's life in Alexandria, of a fact the audience have witnessed in I. i: his reluctance to listen to the Roman messenger. Furthermore we hear:

> Let's graunt it is not
> Amisse to tumble on the bed of *Ptolomy*,
> To giue a Kingdome for a Mirth, to sit
> And keepe the turne of Tipling with a Slaue,
> To reele the streets at noone, and stand the Buffet
> With knaues that smels of sweate: ... (I. iv. 16—21)

Like the preceding speech, this rhetorical flashback serves the double purpose of defining Caesar's critical attitude with regard to Antony's behaviour and of amplifying the impressions we have gathered as spectators of the earlier Egyptian scenes. When Caesar has received the bad news of Pompejus' successes he turns away from Lepidus and the messenger, and invokes the absentee Antony directly, painting a striking word-picture of the latter's former self. We recognize it at once as an elaborate development of one of the key motifs in Philo's opening speech:

> *Anthony,*
> Leaue thy lasciuious Vassailes. When thou once
> Was beaten from *Medena,* where thou slew'st
> *Hirsius,* and *Pansa* Consuls, at thy heele
> Did Famine follow, whom thou fought'st against,
> (Though daintily brought vp) with patience more
> Then Sauages could suffer. Thou did'st drinke

The stale of Horses, and the gilded Puddle
Which Beasts would cough at. Thy pallat then did daine
The roughest Berry, on the rudest Hedge.
Yea, like the Stagge, when Snow the Pasture sheets,
The barkes of Trees thou brows'd. . . . (I. iv. 55—66)

This, and the rest of the speech, is the impassioned plea of the
skilled orator, who knows how to sharpen his listeners' sense of
the disastrous change observable in Antony. It is devoid of gestic
and other acting impulses, and demands the traditional delivery of
the orator. We may add here that this mode of delivery is
thoroughly characteristic for Caesar all through the play; it belongs
to his nature in the same way as a violent form of speech-action is
Cleopatra's favourite and typical mode of expression. Antony is
capable of both these modes, and his turning from one of them to
the other expresses the conflict between his Roman and his
Egyptian self. In the speech before us, and in similar rhetorical
passages, the dramatist sometimes moves quite close to North's
diction, without neglecting his opportunities for heightening it.
North's simple words "to drinke puddle water" are developed
into the unforgettably drastic lines about "the stale of horses" and
"the gilded Puddle / Which Beasts would cough at". But we should
note that also a rhetorical passage like Caesar's speech, though
clearly different from the speech-action predominating in the play,
is subtly attuned to the peculiarly dynamic mode of the whole.
This is achieved by imagery conceived in the spirit of dramatic
and theatrical representation. There is an instance of this in our
quotation: "at thy heele / Did Famine follow, whom thou fought'st
against".

Further additions to the spectators' conception of Antony's life
in Egypt are made by Pompey in II. i. He looks at it from a new
point of view, hoping that Cleopatra's beauty and witchcraft will
prolong the general's inactivity indefinitely. Thus the description
of a situation is given a sharp dramatic edge. Some of the most
striking details in Shakespeare's source are used in the conversation
between Enobarbus and Maecenas in the following scene.
Maecenas retails a slightly distorted version of the story about the
eight roasted wild boars, and Enobarbus boastingly vouches for

its truth. He does so in the jocular colloquial tone that is *de rigueur* among the courtiers, and, in the same manner, he says of Cleopatra "she purst vp his heart vpon the Riuer of Sidnis". Then, with an abrupt transition, he changes his tone and manner, and recites the famous description of her arrival on her barge. North's diction is retained once more, but it is again heightened, and made into poetry by an art that has been analysed, and praised for its masterful simplicity, often enough. Where Shakespeare goes his own way, omitting, adding or changing words, introducing new imagery, he again attunes the description to the dynamic quality of the play, cf. the love-sick winds, the oars,

> Which to the tune of Flutes kept stroke, and made
> The water which they beate, to follow faster;
> As amorous of their strokes, (II. ii. 199—201)

the perfume that "hits the sense", the city that "cast her people out". In spite of this tuning the passage preserves the quality of a polished piece of poetic rhetoric, requiring once more a declamatory delivery, radically different from the acting style demanded by the preceding and the following speeches. This should not be interpreted as a stage-weary author's momentary return to his native country of poetry, but as evidence for an accomplished playwright's delight in contrasts, for his awareness of the possibility that the change from speech-action to declamation, and back again, can intensify both these modes of theatrical representation.

Another of Plutarch's Egyptian anecdotes also takes the form of a reminiscence, but it is completely absorbed by the speech-action of a typical Cleopatra scene (II. v.). The amusing fishing incident receives a very peculiar and moving emotional colour because it is recounted when Cleopatra, disconsolate and impatient without Antony, is at a loss how to while away her hours. We follow her rapid and incalculable mind, as it leaps from music to billiards and then to angling; the thought of catching fish stirs up her desire to catch Antony, and at this moment, to cheer her mistress up, Charmian tells the fishing incident.

Is there no example of one of Plutarch's anecdotes being actually staged by Shakespeare? There is a striking one in the scene on Pompey's galley (II. vii), where Menas tempts his master with the proposal to cut the cable and afterwards the throats of the three world-sharers and so to become the earthly Jove. Here Shakespeare's treatment is remarkable by the way he discovers the acting values in Plutarch's lively story, and makes the most of them. His Menas does not simply tell Pompey of his plan. He finds it extremely difficult to approach his master, who is enjoying the conviviality and the drinking, and can hardly be made to listen. The passage abounds in impulses towards movement and gesture, as the following fragment of it will show:

POMP. Go hang sir, hang: tell me of that? Away:
     Do as I bid you. Where's this Cup I call'd for?
MEN. If for the sake of Merit thou wilt heare mee,
     Rise from thy stoole.
POMP. I thinke th'art mad: the matter?
MEN. I haue euer held my cap off to thy Fortunes.
POMP. Thou hast seru'd me with much faith: what's
     else to say? Be iolly Lords. (II. vii. 52—58)

These words are mainly important as pointers to fascinating and somewhat complicated stage events, which count for much more in the performance of the play than the words themselves. We cannot undertake their scenic interpretation here; if we could, we should derive considerable help from the piece of stage property mentioned in "Rise from thy stoole".

We hope that our study of some of the uses made by Shakespeare of Plutarch's historical account has shed some light on his methods as a dramatic and theatrical artist as well as on the ways of his actors and the functions of his stage. If a critic objects that dramatic and theatrical points have not been properly kept apart, our answer must be that, according to our conception of Elizabethan drama, such separation is neither possible nor desirable. But we have found that the comparison between a play and its epical source renders us particularly sensitive to all those features in it that characterize it as a text intended for stage performance. We have observed how a theatrical opening takes the place of a lengthy historical exposition, how the dramatist uses much of Plutarch's introductory material later in the play in order to create, by a variety of methods, a striking conception of his hero's existence in

Egypt and in Rome; we have noted the appearance of direct and of indirect acting impulses in the speeches of many scenes, but also the juxtaposition of speech-action and declamation. The fact that we have not had much to say about the use of word-scenery is thoroughly characteristic of *Antony and Cleopatra*. The play is famous for its many scenes, but Shakespeare hardly ever finds it necessary to give his places any local qualities and atmosphere. This is different in *Julius Caesar*, where the information offered by Plutarch, and amplified from other sources, concerning the atmospheric horrors and strange portents of the night before Caesar's assassination is important for a whole series of scenes, in which the strategy of word-scenery can be beautifully studied. In *Romeo and Juliet*, to mention a play of an entirely different order, Shakespeare's treatment of the local and atmospheric descriptions in Brooke's poem is a new and individual problem again. Our glance at these two plays tempts us to stress once more, by way of conclusion, the necessity of repeating the study of theatrical physiognomy, and of what we can learn about it from the comparison with the sources, in the case of every individual play.

(1959)

II.

Sir William Davenant and Shakespeare's Imagery

I

ALTHOUGH THE FRIENDS of the poetical drama agree that, in adapting some of Shakespeare's plays to the taste of Restoration audiences, Sir William Davenant toned down powerful creations of the highest order to a level of commonplace mediocrity, the study of his versions has proved attractive to Montague Summers, Hazelton Spencer, and several other scholars.[1] Their main interest belonged to the fate of Shakespeare's plays, but they were fully aware of other possibilities of their subject. The change in the ideals of style which makes itself strongly felt after 1660 is among the most significant facts for any student of 17th century literature because it reflects an all-pervading change of spirit. It is visible in many original works of the period, of course, but it does not appear anywhere more strikingly and clearly than in some adaptations of older plays, where an attempt has been made to transpose some given material from the old style to the new. A wealth of illuminating hints concerning the aims of the new age is brought to light in comparing the new versions with the original texts. The scholars we have mentioned made use of many of these hints, when they discussed how the characters, the plots, the structure, and the language of Shakespeare's plays were treated by the younger dramatists. This paper is not going to cover the same ground

[1] Cf. Nicolaus Delius, "Shakespeare's Macbeth und Davenant's Macbeth", *JDGS*, XX, 1885, 69—84; Georg Jllies, *Das Verhältnis von Davenants 'The Law against Lovers' zu Shakespeares 'Measure for Measure' und 'Much Ado about Nothing'*, Diss., Halle 1900; Gustav Weber, *Davenants Macbeth im Verhältnis zu Shakespeares gleichnamiger Tragödie*, Diss., Rostock 1903; J. D. E. Williams, *Sir William Davenant's Relation to Shakespeare*, Liverpool (1905); Montague Summers, *Shakespeare Adaptations*, London 1922; Hazelton Spencer, "D'Avenant's Macbeth and Shakespeare's", *PMLA*, XL, 1925, 619—644; Hazelton Spencer, *Shakespeare Improved*, Cambridge, Mass. 1927.

again; it is given to the study of the fate of Shakespeare's imagery in the hands of one of the Restoration adapters. Although this part of the subject has by no means been totally neglected before now, a new and exclusive approach to it promises good results, especially since we have learned a good deal concerning imagery from a surprising number of careful and voluminous treatises devoted to Shakespeare's use of it in recent years. Whatever may be said against the methods and results of some of these studies, they have clearly shown that the investigation of a poet's imagery, if undertaken by scholars with a light touch and resourceful spirit like George H. W. Rylands, Wilson Knight, Wolfgang Clemen and, often, Caroline Spurgeon, will reveal intimate artistic processes, characteristics of style, of the way of seeing and experiencing the world, that cannot be reached as well by any other method. The question arises, whether an approach that has led to valuable results in the case of one of the masters of poetry is valuable also when we are dealing with a secondary poet like Davenant, who never achieved a pure and clear style of his own, whose vision, as preserved in his imagery, was far from extraordinary. This study is undertaken in the belief that, when we are looking for the characteristics of a period, a poet of Davenant's type is, with all his weaknesses, a better witness than one of the masters, whose glory it is to have outgrown, in their maturity at least, those modes of experience and expression which are most typical of their age.

For various reasons Sir William Davenant appears to be a particularly instructive representative of Restoration taste. A survey of his interesting career reveals a man of quite unusual vitality and resourcefulness, an extrovert, who always tried to take his direction from the currents into which he found himself plunged.[2] He began his dramatic adventures on paths beaten by the Elizabethan and Jacobean masters, being first attracted by the sensational horror drama cultivated by Webster, Fletcher, and Ford. His own horror tragedies — *The Tragedy of Albovine, King of the Lombards* (published in 1629), *The Cruel Brothers* (1630)

[2] Cf. Alfred Harbage, *Sir William Davenant*, Philadelphia 1935; Montague Summers, *The Playhouse of Pepys*, London 1935; Arthur H. Nethercot, *Sir William D'Avenant, Poet Laureate and Playwright-Manager*, Chicago 1938.

and *The Unfortunate Lovers* (1643, acted in 1638) — are above all fair representatives of a certain type of play. The same is true of his tragicomedies, *Love and Honour* (1649, acted in 1634) especially, where he adopts the code of Platonic love, as introduced by Queen Henrietta into the respectfully startled court. The masques, produced in collaboration with Inigo Jones, again show how easily Davenant accepted the conventions of a given mode, how readily he could meet the requirements of the court stage. If we turn to the period after 1660, we find him successfully catering for a new generation of theatre-goers with new ideals and new interests. Though six years older than Thomas Killigrew, the director of the King's Players, he felt much more at home in the new atmosphere, and managed his own company, the Duke's Players, with better success than his rival. His acute sense of the needs of his audience led him to produce his own versions of old plays, whereas Killigrew often revived the old texts unchanged. This difference was not without influence on the public's attitude towards the two theatres. This account, which gives the impression that Davenant was a chameleon, an artistic time-server, does not contain the whole truth. His affinity with the Restoration spirit was more intimate than his relations to pre-commonwealth tendencies had been. This is shown by the fact that he did not merely follow the taste of the new age, but helped to form it. He was no longer forced to run after the modes created by other people, but was among the originators of the heroic drama and the opera, both dear to Restoration audiences. The part played by him in the creation of the new stages of the Restoration was often fully recognized; his dramatic influence, however, was long misunderstood. This was mainly due to the peculiar angle under which his contribution was viewed in Dryden's *Essay of Heroick Playes* (1672). Dryden states explicitly: "For Heroic Plays (. . .), the first light we had of them, on the English theatre, was from the late Sir William D'Avenant."[3] Then he describes Davenant's procedure so as to create the impression that he began a new genre in the "Rebellious Times" merely by following Italian and French examples. This was an incomplete account of what really had

[3] *Essays of John Dryden*, ed. by W. P. Ker, Oxford 1900, I, 149.

happened. The influence of Italian and French examples on the English cavalier writers was certainly particularly strong during the "Rebellious Times", when they were forced to spend many years abroad, but it had been considerable during the preceding decades already. Alfred Harbage discovered it again and again when he studied the Cavalier Drama.[4] The abbreviation of a long process of foreign influence is not the most important shortcoming of Dryden's account of the matter. He failed to mention that native English tendencies also went to the making of the heroic drama, and thus prevented later students from looking for the fore-runners of the *Siege of Rhodes* in the most natural of all places: in Davenant's own earlier works. Recent authors have corrected the mistake. When Allardyce Nicoll opens his chapter on *The Rimed Heroic Tragedy* with the words: "The chief channel through which these streams of influence descended to the Restoration period was undoubtedly D'Avenant,..."[5] he does not think of foreign streams only, but of a very strong Elizabethan one as well.

In order to understand Dryden we have to remember the dif-ference between our own point of view and that of a young critic and poet in the first decade of the Restoration. For him a new age had begun in 1660, an age in which he felt exciting possibilities. The traits by which it differed from what had been before the revolution struck his eyes, whereas the connecting links escaped him. He strongly expressed his faith in that new age of his own in the defence of his epilogue to the *Conquest of Granada* (1670). One of its characteristics, according to him, was a critical attitude towards tradition: "For we live in an age so sceptical, that as it determines little, so it takes nothing from antiquity on trust; and I profess to have no other ambition in this *Essay*, than that poetry may not go backward, when all other arts and sciences are ad-vancing".[6] He then tries to prove the superiority of the modern writers as against the Elizabethan and Jacobean ones by claiming: "*An improvement of our Wit, Language, and Conversation; or, an alteration in them for the better*".[7] We accept the fact that

---

[4] Cf. Alfred Harbage, *Cavalier Drama*, New York 1936.
[5] *A History of Restoration Drama 1660—1700*, Cambridge 1928, 90.
[6] *op. cit.*, I, 163.   [7] *op. cit.*, I, 164.

Dryden's generation felt a new spirit coming after the Restoration, but we no longer consider it as a kind of spontaneous growth, or an importation from abroad. It was, in part, the coming to the surface of tendencies reaching back to the beginning of the century, at least. For this reason, we think it proper to approach even our restricted subject historically. Before discussing Davenant's handling of Shakespeare's poetry, we are going to look into his own use of metaphors and similes in his original dramatic works composed before 1660. Thus we hope to substantiate the view that there was a certain continuity in his various artistic endeavours and to render his attitude towards Shakespeare more intelligible.

II

In reading Davenant's early plays, those intended for popular audiences as well as those hoping to please courtly spectators, we are struck by two contradictory tendencies, which may puzzle a student who has not learned to except such contradictions in the men of this period.[8] First, there is a strong desire for everything that is extreme, even excessive, in character, plot, and language: inhuman super-villains are opposed to equally inhuman super-heroes; in his tragedies the young author strives to add one horrible situation to another. His Albovine may justly be said to out-Tamburlaine Tamburlaine. The result is usually fairly good sensational food for the theatre, but it is appalling by its unreality. By this we not only mean to say that his characters and plots are improbable; it is more important that they are not really related to the author's inner experience. They correspond to a craving for what has never been, and cannot be experienced, for an enormous canvas filled with huge, gesticulating and declaiming figures, for a fascinating façade without anything behind it. The same cannot be said of the horror dramas by Fletcher and Ford, although these

---

[8] Paul Meissner has convincingly delineated the contradictory tendencies in the most important fields of life and art in the 17th century in *Die geistesgeschichtlichen Grundlagen des englischen Literaturbarocks*, München 1934.

authors were no more afraid of the extraordinary and sensational than Davenant. They never for long overstepped the boundaries of their imaginary experience. In Davenant's works this faculty seems to have played a very modest part. This brings us to their second outstanding tendency. Their author satisfied his expansive craving by an inventive and constructive reasoning power. He deliberately invented characters and constructed plots that would produce the tremendous theatrical effects he desired. One-dimensional figures, rather silly plots satisfied him, provided a series of effective situations could be strung together with their help. This is certainly true of his first dramas; in his later works we may observe that his inventive reason ceased to be merely sub-servient to his craving for strong effects; it began to dominate the expansive tendency, to regulate the whole fabric of the drama. *Albovine, The Unfortunate Lovers* and *The Siege of Rhodes* are three steps in this development.

The desire for what is enormous, beyond experience, has moulded the language of King Albovine. His fulminations are never more extraordinary than in the scene where his drunken madness makes him ask his wife Rhodalinda to drink from the famous cup made of her father's skull. His expression of devotion to her he will presently wound so deeply sounds as follows:

> Shall the world bleed, but frown, and thou renew'st
> A chaos.[9]

Thus he calls for drink:

> Fill me a bowl, where I may swim
> And bathe my head, then rise like Phoebus from
> The ocean, shaking my dewy locks.[10]

It is difficult for him to find expressions strong enough to do justice to his sense of importance:

---

[9] Quoted from *The Dramatic Works of Sir William D'Avenant* in 5 vols., Edinburgh and London 1872—74, I, 37. This edition belongs to the series *Dramatists of the Restoration*, edited by James Maidment and W. H. Logan. The abbreviation *ML* will be used for it.
[10] Ibid.

> I am the broom of heaven; when th' world grows foul,
> I'll sweep the nations into th' sea, like dust.[11]

Soon, he cannot help noticing that his wife has turned from him:

> She's lost, my boy; blown from my fist; her wings
> Have gather'd wind, they fly (like those of Time)
> Swiftly forward, but never back return.[12]

What is our impression of the imagery by which Davenant attempts to suggest to us the gigantic movements of Albovine's soul? We comprehend its intention, but, at the same time, it makes us smile because it appears far-fetched. This is a severe judgment on any use of imagery, since it implies that the poet studiously searched for the means of producing a desired effect. It does not occur to us if an image, however unusual and startling, is used with precision. In what sense may the above images be said to lack precision? Certainly not in the sense that the link between image and primary idea cannot be easily understood. An image used with precision is the necessary expression of a state of mind, a feeling, an idea plus its emotional aura.[13] By no other method could the same effect be produced. This can only be achieved by a poet who moves within the sphere of what he is himself able to experience in reality or imagination. A great poet only — that is, a man whose power of experience is intense and whose gift of expression is equal to it — can use strange, enormous imagery with precision. Young William Davenant was nothing of the sort. His choice of images appears more or less accidental; it betrays a conscious straining to get beyond the limits of his real and imaginary experience. It is sometimes clever (shall the world bleed), more often incongruous (the broom of heaven; a bowl where I may swim). In spite of all their studied vehemence his sentences remain cold and declamatory.

We are not going to base a general conclusion on our consideration of a few of raving Albovine's speeches. Gentle, unhappy Valdaura uses the same extravagant imagery when she threatens:

[11] *ML*, I, 38.
[12] *ML*, I, 48.
[13] The word is John Middleton Murry's, who uses it in his excellent essay on "Metaphor", *Countries of the Mind*, Second Series, 1931.

> Sir, the king is cruel. Should you prove so
> To me, I'd soon distill my soul to tears,
> And weep an ocean deep enough to drown
> My sorrows and myself.[14]

Even more extraordinary is a speech by Hermegild:

> What should such white and harmless souls as we
> Do crawling o'er this mountainous earth? Alas,
> We cannot drink, till we intoxicate
> A whale; nor surfeit, till our greasy cheeks
> Do swell like th'udders of a cow.[15]

The same sort of thing may be frequently met with in *The Cruel Brother* and *The Just Italian*. Two specimens must suffice. Foreste, in the first of these plays, says:

> For I would eat your heart, should it contrive
> A way in thought how to cheat my sister
> Of her pure chastity.[16]

Altamont vociferates in the second:

> The news hath taught her boil her heart
> In her own blood. She now weeps vinegar;
> Boasts of revenge, as if the thunder were
> Her own.[17]

Thus, quite frequently, Davenant's chase after the tremendous ends in a humorous catastrophe. Being aware of his possibilities in this respect, he supplemented his involuntarily humorous imagery by quite effective intentional humour. It can be found in the speeches of Grimaldo and his companions in *Albovine:*

> I would not starve; look like a parch'd anatomy
> Sewed in a kid-skin.[18]

> Must they still walk in wealthy furs, whilst men
> Of merit here are cloth'd in cabbage leaves?[19]

[14] *ML*, I, 41.
[15] *ML*, I, 68.
[16] *ML*, I, 120.
[17] *ML*, I, 220.
[18] *ML*, I, 33.   [19] *ML*, I, 50 f.

Davenant found no difficulty in producing crude effects of this type. Do the serious specimens 14—16 bear out our view of his early method? I think so. Again there is all the purely intellectual clarity that can be desired, again there is little of the precision we are looking for. Specimen 14 happily illustrates a tendency which characterizes Davenant's usage in all his periods. The idea "I shall weep a long time" is rendered by the phrase: "I shall distill my soul to tears", an artificial image, which bears the stamp of conscious preciosity, and seems the result of an arbitrary choice made in an intellectual game. A second, more common-place, image follows: "I shall weep an ocean"; it is straightforward, crude, without subtlety. It is further elaborated; the ocean thus formed is going to be deep enough to drown both Valdaura's sorrows and herself. The result of this elaboration, again, is an artificial conceit, an exhibition of cleverness, sounding well enough, to be sure, in the ears of a superficial hearer. But who would pretend that a clearly apprehended grief has found its necessary expression here? Such elaboration, following purely logical lines, is Davenant's besetting sin. With its help he develops his images into large, sometimes heavy, sometimes elegant ornaments, devoid of that poetic power which only strict adherence to experience, absolute precision, can give. His elaborate imagery often sounds like a weak echo of the conceits of the metaphysical school. At the sight of the fatal cup, from which Albovine drinks, Valdaura exclaims:

> Hide me, Paradine! the object doth so
> Penetrate, that when I wink I spy it
> Through my lids.[20]

In *The Just Italian* Altamont receives the first sign of his unruly wife's becoming tame with the words:

> Dost weep? I sooner thought t'have seen the flint
> Supple as spunge; th'obdurate diamond melt
> At the glow-worm's pale eye.[21]

The importance of the ornamental function of the far-fetched second image is particularly clear. The idea of calling a courtier a

[20] *ML*, I, 39.   [21] *ML*, I, 246.

"court earwig" gives rise to the following dialogue:

GRIMOLD: The king's head must now convert to rotten wood.
GONDIBERT: Why, Grimold?
GRIMOLD: That court earwigs may live there, and devour
              His brains. Dost not perceive how they begin
              To creep into his ears?[22]

The possibilities of the simile are exploited to the utmost; consequently it loses the better part of its effectiveness.

The images we have considered so far all belong to a rather violent kind. Davenant knew how to use metaphors and similes in a quieter way, too. Here is a specimen from *The Just Italian:* Altamont confirms his intention of never seeing his wife again:

> Two neighbouring lillies, whom rude winds disperse
> 'Mongst restless dust, may sooner meet upon
> Their stalks again, and kiss each other in
> A second growth, than we our loves renew.[23]

The passage shows Davenant at his best. The simile is carefully worked out, but not over-drawn. The tender, melancholy determination it suggests is on the whole dramatically appropriate. Only a critical reader will be slightly annoyed by a feeling that the dramatist covets mellifluence and colour for their own sakes. Here, and elsewhere, this suspicion is aroused by the liberality with which Davenant scatters epitheta ornantia over his lines. The specimen offers a good opportunity for a tentative definition of the kind of imagery he could handle successfully. A somewhat vague state of mind is represented with sufficient precision by a simile, carefully worked out along logical lines. The result satisfies the demands of our reason; at the same time it touches our other faculties so as to recreate in us the state of mind intended by the poet. This is not to say that we are dealing with poetry of the first order: what we receive is fairly conventional; there is nothing in it of the strangeness and sharpness we find in original representations of newly acquired, personal visions.

[22] *ML*, I, 28.
[23] *ML*, I, 248.

Although we never can trust young Davenant's conscientiousness and artistic tact for long, there is a fair number of successful short metaphors in his pages. When Paradine tells Valdaura to "sweeten (Rhodalinda's) censure of this act, and mediate for the king" (*ML*, I, 39), and when Rhodalinda complains that all her hopes "are widowed by the king" (*ML*, I, 47), the metaphors work satisfactorily. However, they are by no means always original. The above use of "sweeten", for instance, has parallels in Shakespeare.

Finally we may point out that Davenant had a strong predilection for personification, even in this early period. In one of his fits of exasperation Altamont cries:

> Is this the help divinity gave man?
> Snuff the moon! She burns dim. The spheres are now
> Ill tun'd, and aged nature backward reels.[24]

This, uttered in the middle of one of his squabbles with his wife, has a purely ludicrous effect. It is meant seriously, however: an effect of the author's tendency to people an imaginary stage above the real one with huge allegorical shadows going through impressive movements and gestures. Time is a favourite occupant of that transcendental world:

> Old Time hath thrown his feathers from his heels,
> And slowly limps in's motion to prolong
> This triumph:[25]

> No masks! no epithalamion now!
> Call for a bone-setter, for time hath sprain'd
> His feet, and goes awry.[26]

The elaboration in both these specimens goes very far; a grotesque effect is sought and successfully produced in the second.

At this point it will be found useful to open the question, how closely young Davenant's usage resembles that of such masters as Fletcher and Ford. As we have pointed out their tragedies have many features in common with Davenant's attempts. Their language and use of imagery, however, do not exhibit the faults we have enumerated above. Their taste is much more reliable; their

[24] *ML*, I, 216. [25] *ML*, I, 35. [26] *ML*, I, 40.

straining after the exceptional is checked by their sense of the poetically possible; their imaginative work does not show intrusive elaborations by an over-developed reasoning power. A specimen from Beaumont and Fletcher's *Maid's Tragedy* (acted in 1611) is given here for comparison's sake. In the third act Melanthius swears to revenge himself on the lustful king:

> But from his iron den I'll waken Death,
> And hurl him on this King: my honesty
> Shall steel my sword; and on its horrid point
> I'll wear my cause, that shall amaze the eyes
> Of this proud man, and be too glittering
> For him to look on.[27]

The poet moves nimbly from one image to the other; each is just given time and prominence enough to do its work of evocation. It is not elaborated into an ornament, although the author evidently does not despise its ornamental effect. The image and its spiritual equivalent are both controlled and adequate, though by no means of the precision of very great verse.

The following passage is from Ford's *'Tis Pity She's a Whore* (published in 1633), a play of horror and unnatural love, which certainly helped to form Davenant's taste. Tormented by pangs of conscience, Annabella, at the beginning of the fifth act, salutes the friar who has often admonished her:

> That man, that blessèd friar,
> Who join'd in ceremonial knot my hand
> To him whose wife I now am, told me oft
> I trod the path of death, and show'd me how.
> But they who sleep in lethargies of lust
> Hug their confusion, making Heaven unjust;
> And so did I.[28]

This speech has more immediacy and power than that from the *Maid's Tragedy*, not to speak of Davenant's attempts. Ford uses

---

[27] *The Mermaid Series: Beaumont and Fletcher*, ed. by J. St. Loe Strachey, I, 53.

[28] *The Works of John Ford*, ed. by Alexander Dyce, London 1869, I, 189.

imagery sparingly, despising concessions to the mere desire for writing beautifully. He has a forceful style of his own, and need not search for extraordinary images. Here, he first uses a very unpretentious one: "the ceremonial knot"; then a traditional Christian one: "to tread the path of death". They belong to the comparatively quiet part of the speech, and are perfectly adapted to its tone and natural flow. Then, there is a sudden tension, where two of Ford's own mighty metaphors occur: "those who sleep in lethargies of lust hug their confusion". This mixing of the spiritual and the physical, this neglect of the intellectual link between image and original idea, this relying on the aura of the image rather than on its optical or notional value, reminds us of Shakespeare's ripe style and of the metaphysical school. It is a thing Davenant could neither do, nor fully understand. Ford's masterly handling of it is a useful indication as to the tradition to which he belonged. Davenant's different method appears, in the light of what is to follow, to be more than the result of personal failings. It may be considered that of an as yet weak forerunner of a new tradition.

As we should expect, the study of the language of *Love and Honour* does not reveal anything that is really new. The old traits are all there again, though their relative importance has somewhat changed. The tone of the whole work is slightly more subdued; the glaring type of image is less frequently met with, although it is still present. Often the measured and stately movements of Davenant's patiently suffering heroes require the accompaniment of dignified language. The noble lovers in the play have both styles at their command. Facing the wall that prevents them from rescuing their beloved Evandra from imminent death, they shout:

LEONELL: Would I were in a cannon charg'd, then straight
Shot out to batter it, and be no more.
PROSPERO: Would all the stones might be ordain'd my food
Till I could eat their passage out.[29]

This is the ranting tone we know from *Albovine*. Alvaro, however, the third of the lovers, has other views as to the behaviour befitting a hero under such extraordinary circumstances. He expresses

[29] ML, III, 175.

them in the elevated and ornate style that is characteristic of *Love and Honour* and much of Davenant's later work:

> Let us with fix'd and wat'ry eyes behold
> These ladies suffer, but with silence still,
> Calmly like pinion'd doves; and, when we see
> The fatal stroke is given, swell up our sad
> And injur'd hearts until they break.[30]

The poet luxuriates in a vague emotion of readiness for heroic suffering. He tries to communicate it by a purely external method, presenting a picture of his three heroes at the moment of Evandra's and Melora's death. Numerous adjectives and one all too obvious simile give it its rich colouring. There is no difficulty in understanding all there is to the passage. The words are used with their central, conventional meanings; they follow one another in regular grammatical order, and cannot be said to possess any unusual, new power of suggestion. Davenant aims at the communication of ordinary human emotions, not concentrated, clarified and particularized by his own experience, but generalized, simplified, rendered more overwhelming, and, inevitably, vaguer by an intellectual transposition to a superhuman scale. His faculties do not work together in a spontaneous act of creation: his intellect stands apart, observing his emotions, exaggerating them, trying to prove its agility and resourcefulness. Occasionally this tendency is so marked that the intellectual activity all but smothers the emotion to be communicated. Another speech of Alvaro's may illustrate this point. Again he revels in a description of the sad plight he and Evandra's other lovers will be in after her execution:

> And now let me embrace you both, for we
> Are lovers all; though when the morn must rise
> To see and blush at th'actions of the world,
> Like sad distressed turtles we shall want
> Our mate: then we may sit and mourn beneath
> The willow that o'ershadows every brook;
> There weep, till we are vanisht quite in tears
> T'increase the stream, whose senseless murmurings
> Will be excus'd hereafter in our cause.[31]

[30] *ML*, III, 176.   [31] *ML*, III, 169.

This has a certain charm and finish for all its superficial sentimentality. The personified morning, which rises and blushes at the actions of the world, is good. Then, sad, distressed turtles move across the stage again, as conventional symbols of faithful love as the willow of mourning. In the willow-passage there is the telltale word "every"; it is probably admitted for metrical reasons. Davenant does not notice that it weakens and cools his line by stressing the purely conventional nature of the willow-symbol. No less characteristic is the rendering of the idea of passionate weeping which follows. A fine example of logical and cold elaboration of a conceit: Step one: We shall weep till we are vanished in tears (a hyperbole, interesting, even piquant intellectually, but too logical for an equivalent of true emotion). Step two: Having become tears, we shall increase the stream (a mere piece of cleverness, diluting what emotional power the rest of the passage might have had). The same holds good of step three: "whose senseless murmurings, etc.", an afterthought Davenant was not poet enough to suppress.

The desire for elaborate and ornate renderings of easy feelings ends quite often in mere preciosity:

> One that
> Attends, by your command, these hidden walks,
> In breathless haste just now distill'd
> The poisonous news through my sick ear.[32]

It is not necessary for us to illustrate Davenant's usage in further pre-Commonwealth plays. They all exhibit the characteristics we have observed thus far: the tendency towards the excessive in good and evil, mirrored in plots, characters, and imagery. The imagery is often subservient to a desire for effective ornament at all costs; its elaboration is the work of an agile, resourceful intellect; it corresponds to vague and facile emotions only; it is often involuntarily grotesque and in bad taste. Not infrequently, however, especially in Davenant's minor flights, we encounter imagery that combines logical clearness with emotional effective-

[32] *ML*, III, 166.

ness,[33] proof that it would not do simply to say that he was no poet at all.

Davenant's original Restoration play, *The Siege of Rhodes* (1656–62), so important in the history of the opera and the heroic drama, will now be considered. It is not a very good play, however, for a study of his style. He had to adapt himself to so many new conditions in writing it — the demands of a new stage, of musical composers, of the rhymed couplet — that he had to neglect his plot and his language to a certain extent. The characters are of the same cast as those in *Love and Honour;* the plot and the language are thinner. The imagery is usually simple; the tendency towards elaboration and ornament appears subdued. This is no cause for wonder: the heroic couplet is a difficult form to master, even if passages of free, or Pindaric, verse offer some relief now and then. An occasional attempt at grand imagery shows that the poet's hand had by no means grown steadier at this kind of work since the production of his earlier plays. Mustapha's introduction of Ianthe to Solyman was rightly derided in Buckingham's *Rehearsal* (III, 5):

SOLYMAN: What is it thou wouldst shew, and yet dost shroud?
MUSTAPHA: I bring the morning pictur'd in a cloud.[34]

There are passages full of Davenant's old vehemence: but it is by the sweep of his rhymed lines, not by extraordinary imagery, that he tries to produce his effect. Alphonso, wounded, full of passionate regret for his former jealousy, exclaims:

> Turn to a tempest all my inward strife:
> Let it not last,
> But in a blast
> Spend this infectious vapour, life![35]

[33] See two further examples from *The Unfortunate Lovers.* Galeotto, the criminal father, apostrophizes his virtuous daughter Amaranta, who is trying to thwart his black designs: "thou troublesome delight of holiness" (*ML*, III, 59). A simple, very effective metaphor is in a report by Brusco:

No, some small spy, that watch'd
Which way the current of his discontents
Would run, convey'd it to Court ... (*ML*, III, 29).

[34] *ML*, III, 269.   [35] *ML*, III, 297.

Occasionally much is made of an opportunity for elaboration: a discussion of Alphonso's jealousy by Villerius and the Admiral may serve as an example. The simile jealousy — celestial fire is worked out at great length:

VILLERIUS: Examine jealousy and it will prove
To be the careful tenderness of love.
It can no sooner than celestial fire
Be either quench't, or of it self expire.

ADMIRAL: No signs are seen of embers that remain
For windy passion to provoke.

VILLERIUS: Talk not of signs; celestial fires contain
No matter which appears in smoke.[36]

Though many of Davenant's heroic couplets are clumsy there are some lines that show him mastering the new form with ease. In the following stichomythic dialogue between the Admiral and Villerius the main idea and a simile make an elegant contrast:

ADMIRAL: Where'er she moves she will last innocent.
VILLERIUS: Heaven's spotless lights are not by motion spent.[37]

Superficially, the simile is colourful. A careful inspection, however, shows that it seems to fit better into its place than it actually does. The point of the first line is that Ianthe will remain innocent, even when moving in the sphere of temptation. To say that heaven's lights are not spent by motion, is a rather inadequate rejoinder. The following couplet, too, is smooth and pleasing on the surface, but the difficult metaphorical double antithesis in the second line is hardly convincing:

Crawl to my Sultan, still officious grow!
Ebb with his love, and with his anger flow.[38]

Another outstanding trait of *The Siege of Rhodes* is the important part played by personification in it. It is hardly an exaggeration to say that Love, Hope, Honour, Valour, Jealousy, and so on, are phantom protagonists, acting their own drama in some

[36] *ML*, III, 313.
[37] Ibid.
[38] *ML*, III, 336.

heaven above the human sphere. They belong to a mythology of the reason, and are worthy to play the parts of the Greek gods among mortals that are themselves constructions of the same reason. When Roxolana is afraid that Ianthe, sent from Rhodes to negotiate a peace with Solyman, will become her rival in the sultan's love, she relieves her seething mind in the following tirade:

> Hope thou grow'st weak, and thou hast been too strong.
> Like night thou com'st too soon, and stay'st too long.
> Hence! smiling hope! with growing infants play:
>> If I dismiss thee not, I know
>> Thou of thy self wilt go,
> And canst no longer than my beauty stay.
> I'll open all the doors to let thee out:
> And then call in thy next successor, doubt.
> Come doubt, and bring thy lean companion, care,
> And, when you both are lodg'd, bring in despair.[39]

This method of describing emotion suits Davenant's mind, and takes the place of a more immediate communication. Occasionally, he introduces all too concrete traits into his world of abstractions, producing a rather grotesque discordance, cf. the line: "I'll open all the doors ...". The final speech in the play, spoken by high-minded Solyman, contains, very appropriately, a complete cortège of Davenant's abstract favourites:

> From lover's beds, and thrones of monarchs, fly
> Thou ever waking madness, jealousy.
>> And still, to nature's darling, love
>> (That all the world may happy prove)
> Let giant-virtue be the watchful guard,
> Honour, the cautious guide, and sure reward:
> Honour, adorn'd in such a poet's song
>> As may prescribe to fame
>> With loyal lovers' name
> Shall far be spread, and shall continue long.[40]

All we have said concerning *The Siege of Rhodes* goes to show that the novelties of the play do not really affect Davenant's

[39] *ML*, III, 334.
[40] *ML*, III, 364.

method of using imagery. Some old characteristics appear less, some more pronounced. The attempts at bold, original metaphors and similes, which abound in the early plays, are rarer in his later ones. The ornamental image, the logically elaborated conceit, stately personifications take their place. This meant nothing more than giving up something he could not do well and following a line that was thoroughly in accord with his personal possibilities. Essentially, there was very little development in his usage. This supports our view that he was by no means a chameleon, moving from one style to the other in his desire for success, although he may have tried to be one. He was born with a strongly rationalistic type of mind, which has left its stamp on all his writings. In the first decades of the 17th century this type of mind was comparatively rare in England. Though Davenant tried to adapt himself to his audiences he was only half successful before the Restoration. After that event his own mentality predominated, and, therefore, he found himself one of the great old men, a source of inspiration for much younger authors, an executor of the new age's wishes in his dealings with the greatest plays of the earlier period. By this we do not withdraw the many severe judgments of value we felt obliged to pronounce while observing the details of Davenant's poetry. The fact that his peculiar mind fitted best into the Restoration environment made it possible for him to win a full measure of late success, but it did not make him a better poet than he had been before. We are not to forget this in approaching his treatment of Shakespeare's poetry; its general tendency is, doubtless, characteristic of the new age; many particular changes and questionable improvements, however, are expressions of Davenant's personal preferences and failings.

III

We are going to base the following examination on two of Davenant's Shakespearian versions: *The Law against Lovers* (acted in 1661/2), his rendering of *Measure for Measure*, enriched by scenes from *Much Ado about Nothing*, and his *Macbeth* (acted in 1672/3).

I cannot think of a better introduction to Davenant's treatment of Shakespearian imagery than a close analysis of a passage in *The Law against Lovers*, where the contrast between the two manners appears more clearly than anywhere else. In *Measure for Measure* (Act III, Scene i) Isabella informs her brother of the price Angelo demands of her, if he is to spare Claudio's life. She expects Claudio to prefer death to his sister's dishonour. He, however, hesitates, tormented by the fear of death, and expresses his terrible emotions in the following speech:

> Ay, but to die, and go we know not where;
> To lie in cold obstruction and to rot;
> This sensible warm motion to become
> A kneaded clod; and the delighted spirit
> To bathe in fiery floods, or to reside
> In thrilling region of thick-ribbed ice;
> To be imprison'd in the viewless winds,
> And blown with restless violence round about
> The pendent world; or to be worse than worst
> Of those that lawless and incertain thought
> Imagine howling: 'tis too horrible!
> The weariest and most loathed worldly life
> That age, ache, penury and imprisonment
> Can lay on nature is a paradise
> To what we fear of death.[41]

Davenant had been struck by the force and beauty of this passage before he began his work of reforming *Measure for Measure*. There are two speeches by Alvaro in *Love and Honour* which unmistakably echo it. Before investigating Davenant's literal translation into his own idiom, it is interesting to observe how he worked under the indirect spell of Shakespeare's voice. It cannot be said that his passages on death are as appropriate to the dramatic situation as Shakespeare's is. Alvaro has decided to become the victim of his father's anger in order to save Evandra. Before he executes his plan he takes his last farewell of her. He makes no

---

[41] *The Arden Shakespeare: Measure for Measure*, ed. by H. C. Hart (= *MM*), III. i. 117—131.

direct answer to her anxious question where he intends to go, but lets her guess it by talking of death in a round-about way:

EVANDRA: Ha! whither do you go?
ALVARO: Where shadows vanish, when the world's eye winks,
             Behind a cloud, and they are seen no more.
             The place of absence where we meet, by all
             The guess of learned thought, we know not whom,
             Only a prompt delight we have in faith
             Gives us the easy comfort of a hope
             That our necessity must rather praise
             Than fear as false.

As she has not yet grasped his meaning he continues:

             That you mayst live here safe, till Prospero
             Restore thee unto liberty and light
             I must to darkness go, hover in clouds,
             Or in remote untroubled air, silent
             As thoughts, or what is uncreated yet.
             Or I must rest in some cold shade, where is
             No flow'ry spring nor everlasting growth
             To ravish us with scent, and shew, as our
             Philosophy hath dreamt, and rather seems
             To wish than understand.[42]

It would be very inconsiderate of him to brag of his intended sacrifice in this manner if there were any reality in this scene, these figures and their emotions. Since there is none, Davenant could use this opportunity for a superficial imitation of a striking Shakespearian passage as well as any other. Some of his lines remind us of the emotion communicated by Claudio's speech. The author was evidently pleased by this effect, and did not care whether it fitted in here, or not; again a sign of his utter lack of poetic precision. Where the passage does not echo Shakespeare, it has no power over our emotions; it is a kind of riddle, clever and elegant talk about a mystery whose importance for a man facing death is known only, not felt.

That Davenant was impressed by Claudio's speech is shown

[42] *ML*, III, 145 f.

also by his version in *The Law against Lovers*. Usually he abridged passages where Shakespeare interrupts the action of a play in order to communicate his heroes' emotions in long speeches. In the case before us, the fifteen lines of Shakespeare's text are preserved in the new version, but only two of them are admitted unchanged. This is what Davenant's Claudio says:

> Oh sister, 'tis to go we knew not whither.
> We lie in silent darkness, and we rot;
> Where long our motion is not stopt; for though
> In graves none walk upright, proudly to face
> The stars, yet there we move again, when our
> Corruption makes those worms in whom we crawl.
> Perhaps the spirit, which is future life,
> Dwells salamander-like, unharm'd in fire:
> Or else with wand'ring winds is blown about
> The world. But if condemn'd like those
> Whom our incertain thought imagines howling;
> Then the most loath'd and the most weary life
> Which age, or ache, want, or imprisonment
> Can lay on nature, is a paradise
> To what we fear of death.[43]

Davenant changes "to lie in cold obstruction" into "we lie in silent darkness". Shakespeare's metaphor is one of those that cannot be fully apprehended by being visualized, or submitted to rational analysis. The important thing is the emotional aura of the words "cold" and "obstruction" as here combined. This type of metaphor is frequent in Shakespeare's mature works. It is not the result of a conscious choice, of a rational construction with a purpose; it is the inevitable symbol through which the poet's experience expressed itself. We have never found this intuitive usage in Davenant's works. He desires metaphors that can be visualized and analysed. His "silent darkness" is smooth, elegant, not without suggestive power, but it does not bear comparison with the original. There is nothing in it of the shuddering back of the instincts from a thought that is repulsive and hard to bear.

Then Shakespeare has the sentence: "This sensible warm

[43] *ML*, V, 160 f.

motion to become a kneaded clod; . . ." An elementary reaction is powerfully expressed: utter disgust at the physical consequences of death. These consequences are more than sufficiently hinted at in the words "a kneaded clod". Davenant was not of this opinion; he found Shakespeare's words too indistinct and allusive, and gave the idea a more explicit expression. It is no exaggeration if we term the result of his operation a catastrophe. Shakespeare's one and a half lines are expanded into four:

> Where long our motion is not stopt; for though
> In graves none walk upright, proudly to face
> The stars, yet there we move again, when our
> Corruption makes those worms in whom we crawl.

This is one of the most deplorable elaborations committed by Davenant's forward intellect. The remark that none walk upright in graves proudly to face the stars, though true enough, is simply foolish; the explicit cleverness of the next lines can hardly be called otherwise than nauseating.

Having hinted at the body's fate after death, Shakespeare's Claudio turns to his fears concerning the future state of the soul. Three colourful and highly metaphorical images express some of the vague apprehensions that torment him. It is the poet's aim here to communicate states of feeling that are not accompanied by any clear intellectual notions in the speaker's mind. He chooses telling imaginative symbols with supreme mastery:

> and the delighted spirit
> To bathe in fiery floods, or to reside
> In thrilling region of thick-ribbed ice;
> To be imprison'd in the viewless winds
> And blown with restless violence round about
> The pendent world;

Metaphysical fears are expressed in sensual images: extreme heat, extreme cold, imprisonment in the storm. G. Wilson Knight has devoted a whole volume to the study of tempest imagery in Shakespeare's work[44], and has shown how it is used to suggest physical and mental distress, discord, evil. When we try to explain, or

---

[44] *The Shakespearian Tempest*, Oxford 1932.

rather to feel, the full force of a tempest image like the one before us, we find that Wilson Knight's studies increase our capacity of responding to the poet's intention. Davenant did not understand Shakespeare's fire, ice, and wind images. He intellectualized the passage:

> Perhaps the spirit, which is future life,
> Dwells salamander-like, unharm'd in fire:
> Or else with wand'ring winds is blown about
> The world.

His Claudio, instead of uttering poignant fears, discusses various possibilities. What loss of directness is caused by the introduction of the little word "perhaps"! How little to the point, how absurd even, is the remark here that the spirit will perhaps live unharmed in fire, like a salamander! Why be afraid of the fire, if it will be unable to harm the spirit? This strange change is explained by the fact that Davenant completely misunderstood Shakespeare's drift in these lines. He gave the word "delighted" in "delighted spirit" its modern meaning (entzückter Geist)[45], whereas Shakespeare evidently used it in the sense of "delightful" (entzückender Geist) as he did in several other passages[46]. His reading of "delighted" compelled Davenant to take the fire, ice, and wind images as symbolizing pleasant expectations of the soul and not terrifying ones, in which case the salamander idea is reasonably appropriate. This supposition explains also why Davenant cut out the ice image — he could not discover any pleasant suggestion in it —, and why he toned down the wind passage until there was little positive, or negative, force left in it.

Shakespeare's Claudio passes from the three natural symbols of his fears to an idea that is derived from the Christian doctrine:

> or to be worse than worst

---

[45] He himself used it with this meaning in the following passage:
> yet I have hope I shall
> Be sensible of all her visits to
> My tomb, and ev'ry flower she strews will there
> Take growth, as on my garden banks, whilst I,
> Delighted spirit, walk and hover 'bout
> Their leaves, comparing still their scent with hers. (*ML,* III, 149)

[46] See *Othello,* I. iii. 290 and *Cymbeline,* V. iv. 102.

Of those that lawless and incertain thought
Imagine howling:

It renders the obsession almost intolerable: 'tis too horrible! The most elementary fear of a living creature shakes him; he ends with a touching and desperate vow of fidelity to life at any price whatsoever. Davenant followed the original pretty closely in the last part of the passage, though his strong tendency to intellectualize Shakespeare's poetry left its mark on it, too. It is true, he was not disturbed here by high-strung images, which he had to explain, or omit; his meddlesome intellect took exception, however, to the simple paratactical construction of the original lines. He introduced conjunctions (But if condemned ... then), logical relations between the sentences, hypotaxis, a method he had also employed in some of the earlier lines (cf. for though ... yet ... when). Loss of immediacy is the main result of this change. A series of emotions finds a truer and more poignant expression in paratactical sentences than in hypotactical ones, since, in this latter kind, a net of logical relations is thrown over the immediate experience that cannot but weaken its emotional appeal. We realize this when we observe how much of the strength of the last four lines in our passage is lost by making them dependent on a conditional clause. Shakespeare's Claudio simply communicates his feelings; Davenant's Claudio discusses various hypotheses, and states what his feelings would be in case one of them should happen to be true. The same tendency of Davenant's mind appears in these syntactical alterations as in his treatment of the older poet's imagery.

From the study of this key passage we turn to a quick survey of some other operations of Davenant's. First, we look at a few specimens, where he attempts to find clear, logical, and grammatical renderings for Shakespeare's audacious abbreviations of phrase and construction.

Our natures do pursue,
Like rats that ravin down their proper bane,
A thirsty evil, and when we drink we die.

Our nature does pursue
An evil thirst, and when we drink we die.[47]

---

[47] *MM*, 1. ii. 129 ff. & *ML*, V, 125.

The plural "Our natures do pursue" is replaced by the singular: even in this slight change Davenant's predilection for abstraction appears. The contemptuous comparison with rats is dispensed with, probably because it seemed inelegant and in bad taste to an author whose view of mankind was much more comfortable than Shakespeare's had been at the time of the composition of *Measure for Measure*. The daring phrase "pursue a thirsty evil" for "pursue an evil greedily, thirstily" is made easier. With all its superficial advantages, however, "an evil thirst" lacks the precision of "thirsty evil", since human nature cannot be said to pursue thirst, a distressing state of lacking something essential to life; it pursues the means for quenching it.

> Augurs, and understood relations, have
> By magot-pies, and choughs, and rooks, brought forth
> The secret'st man of blood.

> Augures, well read in languages of birds,
> By magpies, rooks, and daws, have reveal'd
> The secret murther.[48]

Davenant avoids the close association of the concrete term "augur" with the abstract "understood relations", which is somewhat startling indeed. The homely verb-adverb combination "bring forth" is thrown out in favour of the elegant Romance compound "reveal". An abstract phrase is preferred at the end of the passage. The unusual Germanic superlative "secret'st" is given up.

> He, to give fear to use and liberty,
> Which have for long run by the hideous law,
> As mice by lions, hath pick'd out an act,
> Under whose heavy sense your brother's life
> Falls into forfeit.

> To frighten libertines, who long have scap'd,
> And silently have run by th' sleeping face
> Of hideous law, as mice by lions steal,
> Lord Angelo has hastily awak'd

---

[48] *The Arden Shakespeare: Macbeth*, ed. by Henry Cuningham (= *M*), III. iv. 124 ff. & *ML*, V, 362.

> A dreadful act, under whose heavy sense,
> Your brother's life falls into desperate forfeit.[49]

Shakespeare's personifications of the abstract terms "use and liberty" are avoided; the single concrete term "libertines" is used in their stead[50]. Consequently, a rearrangement of the lines is necessary. It takes the form of an expansion. Davenant's predilection for rather obvious epitheta ornantia makes itself felt. Again one of Shakespeare's verb-adverb combinations is replaced.

Davenant's tendency to normalize Shakespeare's expressions when he thought them too forced and unusual appears in many other ways. He was unable to appreciate the contemptuous preciosity in the following speech:

> That no compunctious visitings of nature
> Shake my fell purpose, . . .

His version is:

> That no relapses into mercy may
> Shake my design, . . .[51]

Again, in this passage, two nonce-words of Shakespeare's are sacrificed:

> but this sore night
> Hath trifled former knowings.

> but this one night
> Has made that knowledge void.[52]

Here, the allusion in the adjective "stern" is made perfectly clear:

> the fatal bellman,
> Which gives the stern'st good-night.

> The fatal bellman that oft bids good night
> To dying men.[53]

---

[49] *MM*, I. iv. 62 ff. & *ML*, V, 130.
[50] For a similar treatment of a personification see *MM*, I. ii. 10 ff. and the parallel passage *ML*, V, 137.
[51] *M*, I. v. 45 f. & *ML*, V, 330.
[52] *M*, II. iv. 3 f. & *ML*, V, 344.
[53] *M*, II. ii. 3 f. & *ML*, V, 337.

Another expansion in the interest of clearness and grammatical correctness will hardly surprise now:

> This guest of summer,
> The temple-haunting martlet, does approve,
> By his lov'd mansionry, that the heaven's breath
> Smells wooingly here: ...

> The guest of summer, and
> The temple haunting martin by his choice
> Of this place for his mansion, seems to tell us
> That here heaven's breath smells pleasantly.[54]

Here, Davenant is normalizing and explaining without the slightest regard to poetic effectiveness. The unfortunate formula "seems to tell" changes a strong and direct rendering of an impression, and of the state of mind that accompanies it, into the glib talk of a courtier, who cleverly develops a hint thrown out by his royal master.

Having sufficiently illustrated Davenant's general tendencies in smoothing and normalizing the Shakespearian text, we concentrate on his reaction to the older poet's images. He very often found them too abundant, or too daring, and then, usually, adopted one of three methods in dealing with them. He either simply cut them out of his text, or he expressed in simpler and more conventional language as much of a Shakespearian metaphor as can be thus expressed, or he put imagery of his own into the place of Shakespeare's. In illustrating these processes we shall try to define the kind of imagery Davenant avoided and the kind he sought.

Before we approach this subject we do well to remember a few fundamental facts concerning the use of imagery. In comparing the methods of our two authors our attention is drawn towards two opposing linguistic forces, which are active wherever and whenever language is used. Professor Charles Bally has ably characterized them in his *Précis de Stylistique*[55], and other scholars, whose ambition it is to fight for the cause of straight thinking, notably the leaders of the Orthological Institute at Cambridge,

---

[54] *M*, I. vi. 3 ff. & *ML*, V, 331.   [55] Genève 1905.

have studied this duplicity of language in recent years[56]. There is a tendency in it towards the logician's ideal of a means of communication and another one away from it, a tendency towards words with clearly defined, hard, immutable meanings and another one towards words that are strong, suggestive stimuli. The first manifests itself most purely in the language of the scientist, which I propose to call sign language, the second in that of the poet, which we may call aesthetic language. The two types of language deal with the same reality, but their users are interested in different aspects of it. The first serves practical purposes; it symbolizes conditions of the outside world in a way that allows man to control them; the second pursues aesthetic aims by stimulating in man the fullest possible realization of the forms and events of the outside world. The sphere of the first type of language is among the objects around us; the sphere of aesthetic language between the individual soul in search of experience and those objects. Words have not the same function in the two types of language, though the difference between the two ways of using them is one of degree, and not of kind. We may say of words in all sorts of uses that they are stimuli. They are not the notions associated with them; they stimulate those notions in all persons conditioned to the use of a particular word in a particular sense. They induce the hearer, or reader, to undertake a quest after a notion. In sign language the quest will come to an end at once: a conventional notion, which frequent use has proved to be sufficient for the practical purpose in question, will be the automatic response to the well-known stimulus. The response will be almost identical in all the members of the speaking community, and this is evidently in the interest of easy communication. In aesthetic language the quest will not come to an end as quickly as that. There occur stimuli that make the response with a conventional notion impossible. They cause a momentary semantic tension, which compels every individual to form the notion meant anew by having recourse to his own earlier experience of the subject written or talked about.

[56] See C. K. Ogden and I. A. Richards, *The Meaning of Meaning,* New York 1923.

Consequently, the responses made by several persons to what we call a strong stimulus will not be identical.

Metaphors are the strong stimuli par excellence. They force a new approach to the intended notion, and a fuller apprehension of it, on the hearer or reader. Many types of metaphors do more than this: they assist the mind in the rebuilding of the intended notion by drawing attention to some particular trait of it, the trait that connects it with the image in the metaphor. They may even attempt the communication of an entirely new experience. We must add that aesthetic language does not merely appeal to the intellectual powers in man, as sign language does, but to the emotions as well. The poet tries to give form to a complete experience, consisting of inseparably intertwined intellectual and emotional elements. He cannot achieve this with words alone that are normally used in sign language, because they do not possess the emotional aura that accompanies fresh metaphorical expressions. This is not to say that these words are necessarily useless for him; many of them are dead, or dormant, metaphors, capable of revival. By skilful handling, by placing them in appropriate contexts, the poet may endow them with a new and surprising emotional and intellectual force. In spite of this, he will never neglect the marvellous possibilities offered him by new metaphorical expressions. He chooses many of the images that he employs in his metaphors not only because they are intellectually related to the experience he tries to express, but because they lend the emotional colour to his words that is required. He may even cause a number of images to follow one another in so quick a succession as to render it impossible for us to grasp the full intellectual import of each of them. Their emotional suggestions blend, and stimulate in us a delightful experience of rare complexity and uniqueness, whereas their intellectual meanings remain hidden in an indistinct twilight.

In many Shakespearian passages we have quoted, and are going to quote, we find imagery of this kind. When he strives to communicate an emotion precisely and completely the poet is often careless of his grammar and of the intellectual link between an image and the corresponding primary idea, mainly because an adequate primary idea does not exist, because what he wishes to express can be reached by his imagery only, and not by means of conventional thought or language. With this, we have touched the sphere where Davenant began to rebel. It would never do, of course, to class his method of expression with what we have called sign language. This would bring us into too close an alliance with Matthew Arnold, who considered the masters of the school of poetry of which Davenant was a forerunner, prose writers.[57] Davenant was looking for a poetic style that was to combine certain virtues of sign language and aesthetic language. It was to have the clearness of sign language; it was to permit easy and immediate communication; at the same time it was to possess power over the emotions, an elevated tone, and an ornamental variety of expression. His opinion concerning imagery seems to have been about that of Dryden, his collaborator in the rewriting of *The Tempest*. Dryden wrote in his *Preface to Troilus and Cressida* (1679): "It is not that I would explode the use of metaphors from passion, for Longinus thinks 'em necessary to raise it: but to use 'em at every word, to say nothing without a metaphor, a simile, an image, or description, is, I doubt, to smell a little too strongly of the buskin."[58] This by no means restricts imagery to purely external purposes; yet it betrays a certain lack of seriousness in treating of the subject. Dryden, and Davenant, believed that deliberate choice played an important part in a poet's use of imagery. As they saw nothing inevitable and necessary in Shakespeare's metaphorical expression, they were ready to interfere with it when it seemed to lack that clearness and reasonableness which they had learned to demand even in the extreme language of passion. Their respect for the boundaries of conventional language, their profound trust that this language, heightened by reasonable imagery, was able to serve all the purposes of a poet, is highly characteristic in an age which developed a new faith in a universe based on the principles of reason. The followers of this faith accepted reason whole-heartedly as the adequate instrument for exploring the universe, and did not believe an experience that could not be formulated reasonably to be worth communicating at all. It is an important advantage of the new poetry which rose under the

[57] See "The Study of Poetry" in *Essays in Criticism*, Second Series, London 1888.
[58] *op. cit.*, I, 224.

influence of this faith, that it was admirably fitted for its social function. By devoting itself to the experience common to all men and women of fine organization, by avoiding those personal intuitions that are not commensurable with reasonable standards, it could make an immediate appeal to all educated readers and work its effect on them. But, in studying Davenant's treatment of Shakespeare's imagery, we cannot help noticing the limitations of the new poetic method rather than its advantages, simply because so many triumphs of expression were destroyed by the adapter's hand. Davenant followed the original text gratefully enough when he was offered

> What oft was thought, but ne'er so well expressed,

but, whenever Shakespeare caught for us glimpses of his own unique way of reacting to life, Davenant was not interested.

We are now going to observe how he used the pruning-hook. Let us see what the following speech of unhappy Claudio became in his text:

> And the new deputy now for the duke,
> Whether it be the fault and glimpse of newness,
> Or whether that the body public be
> A horse whereon the governor doth ride,
> Who, newly in the seat, that it may know
> He can command, lets it straight feel the spur;
> Whether the tyranny be in his place,
> Or in his eminence that fills it up,
> I stagger in: — but this new governor
> Awakes me all the enrolled penalties
> Which have, like unscour'd armour, hung by the wall
> So long that nineteen zodiacs have gone round,
> And none of them been worn; and, for a name,
> Now puts the drowsy and neglected act
> Freshly on me: 'tis surely for a name.

Davenant reduced this rich speech with its two carefully worked out similes to a bare, but straightforward, piece of information:

> And the new deputy
> Awakens all the enroll'd penalties

Which have been nineteen years unread, and makes
Me feel the long neglected punishment,
By such a law, as three days after
Arrest, requires the forfeit of my head.[59]

Davenant's meaning is much easier to grasp than Shakespeare's, but this advantage is gained by heavy sacrifices. Davenant's Claudio does not ponder over the reasons explaining the new governor's severity. The comparison between the governor and a rider on a new horse is omitted as well as the simile that likens the long forgotten laws to unscoured armour. The very suggestive metaphorical use of "drowsy" is unhesitatingly given up.[60]

In the passage where Macbeth expresses, for the first time in the drama, his sense of the moral, and vital, loss he has suffered through his murderous deed, Davenant dropped a most impressive series of metaphors, evidently because it remains puzzling after a purely intellectual analysis:

There's nothing serious in mortality;
All is but toys: renown, and grace, is dead;
The wine of life is drawn, and the mere lees
Is left this vault to brag of.

There's nothing in't worth a good man's care,
All is but toys, renown and grace are dead.[61]

Davenant was not alone to wonder at the colour metaphors in the following speech of Macbeth:

Here lay Duncan,
His silver skin lac'd with his golden blood;
And his gash'd stabs look'd like a breach in nature
For ruin's wasteful entrance.

I saw Duncan
Whose gaping wounds look'd like a breach in nature,
Where ruin enter'd there.[62]

[59] *MM*, I. ii. 158—172 & *ML*, V, 126.
[60] For a similar reduction see *M*, II. iii. 55 ff. & *ML*, V, 341.
[61] *M*, II. iii. 95 ff. & *ML*, V, 342.
[62] *M*, II. iii. 114 ff. & *ML*, V, 343.

Dr. Johnson called them "forced and unnatural", but he suspected that Shakespeare put them into Macbeth's mouth "as a mark of artifice and dissimulation, to show the difference between the studied language of hypocrisy and the natural outcries of sudden passion."[63]

It is hard to say what unhappy idea led Davenant to eliminate the master-stroke in this speech:

> Can such things be,
> And overcome us like a summer's cloud,
> Without our special wonder?

> Can such things be without astonishment?[64]

We next see the adapter shrinking back from a violent concrete image, expressive of spiritual shock. In his youth he revelled himself in expressions of this type. His platitudinizing treatment of the rest of the following lines is one of his major poetic sins:

> What hands are here? Ha! they pluck out mine eyes.
> Will all great Neptune's ocean wash this blood
> Clean from my hand? No, this my hand will rather
> The multitudinous seas incarnadine,
> Making the green one red.

> What hands are here? Can the sea afford
> Water enough to wash away the stains?
> No, they would sooner add a tincture to
> The sea, and turn the green into a red.[65]

In his desire to give full expression to the king's bitter disappointment and nervous exasperation on hearing that Fleance has not been killed together with Banquo, Shakespeare uses two series of images. Their constituting members follow one another closely and quickly; they are gasps wrung from Macbeth's tormented spirit. Davenant, taking exception to this manneristic method of working an effect through accumulation, combs out more than half of Shakespeare's images, and polishes the rest.

[63] *M*, page 60, note.
[64] *M*, III. iv. 110 ff. & *ML*, V, 362.
[65] *M*, II. ii. 58 ff. & *ML*, V, 339.

Then comes my fit again: I had else been perfect;
Whole as the marble, founded as the rock,
As broad and general as the casing air:
But now, I am cabin'd, cribb'd, confin'd, bound in
To saucy doubts and fears.

Then comes my fit again. I had else been perfect,
Firm as a pillar founded on a rock,
As unconfin'd as the free spreading air;
But now I'm check'd with saucy doubts and fears.[66]

We turn to Davenant's attempts to substitute primary ideas, formulated in conventional language, for Shakespeare's metaphors. It is interesting to see how often he relies on the help of words of Romance origin in solving this problem. These words are ideal tools of sign language. Since they are cut off from their own metaphorical origin for the English speaker, they are thoroughly dead metaphors, hard and immutable counters with conventional meanings attached to them. Their elegance recommended them in the following specimens:

Were such things here, as we do speak about,
Or have we eaten on the insane root,
That takes the reason prisoner?

Were such things here, as we discours'd of now?
Or have we tasted some infectious herb
That captivates our reason?[67]

                my dull brain was wrought
With things forgotten.

I was reflecting upon past transactions.[68]

                honours deep and broad, wherewith
Your majesty loads our house.

Obliging honours which
Your Majesty confers upon our house.[69]

---

[66] *M*, III. iv. 21 ff. & *ML*, V, 359.   [67] *M*, I. iii. 83 ff. & *ML*, V, 323.
[68] *M*, I. iii. 149 f. & *ML*, V, 325.   [69] *M*, I. vi. 17 f. & *ML*, V, 332.

> and the surfeited grooms
> Do mock their charge with snores.

> And, whilst the surfeited grooms neglect their charges
> for sleep.[70]

> So weary with disasters, tugg'd with fortune, . . .

> So weary with disasters and so inflicted by fortune.[71]

> With twenty trenched gashes on his head;
> The least a death to nature.

> With twenty gaping wounds about his head,
> The least of which was mortal.[72]

> Thy crown does sear mine eye-balls.

> Thy crown offends my sight.[73]

> What! will the line stretch out till the crack of doom?

> will they succeed
> Each other still till doomsday?[74]

Of course, Romance words were not the only means by which Davenant tried to tone down dynamic Shakespearian metaphors. Germanic phrases served him, too, when he fled from the expressive intensity of the Elizabethan:

> And rather prov'd the sliding of your brother
> A merriment than a vice.

> And so your brother's guiltiness excused,
> As if it rather might be styl'd
> A recreation than a vice.[75]

---

[70] *M*, II. ii. 5 f. & *ML*, V, 337.
[71] *M*, III. i. 111 & *ML*, 352.
[72] *M*, III. iv. 27 f. & *ML*, V, 359.
[73] *M*, IV. i. 113 & *ML*, V, 371.
[74] *M*, IV. i. 117 & *ML*, V, 371.
[75] *MM*, II. iv. 115 f. & *ML*, V, 148.

As we shall make our griefs and clamour roar
Upon his death?

As we shall make our griefs and clamours loud
After his death?[76]

With bare-fac'd power sweep him from my sight, . . .

With open power take him from my sight, . . .[77]

       did he not straight
In pious rage, the two delinquents tear,
That were the slaves of drink and thralls of sleep?

       did he not straight
In pious rage the two delinquents kill
That were the slaves of drunkenness and sleep?[78]

       Yet my heart
Throbs to know one thing: . . .

       Yet my heart
Longs for more knowledge: . . .[79]

       But I have words
That would be howl'd out in the desert air, . . .

       But I have words
That would be utter'd in the desert air, . . .[80]

In the following specimens we see Davenant dealing with more
elaborate metaphors. He is forced to formulate his interpretations
more freely.

       Ignominy in ransom and free pardon
Are of two houses: . . .

[76] *M*, I. vii. 78 f. & *ML*, V, 335.
[77] *M*, III. i. 118 & *ML*, V, 353.
[78] *M*, III. vi. 11 ff. & *ML*, V, 364.
[79] *M*, IV. i. 100 f. & *ML*, V, 370.
[80] *M*, IV. iii. 194 f. & *ML*, V, 380.

Ignoble ransom no proportion bears
To pardon freely given; . . .[81]

For we are soft as our complexions are,
And credulous to false prints.

For we are soft, as our complexions are,
And soon a bad impression take.[82]

         and destroy your sight
With a new Gorgon: . . .

         and behold the sight,
Enough to turn spectators into stone.[83]

And yet dark night strangles the travelling lamp.

And yet dark night does cover all the sky, . . .[84]

Whose execution takes your enemy off,
Grapples you to the heart and love of us,
Who wear our health but sickly in his life,
Which in his death were perfect.

Which, if perform'd, will rid you of your enemy,
And will endear you to the love of us.[85]

Unsafe the while, that we
Must lave our honours in these flattering streams, . . .

In how unsafe a posture are our honours,
That we must have recourse to flattery, . . .[86]

Time, thou anticipat'st my dread exploits:
The flighty purpose never is o'ertook,
Unless the deed go with it. From this moment
The very firstlings of my heart shall be
The firstlings of my hand.

[81] *MM*, II. iv. 111 f. & *ML*, V, 148.   [82] *MM*, II. iv. 129 f. & *ML*, V, 148.
[83] *M*, II. iii. 73 f. & *ML*, V, 341.   [84] *M*, II. iv. 7 & *ML*, V, 344.
[85] *M*, III. i. 104 ff. & *ML*, V, 352.   [86] *M*, III. ii. 32 f. & *ML*, V, 356 f.

Time, thou anticipat'st all my designs;
Our purposes seldom succeed, unless
Our deeds go with them.
My thoughts shall henceforth in action rise, . . .[87]

         Each new morn,
New widows howl, new orphans cry; new sorrows
Strike heaven on the face, that it resounds
As if it felt with Scotland, and yell'd out
Like syllable of dolour.

         Each new day,
New widows mourn, new orphans cry, and still
Changes of sorrow reach attentive heaven.[88]

That of an hour's age doth hiss the speaker;
Each minute teems a new one.

That of an hour's age is out of date,
Each minute brings a new one.[89]

The devil damn thee black, thou cream-fac'd loon!
Where gott'st thou that goose look?

Now friend, what means thy change of countenance.[90]

It remains for us to observe Davenant's procedure when he was
not content to substitute interpretations in conventional language
for Shakespeare's imagery, but worked images of his own into the
text. Again, we begin with a key passage. When Macbeth, in the
fifth act of the tragedy, receives the news of his powerful enemies'
approach, Shakespeare interrupts the action for a moment, and
puts a monologue into the doomed king's mouth, the contents of
which have no immediate connection with the messenger's words.
The shock makes Macbeth confess the general depression, the loss
of vitality, the feelings of isolation and of a wasted life, which
have gained on him since the time of his first crime.

<hr>

[87] *M*, IV. i. 144 ff. & *ML*, V, 372.   [88] *M*, IV. iii. 4 ff. & *ML*, V, 374.
[89] *M*, IV. iii. 175 f. & *ML*, V, 379.   [90] *M*, V. iii. 11 f. & *ML*, V, 384.

> I have liv'd long enough: my way of life
> Is fall'n into the sere, the yellow leaf;
> And that which should accompany old age,
> As honour, love, obedience, troops of friends,
> I must not look to have; but, in their stead,
> Curses, not loud, but deep, mouth-honour, breath,
> Which the poor heart would fain deny, and dare not.

Davenant leaves out a great part of this speech, and changes the rest into a continuous chain of reasoning, adorning it with two similes of his own:

> I am sure to die by none of woman born,
> And yet the English drums beat an alarm
> As fatal to my life as are the croaks
> Of ravens when they flutter about the windows
> Of departing men.
> My hopes are great, and yet methinks I fear;
> My subjects cry out curses on my name,
> Which like a north wind seems to blast my hopes.[91]

Davenant's similes are of the most harmless and reasonable type. They make use of ideas conventionally connected with croaking ravens[92] and the north wind. They are dignified, well adapted to the situation. It is the comparison with the original that annihilates them. What has become of the still and deadly intensity in Shakespeare's lines!

In looking through the following quotations we find many innovations of the same simple and unassuming kind. Davenant is no longer tempted by those audacious flights which we have ob-

---

[91] *M*, V. iii. 22 ff. & *ML*, V, 385.

[92] Shakespeare used this image *M*, I. v. 38 ff. There, Davenant considerably weakened its effect by introducing one of his unhappy conditional clauses:

> The raven himself is hoarse
> That croaks the fatal entrance of Duncan
> Under my battlements.

> There would be music in a raven's voice,
> Which should but croak the entrance of the King
> Under my battlements (*ML*, V, 330).

served in the plays of his youth. His imagery is reasonable; we judge it too reasonable, too obvious, only because we cannot help looking at the original text.

> And liberty plucks justice by the nose;
> The baby beats the nurse, and quite athwart
> Goes all decorum.

>   and froward liberty
> Does Justice strike, as infants beat the nurse.[93]

> In such a one as, you consenting to't,
> Would bark your honour from that trunk you bear,
> And leave you naked.

> 'Tis such as, should you give it your consent,
> Would leave you stript of all the wreaths of war,
> All ornaments my father's valour gain'd,
> And shew you naked to the scornful world.[94]

> This supernatural soliciting
> Cannot be ill; cannot be good: — if ill,
> Why hath it given me earnest of success,
> Commencing in a truth? I am thane of Cawdor:
> If good, why do I yield to that suggestion
> Whose horrid image doth unfix my hair,
> And make my seated heart knock at my ribs,
> Against the use of nature? Present fears
> Are less than horrible imaginings.
> My thought, whose murder yet is but fantastical,
> Shakes so my single state of man, that function
> Is smother'd in surmise, and nothing is,
> But what is not.

> This strange prediction in as strange a manner
> Deliver'd neither can be good or ill;
> If ill, 'twould give no earnest of success,
> Beginning in a truth: I'm Thane of Cawdor;

[93] *MM*, I. iii. 29 ff. & *ML*, V, 128.   [94] *MM*, III. i. 70 ff. & *ML*, V, 159.

If good, why am I then perplext with doubts?
My future bliss causes my present fears.
Fortune, methinks, which rains down honours on me,
Seems to rain blood too: Duncan does appear
Clouded by my increasing glories, but
These are but dreams.[95]

Davenant sacrifices all the immediacy in Shakespeare's representation of the growth of evil plans in Macbeth's mind. He gets rid of
the unusual, but telling, phrase "supernatural soliciting". Where
Shakespeare's hero carefully explores one possibility after the
other (Cannot be ill; cannot be good), Davenant's Macbeth sums
up a result (neither can be good or ill). The terrible outburst after
"If good", expressive of a soul's fright that senses the horrors to
which it is going to condemn itself, must give way to two cool
and detached lines. Evidently, Davenant was pleased with the neat
antithesis of "My future bliss causes my present fears". Fortune, a
traditional personification, is then introduced. The metaphorical
uses of "to rain", which follow, strike us as incongruous; they
represent the type of metaphor that does not permit of visualization or logical analysis. Davenant is not successful, because he
fails to use these metaphors with the appropriate directness and
speed. His "methinks" and "seems" isolate them, and render them
too conspicuous. We cannot accept them as immediate representations of passion. Thus they attract too much, and the wrong kind
of, attention, and are rejected as absurdities. The metaphor
"clouded by my increasing glories", although accompanied by the
chilling formula "appear", is less awkward.

We observe a few more of Davenant's simplifications:

Sleep that knits up the ravell'd sleave of care, ...

Sleep, that locks up the senses from their care; ...[96]

Come, seeling night,
Scarf up the tender eye of pitiful day,
And, with thy bloody and invisible hand,
Cancel, and tear to pieces, that great bond

[95] *M*, I. iii. 130 ff. & *ML*, V, 324.   [96] *M*, II. ii. 36 & *ML*, V, 338.

Which keeps me pale! — Light thickens; and the crow
Makes wing to the rooky wood;
Good things of day begin to droop and drowse,
Whiles night's black agents to their preys do rouse.

Come, dismal night!
Close up the eye of the quick-sighted day
With thy invisible and bloody hand.
The crow makes wing to the thick shady grove,
Good things of day grow dark and overcast,
Whilst night's black agents to their preys make haste.[97]

Davenant's treatment of the first two full lines is partly to be
accounted for by metrical reasons. The metaphor "seeling" is given
up; "to scarf up" is simplified into "to close up". The personification of "day" is retained; however, it is interesting to observe
how Davenant avoids attributing tenderness and pity to the day.
There is, indeed, no intellectual link to support this attribution: it
is an arbitrary expression of Macbeth's state of mind. Davenant
puts in "quick-sighted"; here, of course, the intellectual link is
obvious enough, although, as an expression of Macbeth's passion,
the phrase has little force. Only a poor rest of the following strong
lines is admitted. The introduction of "shady grove" for "rooky
wood" betrays an awakening to the virtues of what was to develop
into the poetic diction of the 18th century[98]. Finally, Shakespeare's
daring personification of "good things of day" is avoided, and,
with it, the verbs "droop and drowse", replete with the power of
suggestion, fall.

Be this the whetstone of your sword: let grief
Convert to anger; blunt not the heart, enrage it.

Let us give edges to our swords; let your tears
Become oil to your kindled rage.[99]

Shakespeare's series of short exhortations displeased Davenant,
probably because metaphors and direct expressions follow so

[97] *M*, III. ii. 47 ff. & *ML*, V, 357.
[98] See also p. 119 "infectious herb", p. 125 "the wreaths of war", p. 126
"future bliss", and p. 128 "eternal homes".
[99] *M*, IV. iii. 229 f. & *ML*, V, 381.

quickly and abruptly one upon the other. He preferred two sustained metaphors. The second of them recalls the style of his youth: it is a clever conceit, too self-conscious to compare favourably with Shakespeare's passionate imagery. Three further examples follow:

> Go, prick thy face, and over-red thy fear,
> Thou lily-liver'd boy. What soldiers, patch?
> Death of thy soul! those linen cheeks of thine
> Are counsellors to fear. What soldiers, whey-face?

> Go, blush away thy paleness, I am sure
> Thy hands are of another colour: thou hast hands
> Of blood but looks of milk.[100]

> To-morrow, and to-morrow, and to-morrow,
> Creeps in this petty pace from day to day,
> To the last syllable of recorded time;
> And all our yesterdays have lighted fools
> The way to dusty death.

> To-morrow, to-morrow, and to-morrow,
> Creeps in a stealing pace from day to day,
> To the last minute of recorded time,
> And all our yesterdays have lighted fools
> To their eternal homes.[101]

> As easy mayst thou the intrenchant air
> With thy keen sword impress as make me bleed: . . .

> Thou may'st as well attempt to wound the air
> As me; . . .[102]

Having studied this list of specimens, we have a clear idea of Davenant's attitude towards imagery. For him its use had to be subservient to his ideals of reasonableness, easy communication, and elegance. He valued it for its ornamental effect, as a means of expressing passion, and as an opportunity for the poet to show his ingenuity. Conditio sine qua non for the admission of an image

[100] *M*, V. iii. 14 ff. & *ML*, V, 384 f.
[101] *M*, V. v. 19 ff. & *ML*, V, 387 f.
[102] *M*, V. vii. 38 f. & *ML*, V, 391.

was the presence of a clear intellectual link between primary idea and image. Davenant excluded, therefore, images introduced for the sake of their emotional aura only, as well as those attempting to express experiences altogether beyond the reach of conventional language: the most personal and greatest things in Shakespeare's poetry.

This result is thoroughly in keeping with our observations on Davenant's methods in his earlier original dramas. His limitations were the same from the beginning to the end of his career; his positive aims underwent changes of minor importance.

At this point we are tempted to open an investigation to decide how far precisely Davenant's method is representative of Restoration poetry as a whole. We cannot load this paper with it, and conclude by expressing the opinion that his implied theory of imagery is that of the school of Dryden and Pope, whose positive achievements are merely adumbrated in his lines.[103]　　　(1942)

---

[103] To support this view three powerful metaphorical passages from Dryden's *All for Love* (acted in 1677) may be placed here. They keep within the limits demanded by Davenant; at the same time they show that a master of the first order could write great poetry even within those limits. In the first scene of the play Serapion recalls the time when Antony still was powerful:

> While Antony stood firm, our Alexandria
> Rivalled proud Rome (dominion's other seat),
> And Fortune striding, like a vast Colossus,
> Could fix an equal foot of empire here.
> 　　　(*The Works of John Dryden*, ed. Sir Walter Scott
> 　　　and G. Saintsbury, Edinburgh 1882—84, V, 345.)

Alexas complains because Cleopatra clings to her love for a ruined man:

> Oh, she dotes,
> She dotes, Serapion, on this vanquished man,
> And winds herself about his mighty ruins; ... (*op. cit.*, V, 346).

Dolabella has the task of informing Cleopatra that Antony intends to leave her without seeing her again. As he loves her himself he pretends that Antony was angry when he sent him:

> He chose the harshest words;
> With fiery eyes, and with contracted brows,
> He coined his face in the severest stamp;
> And fury shook his fabric, like an earthquake;
> He heaved for vent, and burst like bellowing Aetna,
> In sounds scarce human — (*op. cit.*, V, 401 f.).

III.

George Bernard Shaw and Shakespeare's
Cymbeline

BERNARD SHAW's career as a Shakespearian critic has been studied several times in recent years,[1] and was found to be of considerable interest and importance: an unexpected result for all those Shakespearians who, disgusted by the outrageous statements with which Shaw peppered his important ones, had developed the habit of dismissing the whole subject as unworthy of serious consideration. In a lecture delivered before the members of the *Deutsche Shakespeare-Gesellschaft* in the spring of 1957[2] the present writer tried to define the extent and the limits of Shaw's understanding of Shakespeare's art, and came to the conclusion that, in some important respects, he was a precursor of the modern way of interpreting the plays, both in the study and on the stage. This achievement seems all the more remarkable if we remember that the Irish dramatist's own mind and art were akin to 18th century classicism rather than to Shakespeare's manneristic or, in the last plays, baroque style: a fact that is responsible for the most serious blind spots in an otherwise valuable body of criticism. There are other more superficial and more visible blemishes in it, springing from less fundamental causes.

Many of the limitations and some of the virtues of Shaw's approach are strikingly exhibited by his treatment of one particular play of Shakespeare's, which fascinated him in the middle and towards the close of his life: *Cymbeline*. It is the purpose of the present essay to concentrate attention on this test case, though it proves somewhat difficult to analyse correctly and evaluate justly,

[1] Cf. E. J. West, "G. B. S., Music, and Shakespeare's Blank Verse", *Elizabethan Studies and Other Essays in Honor of George F. Reynolds*, Boulder, Col. 1945, 344–356, and "G. B. S. on Shakespearean Production", *SP*, XLV, 1948, 216–35; Henning Krabbe, *Bernard Shaw on Shakespeare and English Shakespearian Acting*, *Acta Jutlandica*, XXVII, *Suppl. B, Humanistisk Serie 41*, Kopenhagen 1955.
[2] Published in vol. XCIV (1958) of the *Shakespeare Jahrbuch*.

because Shaw's first major encounter with the play took place under very peculiar circumstances.

When, in the summer of 1896, Sir Henry Irving was preparing the most famous nineteenth century production of *Cymbeline* and Shaw had a unique opportunity of observing his preparations at close quarters through the medium of his correspondence with Ellen Terry,[3] and while he was pondering over his article on the first performance for the *Saturday Review*,[4] he was in a strange quandary. Both the play and its production attracted and repelled him at one and the same time, and it was impossible for him to discuss them dispassionately, justly, or even consistently. Everything he put into his letters to Ellen Terry and into his article for the *Saturday Review* was written by an aspiring playwright with several axes to grind and, besides, by a middle-aged philanderer, who had half fallen in love with Ellen Terry and did his best, in the course of a curiously romantic letter flirtation, to impress her by his wit, artistic taste, understanding of the theatrical requirements of Shakespeare's play, and by his general helpfulness. The impulses of the aspiring playwright and the aspiring friend of Ellen Terry were frequently at odds with each other. The author of the early plays, from *Widowers' Houses* to *The Devil's Disciple*, was disgusted by his lack of theatrical success, by the fact that Henry Irving and Ellen Terry expended their genius and their resources on mediocre melodramas or on Shakespeare and, especially, by the great success of their policy. Many of the lines in his letters to Ellen Terry and whole paragraphs in his review are the outbursts of a modern artist, no longer so young, half-conscious of his own potential powers, oppressed by the reigning taste for a classic, and trying to make room for his own work. Many of these outbursts make bad reading nowadays by reason of their vulgar noisiness and manifest wrong-headedness. They should not be held

---

[3] Published by Christopher St. John in *Ellen Terry and Bernard Shaw: a Correspondence*, London 1931 (quoted as *Terry-Shaw*).

[4] The first-night of *Cymbeline* was on September 22nd, 1896, and Shaw's review, entitled "Blaming the Bard", appeared on September 26th. It will be quoted from *Our Theatres in the Nineties (Standard Edition of the Works of Bernard Shaw)*, 3 vols, London 1932, where is appears in vol. II, 195—202.

against Shaw, because they are simply the journalistic counterpart of similar, though usually less outrageous, attacks on established art by growing artists trying to create their own style and the taste for it. We should remember here that a genuine dramatist, unlike a lyrical poet or a novelist, cannot possibly evade the problem of finding producers, actors, and an audience with a taste for his art. But, while Shaw was using his journalistic tricks for the best of egotistical reasons to make Ellen Terry, Henry Irving, and everybody else, feel that they had outgrown Shakespeare and were just about mature for Shaw himself, he was in reality ill at ease because, being the artist that he was, he could not but love and revere the creations of Shakespeare, foreign and far away though they were from his own taste and artistic potentialities. For the time being he resolved the painful tensions in his attitude in a rather desparate way by frequently indulging in see-saw judgments according to the most approved classicist pattern. Formerly it had been "natural genius" versus "want of art"; now it was "miracles of expression" versus "intellectual sterility". Once more, we should not, and shall not, pay too much attention to this impossible separation of form from contents, of expression from thought, because it was merely a makeshift of Shaw's during those years of struggle and is at variance with his more considered statements on this fundamental problem of art.[5]

His awareness of the elementary fact that a work of art cannot be judged by its intellectual contents is already implied in the positive sentences, balancing the wild onslaught at the beginning of "Blaming the Bard", Shaw's public statement of his position, which we may consider briefly before examining the letters to Ellen Terry, although the most interesting among them were written before the review. Those sentences run as follows:

"But I am bound to add that I pity the man who cannot enjoy Shakespear. He has outlasted thousands of abler thinkers, and will outlast a thousand more. His gift of telling a story (provided some one else told it to him first); his enormous power over language, as conspicuous in his senseless and silly abuse of it as in his miracles of expression; his humor; his sense of idiosyncratic

[5] Cf. the lecture mentioned in note 2.

character; and his prodigious fund of that vital energy which is, it seems, the true differentiating property behind the faculties, good, bad, or indifferent, of the man of genius, enable him to entertain us so effectively that the imaginary scenes and people he has created become more real to us than our actual life — at least, until our knowledge and grip of actual life begins to deepen and glow beyond the common."[6]

This promising passage is followed, unfortunately, by a paragraph of slapdash character criticism. A number of characters are dismissed as "nothing": Cymbeline himself, the Queen (she is said to be nothing after Lady Macbeth), Posthumus ("most fortunately, as otherwise he would be an unendurably contemptible hound"), Belarius (seems nothing after Kent in *King Lear*). Iachimo is said to be "not much — only a *diabolus ex machina* made plausible; and Pisanio, less than Iachimo". Again this negative list is balanced by a positive one. It is opened by Cloten, "the prince of numbskulls, whose part, indecencies and all, is a literary masterpiece from the first line to the last". He is followed by the two princes ("fine presentments of that impressive and generous myth, the noble savage"), by Caius Lucius ("urbane among the barbarians") and, of course, by Imogen. In speaking of her the critic makes a further, particularly unhappy, use of his see-saw method of approach. He tries to convince his readers that there are, in reality, two Imogens, tied together "with ropes of blank verse (which can fortunately be cut)". One is "a solemn and elaborate example of what, in Shakespear's opinion, a lady ought to be". She is characterized by chronic "virtuous indignation" and by "her fertility and spontaneity in nasty ideas". The other is "the Imogen of Shakespear's genius, an enchanting person of the most delicate sensitiveness, full of sudden transitions from ecstasies of tenderness to transports of childish rage, and reckless of consequences in both, instantly hurt and instantly appeased, and of the highest breeding and courage".

In spite of some good remarks on several of the characters, the paragraph as a whole is disappointing, because Shaw neglects the meaning of the whole play in relation to which the single figures

---

[6] *Our Theatres*, II, 196.

and their arrangement were viewed by the romantic critics and are viewed by the best modern ones, and chooses his place in the eighteenth century tradition. In that position a plea for cutting and re-arranging the play in order to make it fit for production becomes inevitable. We find a plea of this kind in Shaw's analysis of Imogen's character, but it is more solidly grounded than on an evaluation of the intellectual contents and the characters according to standards absolutely foreign to the Elizabethan drama: "The instinctive Imogen, like the real live part of the rest of the play, has to be disentangled from a mass of stuff which, though it might be recited with effect and appropriateness by young amateurs at a performance by the Elizabethan Stage Society, is absolutely un-actable and unutterable in the modern theatre, where a direct illusion of reality is aimed at, and where the repugnance of the best actors to play false passages is practically insuperable. For the purposes of the Lyceum, therefore, Cymbeline had to be cut, and cut liberally."[7] We should not be discouraged here by the con-descending way in which the Elizabethan Stage Society is mentioned. Shaw was in reality a friend and admirer of William Poel's work, as is shown by the following passage: "I welcome the advent of The Elizabethan Stage Society, founded 'to give practical effect to the principle that Shakespear should be accorded the build of stage for which he designed his plays . . .' It is only by such performances that people can be convinced that Shakespear's plays lose more than they gain by modern staging."[8] In "Blaming the Bard", however, Shaw's point of view is definitely that of the "modern" theatre, proud of being able to create "direct illusion of reality", and his conclusion that Shakespeare's texts are recalcitrant against its style, and vice versa, that this modern theatre is no place for Shakespeare is unimpeachable. If it insists on producing the plays, cutting and re-arranging are inevitable. Here we touch the solid core of Shaw's many violent attacks against Shakespearian performances of the Lyceum type: The modern dramatist is crying: This is my own theatre! Open it to my plays, and give Shakespeare another kind of theatre, another type of performance, really adapted to his plays!

[7] *op. cit.*, II, 197.   [8] *op. cit.*, I, 188 f.

The praise of the practice of cutting we have quoted was meant for the paradoxical undertaking Shaw saw in Irving's production. In reality he was a convinced opponent of the practice,[9] at least as long as the cutting was being done by other people. As to himself, he was far too imperialistic a personality to refrain from it; this is proved both by his letters to Ellen Terry and by his version of the last act of Cymbeline.

Having completed his defence of cutting in the *Cymbeline* review of 1896, he at once starts to belabour Henry Irving for the use he made of the privilege so generously accorded him. The loss of the "antiphonal third verse of the famous dirge", of a great part of "the grotesque character tracery of Cloten's lines", "of the Queen's great speech about the natural bravery of our isle" is vehemently complained of. The rest of Shaw's review consists mainly of two careful appraisals of Henry Irving's and Ellen Terry's achievements in the parts of Iachimo and Imogen. Shaw writes admiringly of Irving's ability to create a fascinating character out of almost nothing: "the author's futility is the opportunity for the actor's masterpiece."[10] Passing briefly over the secondary actors, of whom we learn for instance that "Mr Gordon Craig and Mr Webster are desperate failures as the two noble savages. They are as spirited and picturesque as possible; but every pose, every flirt of their elfin locks, proclaims the wild freedom of Bedford Park",[11] he extols Ellen Terry's Imogen, paying his pen-friend the compliment that she "had evidently cut her own part; at all events the odious Mrs Grundyish Imogen had been dissected out of it so skilfully that it went without a single jar".[12]

[9] An intermediary position between the passage before us and the un-ambiguous declaration of war against the cutters to be found in the *Fortnightly Review*, CVI, 1919, 215—218, is held by an article contributed to the *Saturday Review* (February 1905) and reprinted by the London Shakespeare League in 1920 in a pamphlet entitled *The Dying Tongue of Great Elizabeth*. Here he describes how Herbert Beerbohm Tree used the text of *Much Ado about Nothing* as the mere raw material for a fascinating stage creation of his own, and — half-seriously — defends the ingenious actor-manager on the ground that Elizabethan English is rapidly becoming a forgotten tongue for the average theatre-goer: the Shavian way of approaching a very real and serious problem.

[10] *op. cit.*, II, 199.   [11] *op. cit.*, II, 200.   [12] *op. cit.*, II, 201.

The fun of this compliment, both for its author and for its recipient, lay in the fact that there was an element of self-praise in it. It leads us to a consideration of the series of letters exchanged by the actress and the critic during the weeks and days before the first-night of *Cymbeline*. They are half professional, half personal letters. Shaw wrote them because he was no less fascinated by the woman than by the actress, who replied so intelligently and wittily to his heresies about Shakespeare and Sir Henry, to his advice concerning the cutting of the text, and the acting of her part. His respect and his tender feelings for her made him realize — though he was a tactless man by nature and profession — that it would never do to run down the achievements of Shakespeare and Irving too insistently in his letters to an artist who was devoting all her time and energy to the study of Imogen. Therefore the outbursts against the master dramatist are not too frequent, though no opportunity is lost to offer a broad hint on the possibility of giving up the old plays for the sake of first-rate modern ones. Sir Henry receives an occasional thrashing for two somewhat contradictory reasons: because he has undertaken a Shakespearian, instead of a Shavian, production, and because his acting version of *Cymbeline* seems intolerable to Shaw, who cannot hide from Ellen Terry the fact that he is a very well informed student, even a lover of Shakespeare's art. Nor does he wish to hide it from her. He realizes that there is no better way to her esteem than by assisting her in the difficult work she is doing, and the idea that he can influence Sir Henry's production through her is far too extraordinary not to tickle his sense of the incongruous and, to a certain extent, his vanity.

He objects to Sir Henry's stage version because he thinks that the scissors have not been properly handled by the actor-manager. Ellen Terry is told that he has spoilt every part except his own; "and he has actually damaged his own by wantonly cutting off your white and azure eyelids laced with blue of heaven's own tinct".[13] Shaw raises this protest, and makes many of his other remarks, after having studied a playhouse text that is not identical with the printed version[14] of Irving's arrangement. In this version

[13] *Terry-Shaw*, 56.
[14] CYMBELINE. A Comedy in Five Acts by WILLIAM SHAKESPEARE, As

Iachimo's lines to which Shaw alludes are not omitted: perhaps a result of his timely intercession. According to Ellen Terry's statement[15] he seems to have saved, beside a few other good things, the famous simile "as small a drop of pity as a wren's eye", although it is not contained in the printed stage version. The accusation that Irving tried to increase the relative importance of his own part should not be pushed too far. It is certainly not entirely unfounded, but many of Irving's numerous and sometimes very extensive cuts have no other object than to shorten the play by about one fourth of its original length without rendering any part of it incomprehensible. No part was completely spared, but Belarius and his foster sons, Cymbeline, the Queen, Cloten and Lucius were, relatively speaking, deprived of more lines than Iachimo and Imogen. A few scenes were omitted entirely. Posthumus lost the whole of the vision scene, and the last act of the play was stripped of everything not absolutely indispensable. The trick of transposing speeches from one passage or scene to another was occasionally resorted to. On all these counts Shaw's judgment: "Generally speaking, the cutting of the play is stupid to the last extremity"[16] cannot be accepted. If there must be meddling with the text, Irving's solution would appear to be rather a good one, with the exception of its prudery, however. Shaw's strictures on this weakness are indeed well deserved. Irving had to undertake an incredible amount of pruning in order to make every single speech in the play "nice" and clean, and Shakespeare's diction became thin and pale in the process.

Shaw's own quite numerous proposals for cutting are no less dubious than Irving's, as will appear in the following survey of his theatrical advice to Ellen Terry. She is told, at the encouraging beginning of a letter entitled *The Intelligent Actress's Guide to Cymbeline* that the play "can be done delightfully in a village schoolroom, and cant be done at the Lyceum at all, on any terms".[17]

Arranged for the Stage by *Henry Irving* and Presented at the *Lyceum Theatre* on Tuesday, 22nd September, 1896. Printed for Private Use Only, London, Printed at the Chiswick Press, 1896.

[15] *Terry-Shaw*, 58.
[16] *op. cit.*, 56.
[17] *op. cit.*, 46.

In approaching the character of Imogen the critic introduces his theory of her double nature, and his advice consists, of course, in concentrating on the "natural aristocrat"[18] in her and in extirpating everything belonging to the "Bishopess side of the part".[19] It is difficult to take seriously any of the negative results of this attempt at vivisecting a figure that was created whole and entire by Shakespeare. On the other hand, we observe with interest how Shaw tried to develop his own idea of Imogen in Ellen Terry, who evidently found his letters stimulating, especially since she perused them critically, accepting some suggestions and rejecting others. He offers her, and us, a short-cut to his ideas when he states, rather provokingly, that "there are four good lines in the part".[20] The first is:

> how far it is
> To this same blessed Milford,

a passage in which he seems to have appreciated the poignant note of tragic irony produced by the simplest of words. The second is:

> Such a foe! Good heavens!

Again an ironic remark, dear to Shaw because of "its touch of vernacular nature". Thirdly, we find:

> I'll hide my master from the flies,

a line of drastic realism, one of those simple sayings which, no less than the passionate, imaginative, and highly metaphorical speeches, were part of Shakespeare's art in his maturity. Shaw's appreciation of such strokes of racy realism is also apparent in his defence of the "clouted brogues".[21] The last of his favourite lines is:

> Fear not: I'm empty of all things but grief,

called "the only good line of pure rhetoric in Mrs Siddons's style". He likes this line, but he is distressed by its complement:

[18] *Ibidem.*
[19] *op. cit.*, 56.
[20] *op. cit.*, 46 f.
[21] *op. cit.*, 56.

> Thy master is not there, who was, indeed,
> The riches of it.

He says of the first line: "Only, Shakespear, like an ass, spoils that line by adding, in words, all that the delivery of the line itself ought to convey", a piece of criticism that reminds us once more of Shaw's affinity with the classicist taste for simplicity and economy. The same affinity is more fully revealed in his discussion of the whole scene (III. iv) to which our last Shakespearian quotation belongs. One of its main topics is the letter handed by Pisanio to Imogen and read aloud by her. Using much wild rhetoric himself, Shaw tries to dissuade Ellen Terry from following Shakespeare's arrangement: "And oh, my God, dont read the letter. You *cant* read it: no woman could read it out to a servant",[22] a strangely snobbish argument on the part of Shaw, considering that Pisanio is the only friend and ally left to Imogen after her husband's banishment. In spite of the fervour with which he acts the part of the *avantgardiste* in this correspondence and elsewhere, he cannot help occasionally being shocked by Shakespeare, not so very unlike any other middle class Victorian. His opposition against the original arrangement has also a purely theatrical basis. He proposes to have the letter read out by Pisanio earlier in the play (III. ii), so that there should be no need for repeating it in the present scene. This would permit Ellen Terry to act the impact of the letter without reading it aloud. Knowing how well she could perform a task of this kind, Shaw wants to give her a splendid chance, although this proposal is out of harmony with his own important idea that, in Shakespeare, one should not act between the lines, but to the lines and through the lines.[23] His advice was not accepted by the actress, who remained convinced that she could get through the reading of the letter successfully.

The cuts envisaged by Shaw in the following conversation between Pisanio and Imogen are radical indeed, but there is a certain consistency in them. He wants to get rid of everything not directly connected with the events of the scene and the emotions of the characters. Everything of the nature of a commentary, of

[22] *op. cit.*, 47.
[23] Cf. below, p. 142.

generalizing reflection, all the rhetorical heightening and baroque rounding-off of the speeches must go. There is no room for Pisanio's

> No, 'tis slander,
> Whose edge is sharper than the sword, whose tongue
> Outvenoms all the worms of Nile, whose breath
> Rides on the posting winds, and doth belie
> All corners of the world. Kings, queens, and states,
> Maids, matrons, nay, the secrets of the grave
> This viperous slander enters,

nor for Imogen's

> Thou didst accuse him of incontinency;
> Thou then look'dst like a villain: now, methinks,
> Thy favour's good enough. Some jay of Italy
> (Whose mother was her painting) hath betray'd him:
> Poor I am stale, a garment out of fashion,
> And, for I am richer than to hang by th' walls,
> I must be ripp'd: — to pieces with me! — O,
> Men's vows are women's traitors! All good seeming,
> By thy revolt, O husband, shall be thought
> Put on for villainy; not born where't grows,
> But worn a bait for ladies.[24]

Instead of this whole speech Shaw recommends its introductory line only:

> I false? Thy conscience witness:

adding that "everything can be conveyed in these four words". Evidently, the dramatic ideal he has in mind is very different from Shakespeare's. Shaw is on safer ground where he criticizes Irving's arrangement, or rather destruction, of the same speech, the actor-manager having retained no more than the four words "To pieces with me!", cutting them loose from their metaphorical context and thus giving them an incongruous meaning not intended by Shakespeare.

---

[24] *Cymbeline*, ed. by J. M. Nosworthy *(Arden Edition)*, London 1955, 94 ff.

Another key-passage of his advice to Ellen Terry deals with the scene between Imogen and Iachimo in Irving's second, Shakespeare's first act (I. vii). Here he combats the notion that the young woman could be capable of "half affections or half forgivenesses".[25] "It is quite easy for Iachimo to put her out of countenance by telling her that Posthumus has forgotten her; but the instant he makes the mistake of trying to gratify her by abusing him — 'that runagate' — he brings down the avalanche. . . . And Iachimo has nothing to do but praise Posthumus, and lay the butter on thick, and she is instantly as pleased as Punch, and void of all resentment."[26] This is an excellent elucidation of her character. Shaw has quite a number of similarly useful hints to give. His idea of how to perform Imogen's

> O the gods!
> When shall we see again? (I. ii)

and his warning against making Pisanio's "and too much too" (III. ii) a comic aside, do honour to his dramatic and theatrical good sense. What he says on the words last quoted above is among those fine passages in his Shakespearian criticism that help us to forget and forgive many a wrong-headed remark on the great Elizabethan: "It is a perfectly serious, tender, *nurselike* thing to say. Any Irish peasant would say 'and too much too, darlint', quite naturally."[27]

The scene that caused most trouble to Shaw, to Ellen Terry, and to Henry Irving himself, is Imogen's soliloquy in IV. ii, in the course of which she wakes up near the gory and headless trunk of Cloten, and mistakes it for the body of her husband. This is another event that strikes Shaw as brutal and foolish, as he cannot accept it as a gruesome incident in a fairy-tale should be accepted, but tackles it with the ideals of realistic verisimilitude and classicist decorum somewhere in his mind. However, once he buckles down to the task of devising a way of speaking and acting the scene, he has many worthwhile remarks to make. It is in connection with this soliloquy that he offers his one severe criticism of Ellen

[25] *Terry-Shaw*, 54.
[26] *Ibidem.*
[27] *op. cit.*, 55.

Terry's interpretation in a letter written shortly after the successful first-night of *Cymbeline:* "You made one AWFUL mistake.
You actually bawled out the words 'a headless man!' before you
had half seen him. Good heavens! you mustnt do that: it's ridiculous. You must simply start in horror, give the audience time to
see in your face what is the matter, and then say 'a headless man'
in a frozen whisper. If you must make a noise, screech like mad
when you start. Then it will be all right."[28] This exhortation leads
Shaw up to one of the best passages he ever wrote on Shakespearian acting. It reveals an awareness of the characteristic
theatrical physiognomy of a Shakespearian play, an awareness that
was not always his, but which certainly was in his best moments
as a critic: "In playing Shakespear, play *to* the lines, *through* the
lines, *on* the lines, but never between the lines. There simply isnt
time for it. You would not stick five bars rest into a Beethoven
symphony to pick up your drumsticks; and similarly you must not
stop the Shakespear orchestra for business. Nothing short of a
procession or a fight should make anything so extraordinary as a
silence during a Shakespearean performance. All that cave business
wants pulling together: from the line about 'tis some savage hold'
to 'Such a foe! Good Heavens!' You ought to get all the business
of peeping and hesitating and so on packed into the duration of
the speech, spoken without a single interval except a pause after
the call. Otherwise it drags. Mind, I dont propose that you
should omit or slur anything, but only that you should do it with
the utmost economy of time."[29]

In looking over this critical effort as a whole, we conclude that
Shaw's approach to Shakespeare was limited by a number of
doctrinaire opinions, but much more by the nature of his mind and
taste which belonged in the classicist tradition. He was unable to
conceive of the plays as being organic wholes; he had hardly
anything useful to say on their complete meaning and aesthetic
quality, but he was a shrewd interpreter of certain details, details
of speeches, of characters, and of situations. Above all, he had the
born dramatist's flair for the theatrical physiognomy of the plays.

[28] *op. cit.,* 78.
[29] *op. cit.,* 78 f.

He understood the conditions in which they had been created; he saw how the theatrical potentialities of individual lines and situations could become effective on the stage. He knew about the proper speed for the speaking of Shakespeare's verse and about the proper relation between speech and action. All this made him a forerunner of present-day conceptions.

Late in his life, in 1945, Shaw returned to the subject of *Cymbeline*. At that time he did not resist the temptation to compose "A Variation on Shakespear's Ending" when somebody suggested this idea to him. After all we have said about his connection with the classicist tradition, there is nothing surprising in this. His foreword to *Cymbeline Refinished*[30] is a curious document. The improver upon the Elizabethan play justifies himself by saying that "Cymbeline, though one of the finest of Shakespear's later plays now on the stage, goes to pieces in the last act".[31] But he does not leave it at that. He confesses that, when he actually re-read the condemned act after many years, he found his former notion that it was "a cobbled-up *pasticcio* by other hands" an "unpardonable stupidity". He continues: "The act is genuine Shakespear to the last full stop, and late phase Shakespear in point of verbal workmanship."[32] He even accepts the masque as an appropriate device, characteristically judging it from the point of view of theatrical expediency. He does not think of relating it to the meaning of the whole play. What happens in the course of this foreword is almost the contrary of what he has set out to do: Instead of justifying his own version he comes near to justifying Shakespeare's original fifth act. Nevertheless, he has something to say for himself as well. Understandably and amusingly enough, he prefers to compare his own endeavour to "additions made by Mozart to the score of Handel's Messiah", to "trombone parts added by Wagner to Spontini's choruses", and similar highly respectable musical undertakings rather than to the operations performed on Shakespeare's texts by William Davenant, Nahum Tate, Colley Cibber, David Garrick and his other English forerunners. In spite of these high

[30] *Geneva, Cymbeline Refinished, & Good King Charles (Standard Edition of the Works of Bernard Shaw),* London 1946.
[31] *op. cit.,* 133.
[32] *op. cit.,* 134.

aspirations he recommends his version, modestly enough, to such producers only as lack the good sense to present "the original word-for-word as Shakespear left it, and the means to do justice to the masque".[33]

Shaw's version of the fifth act is very short. It contains 89 lines by Shakespeare and a little more than twice that number by himself. The act is an aesthetic impossibility, as there is no connection between it and the all-pervading fairy-tale quality of the play as a whole, the only quality permitting the leisurely unravelling of mysteries which have ceased to be mysteries for the audience before the beginning of the act. Shaw tries to give his act a new interest by making the most important characters react to the expected revelations in an unexpected post-Ibsen manner. Forgetting everything he wrote about the character of Imogen to Ellen Terry in the old days, he turns Shakespeare's heroine into a modern problem woman. She cannot forget and forgive her husband's cruel and impossible behaviour, and leaves the stage with the resigned remark:

> I must go home and make the best of it
> As other women must.[34]

The event of regeneration, the core and centre of Shakespeare's ending, is unknown to Shaw and to his Imogen. His Posthumus behaves like an ass — if we may permit ourselves, for once, Shaw's own way of putting such things — after having discovered that his wife is alive and with him. Instead of repenting and looking with horror at his former self, he offers exasperatingly lame excuses:

> Well, my dearest,
> What could I think? The fellow did describe
> The mole upon your breast.[35]

He even asks Iachimo to pay him ten thousand ducats, since he has lost the wager after all. Having to go on living with a Posthumus of this kind, Shaw's Imogen can hardly be expected to be overjoyed and generous. Another innovation consists in making

---

[33] *op. cit.*, 138.
[34] *op. cit.*, 149.
[35] *op. cit.*, 145.

Guiderius and Arviragus two angry young men, proudly refusing the conventional tasks connected with their new status as the King's sons. These tricks and some others characterize Shaw's version as a *jeu d'esprit*, which we should not judge too severely. We cannot help adding, however, that Shaw's blank verse, which, according to the foreword, came very easily to him, convinces us of his wisdom in having written in this style on very rare occasions only. It is unpretentious, but also flat: verse written by a clever imitator in a worn-out-form. His imagery consists of similes in the conventional manner of the second-rate classicists. The following protestations of Posthumus are a good specimen:

> Sweet, I dare
> Anything, everything. Mountains of mortal guilt
> That crushed me are now lifted from my breast.
> I am in heaven that was but now in hell.[36]

Occasionally, to be quite fair, he hits on a better line, e. g. when he makes Philario (a character quite forgotten in Shakespeare's last act, but benevolently given another chance in Shaw's) speak of

> this witless savage Cymbeline,
> Whose brains were ever in his consort's head.[37]

Nobody will deny that this dramatic exercise of Shaw's old age contains some amusing points, and is an elementary object lesson on the differences between Shakespeare's and his own style. And yet its main virtue consists in its sending us back to the original ending of *Cymbeline* with a sharpened sense for its beauty and vigour and a new appreciation of an art capable of telling the conclusion of a wonderful fairy-tale the way it should be told to children, eager to hear all the details, including the long-expected ones, and of making it, at the same time, a moving expression of faith in the possibility of human regeneration through the intervention of divine grace.   (1957)

---

[36] *op. cit.*, 143.
[37] *op. cit.*, 140. It has also struck J. M. Nosworthy, who quotes it in the introduction to his edition of *Cymbeline*, p. lii.

IV.

Hamlet in Richard Flatter's Translation

I

THE MAIN difficulty in the criticism of a translation lies in the danger of becoming involved in the discussion of particular passages and of thus losing sight of the translator's achievement as a whole. Therefore it seems useful to state at the beginning of this article what its author's impressions were when he saw a performance of a Shakespearian play in Flatter's version for the first time. He found that the actors impersonating the characters in *Measure for Measure* spoke the lines provided for them by the translator with ease and enjoyment; he obtained a sense of freshness and spontaneity in listening to the give-and-take of Flatter's dialogue, coloured by the suspicion that it had to be paid for by a loss of some of the sudden surprises and the strange power of Shakespeare's metaphorical language. But nowhere more clearly than in the translator's necessary and ungrateful trade gains are only to be had at the cost of losses, and the great translator's art consists in making the proportion of gains to losses as reasonable and convincing as possible. It is the purpose of these pages to study that proportion in Flatter's version of *Hamlet*. This has appeared in the series of five volumes of translations[1] — to be completed by a sixth —, which Flatter has devoted to twenty of Shakespeare's plays. The whole series is a massive achievement, deserving our serious consideration, especially since Flatter has begun his work only after an intimate personal experience of the theatre and its requirements and after a careful preparation, in the course of which he has familiarized himself with the findings of Shakespearian scholarship. His relation to this field of knowledge has nothing in common with that superficial contact which can be used by an irresponsible translator in order to hide his arbitrary operations on the texts from the ignorant and the gullible. In fact,

---

[1] *Shakespeare, neu übersetzt*, Walter Krieg Verlag, Wien — Bad Bocklet — Zürich, 1952—1955.

it has led to Flatter's own well-known contributions to the interpretation of the texts in the First Folio and of some individual
plays.[2]

In spite of all this work of preparation Flatter modestly uses a
series of disclaimers in defining the aims of his translation:

> Sie will nicht modern sein, nicht in der Sprache und noch
> weniger in Gesinnung oder Auslegung. ... Sie hält sich auch
> fern von jener Respektlosigkeit, die vermeint, paraphrasieren,
> ändern, hinzufügen zu dürfen; sie will lediglich übersetzen, d. h.
> sie will ausschließlich das, was im Original vorhanden ist, nicht
> mehr und nicht weniger, und das mit möglichster Treue, ins
> Deutsche herübersetzen. Sie will auch keinen Stil haben; sie will
> lediglich den Stil Shakespeares mit all seinen Schwankungen
> und Wandlungen von Zeile zu Zeile nachbilden. Sie will weder
> mildern noch verstärken noch andre Farben auftragen. Ein
> Kopist, der etwa ein Rembrandt-Bild kopiert, hat selbst keinen
> Stil zu haben.[3]

His main positive aim is mentioned at the end of this introduction
only:

> Hier nun, in einen Satz zusammengefaßt, sei die Frage be-
> antwortet, was es denn ist, das die neue Übersetzung als Grund-
> lage ihrer Existenzberechtigung in Anspruch nehmen möchte:
> es ist das Schauspielerische ihrer Diktion, mit der sie die Diktion
> des großen Schauspieler-Dichters zu kopieren bemüht ist.[4]

Flatter's position is further elucidated by his incidental criticism
of his great forerunner August Wilhelm Schlegel. His admiration
for this master of the German language and lover of Shakespeare,
whose struggle for a faithful and poetically adequate translation
was so astonishingly successful, has increased during his own
work, and he is grateful to him for having laid the foundation on
which he can raise his own structure. If he thinks a new structure
necessary at all, it is for four different reasons:

---

[2] Cf. *Shakespeare's Producing Hand*, London 1948; *Hamlet's Father*,
New Haven 1949; *The Moor of Venice*, London 1950, and numerous
articles and reviews.
[3] *op. cit.*, I, 23.
[4] *op. cit.*, I, 25.

1. Schlegel's language is grounded on the usage of a past period; although Flatter, very wisely, does not aim at any particular modernity in his language and style, he bases his version, which is intended for the actors of our period, on our living speech.

2. Schlegel had an 18th century text before him, and lacked much of the equipment of a modern translator; accordingly, there are imperfections in his version that a new translator must do his best to remove.

3. In spite of his remarkably faithful rendering of many of the most important characteristics of the original, he was governed by the taste of his own age where he took off some of the sharpest edges of Shakespeare's language and smoothed down some of his extreme expressions. Here, too, the new translator wants to do full justice to the original.

4. Schlegel is, according to Flatter, a translator for the reader, rather than for the speaker, a translator of a poetical rather than a theatrical text. Flatter himself tries to preserve in his version all those hints and indications for the speaker and actor which he discovers in the Folio texts rather than in the Good Quartos. He suspects the latter of having been edited for the purposes of the Elizabethan reader.

This is not the place for a discussion of Flatter's views concerning Shakespeare's theatrical language and the traces it is supposed to have left in the early prints;[5] but two *caveats* should be mentioned nevertheless: Flatter has discovered, from the producer's and the actor's point of view, very interesting functions of broken-off and otherwise incomplete lines; but it would be a mistake to suppose that Shakespeare indicated intended pauses and openings for stage business by using such lines under all circumstances. Normally he was perfectly capable of expressing whatever he wanted to express within the extremely plastic and elastic metrical form he developed for himself in the course of his creative life, and his actors were certainly trained to take and to react to much subtler hints than broken-off lines. Many of those subtler hints are contained in his rhythms.

[5] Cf. the useful review of *Shakespeare's Producing Hand* by Peter Alexander: *RES*, N. S., I, 1950, 66 ff.

Flatter has a keen ear for Shakespeare's use of the iambic scheme of his blank verse and, especially, for his departures from it. In many cases he thinks it important to find the closest possible German equivalent to them. His delight in this achievement makes him somewhat unfair towards Schlegel, who, in Flatter's view, was a great stickler for metrical correctness and therefore did not admit Shakespeare's irregularities or, better, variations to his German lines. Though, doubtless, his verses are more regular than Shakespeare's, he had nevertheless many subtle variations at his command. Even in two examples, quoted by Flatter himself in order to illustrate the difference between Schlegel's and his own method,[6] the great Romantic is far more flexible than he believes him to be.

The line:

To give them seals never, my soul, consent!

is scanned: ∪ — ∪ — | — ∪ ∪ — ∪ —, and compared with Schlegel's:

Nie will'ge drein, sie zu versiegeln, Seele!

Flatter's scansion of this (∪ — ∪ — ∪ — ∪ — ∪ — ∪) is wholly inadequate. This inadequacy is partly due to the fact that the critic fails to distinguish between full stresses and half stresses (symbolized here by the sign ✕), a simplification that makes it impossible to do justice to the less obvious characteristics of a verse. But apart from this, we cannot possibly read this line in Flatter's way; it must be scanned: — — ∪ — | ✕ ∪ ∪ — ∪ — ∪. This must be compared with the rhythm of Shakespeare's line, imitated so carefully by the modern translator:

Das Siegel "Tat" — nie laß es zu, mein Herz!

∪ — ∪ — | — ∪ ∪ — ∪ —

This example, incidentally, points to the kind of price Flatter is ready to pay for his rhythmical fidelity.

The second instance of a misrepresentation of Schlegel's scansion is:

Das zwingt uns, still zu stehn. Das ist die Rücksicht,

translating:

Must give us pause. There's the respect . . .

6 Cf. *op. cit.*, I, 15 & 17 f.

Here again Flatter complains of Schlegel's failure to reproduce the rhythm: ∪ — ∪ — (—) — ∪ ∪ —, with the striking pause in the middle. All he can see in the older translator's line is an absolutely regular iambic pentameter: ∪ — ∪ — ∪ — ∪ — ∪ —. What we find, however, if we read it properly in its context, is: — — ∪ | — ∪ — ‖ — ∪ ∪ — ∪. Although there are no syllables missing here, there is a very strong caesura, which is certainly very effective, too, and the question arises whether Flatter's rhythmically more faithful version:

> Das läßt uns zaudern — das ist die Scheu

is really better, considering that it replaces the excellent word "Rücksicht" by the less satisfactory "Scheu". However this may be, Schlegel's rhythms are certainly much subtler than Flatter's report on them suggests.

But, generally speaking, we do not hesitate to say that Flatter's principle of according to the reproduction of rhythmical patterns as well as of sound qualities and onomatopoeic effects an important place among the Shakespearian translator's tasks is a sound one. Rhythm is a most essential connecting link between dramatic speech with all its emotional and intellectual contents on the one hand and an actor's gestures and behaviour on the stage on the other, and Shakespeare used it accordingly. Flatter creates an erroneous impression, however, especially in his essay: *Das Schauspielerische in der Diktion Shakespeares*,[7] by suggesting that expressive departures from the rigid iambic pattern are peculiarities of Shakespeare's theatrical language and that the normal thing for a "poet" to do is to follow the ∪ — ∪ — ∪ — ∪ — ∪ — pattern obediently and unflinchingly.[8] In reality they are a common practice

---

[7] *Shakespeare-Schriften*, hrsg. von Richard Flatter, 1. Heft, Wien — Bad Bocklet — Zürich, 1954.

[8] Cf. the following passages (*op. cit.*, 16 & 19): "Worin nun liegt 'das Schauspielerische' der Sprache Shakespeares?
Es liegt in der Lautmalerei ebenso wie in der Wortstellung, in Verslücken ebenso wie in regelwidrigen Betonungen, in hüpfenden ebenso wie in schwerfällig schleichenden Rhythmen und in manchem andern. Es gibt kein sprachliches Ausdrucksmittel, das der große Schauspieler-Dichter nicht zu seinen schauspielerischen Zwecken verwendet hätte ...

of all the English masters of iambic verse,[9] so much so that it will hardly do to class a trochaic beginning of a line, groups of two or more stressed or unstressed syllables, lines with more or less than five stresses as irregularities. They are present in Milton and Pope, in Wordsworth and Keats, in Yeats and Eliot, and cannot possibly be claimed as peculiarly "theatrical" or "Shakespearian". What is "theatrical" in Shakespeare's use of them is simply that he charges them with acting as well as with speaking impulses. The case of severely curtailed and broken-off lines is different; they are certainly not common outside of the body of plays with which Flatter is dealing.

II

But Flatter's theories, interesting though they are, are not to detain us any longer from our scrutiny of one of his translations. We have chosen *Hamlet* for our purpose because of the central position of this play among Shakespeare's works and Schlegel's translations. In consequence of his conviction that the Folio version is much more of a playhouse text than Q2, Flatter follows the Folio wherever this is possible, and adopts Q2 readings only when they are inevitable. Most of the passages preserved in Q2 only are not included in the main text of the translation, but relegated to an appendix.

The basis of the following remarks is a comparison of Flatter's

---

Nun war jedoch Shakespeare, je mehr er sich seiner Reifezeit näherte, immer mehr von den Postulaten der Prosodie abgewichen. Wenn er eine schauspielerische Nuance erzielen wollte, setzte er sich mit selbstverständlicher Gleichgültigkeit über die Vorschriften des jambischen Verses hinweg. Er läßt Verse mit einer Hebung beginnen, läßt zwei oder auch drei Hebungen zusammenstoßen, läßt eine Silbe ausfallen, wodurch ein kurzer Hiatus entsteht, und so fort."

[9] In German poetry a similar, though more restricted, latitude exists, and Schlegel makes a masterly use of it. Cf. e.g.:

Schlafen! Vielleicht auch träumen! — Ja, da liegt's:

$$(- \smile \| \smile - \smile - \smile \| - | - -)$$

text with the original[10] and with Schlegel's version.[11] They are arranged so as to permit the illustration and evaluation of the methods by which Flatter tries to create a rendering that is new, faithful, and more stageworthy than Schlegel's.

To begin with we wish to insist on the point that he is not merely an innovator à tout prix: Many of Schlegel's memorable phrases, such as

> Dies über alles: sei dir selber treu,

> Engel und Boten Gottes steht uns bei!

> Die Zeit ist aus den Fugen:

> Der Rest ist Schweigen.

are preserved, because they cannot be bettered. In other cases a manifest improvement results from a minor change:[12]

> This gentle and vnforc'd accord of *Hamlet*
> Sits smiling to my heart; (I. ii)

> Dies will'ge freundliche Nachgeben Hamlets
> Sitzt lächelnd um mein Herz;

> Dies zwanglos freundliche Sich-Fügen Hamlets
> Sitzt lächelnd mir ums Herz.

> for they are the Abstracts and breefe Chronicles of the time.
> (II. ii)

> denn sie sind der Spiegel und die abgekürzte Chronik des
> Zeitalters.

> Denn sie sind der Auszug und die abgekürzte Chronik der Zeit.

The wish to get away from the slightly misleading "Spiegel" is

---

[10] *Hamlet. Parallel Texts of the First and Second Quartos and the First Folio.* Ed. by Wilhelm Vietor, *Shakespeare Reprints*, II, Marburg 1891.

[11] *Hamlet, Prinz von Dänemark.* Übersetzt von A. W. Schlegel. *Shakespeares sämtliche dramatische Werke*, Stuttgart (o. D.), VIII.

[12] English quotations without reference are Folio readings. They are followed first by Schlegel's and then by Flatter's rendering.

justified; "Auszug" has the disadvantage that the intended meaning can hardly be apprehended immediately. The word "Summe", which we venture to suggest, has its drawbacks, too.

> That suck'd the Honie of his Musicke Vowes: (III. i)

> Die seiner Schwüre Honig sog,

> Die seiner Eide süßen Wohllaut sog,

Here, the absolute metaphor in "Honie" becomes an echo only in "süß" in order to admit the musical touch both in the word "Wohllaut" and in the whole sequence of sounds. An operation that can be unhesitatingly commended will be found in the following example where the modern translator gets closer to the Shakespearian metaphor than his predecessor:

> And with a larger tether may he walke, (I. iii)

> und habe freiern Spielraum,

> Und daß er an viel längrer Leine gehn darf

Another group of three quotations is to illustrate Flatter's tendency to eliminate phrases in Schlegel that seem hard and unusual for no good reason and thus to achieve fluence and ease:

> But with much forcing of his disposition. (III. i)

> Doch that er seiner Fassung viel Gewalt.

> Doch tat er seiner Laune sehr Gewalt an.

> Be thy euents (Q2: intents) wicked or charitable, (I. iv)

> Sei dein Beginnen boshaft oder liebreich,

> Ob du auf Segen aus bist oder Fluch,

> and that should teach vs,
> There's a Divinity that shapes our ends,
> Rough-hew them how we will. (V. ii)

> und das lehr' uns,
> Daß eine Gottheit unsre Zwecke formt,
> Wie wir sie auch entwerfen —

> und das lehr' uns:
> Es lebt ein Gott, der für uns formt und ausführt,
> Was wir nur roh behaun.

In the third example Flatter's version is striking by its smooth movement, its definiteness and its fine translation of the unique phrase "Rough-hew". At the same time it is undeniable that the modern translator has become an interpreter here, whereas Schlegel modestly accepted a certain darkness and difficulty, because he found them in the original. For Flatter it is sometimes difficult to resist the temptation of telling us what Shakespeare really meant instead of faithfully reproducing his words. Another instance of this:

> vse them after your own Honor and Dignity. (II. ii)

> Behandelt sie nach Eurer eignen Ehre und Würdigkeit:

> Behandelt sie nach Euerm eigenen Wert und Verdienst:

Usually this interpretative kind of work is done in order to give the lines the qualities of current and living speech, a tendency that certainly recommends itself in a stage version, but which can also lead to the loss of a number of definitely Shakespearian touches, of more of them perhaps than Schlegel's hesitations before what he considered low and crude expressions. A few passages will enable us to measure such gains and losses:

> Vnhouzzled, disappointed, vnnaneld, (I, v)

> Ohne Nachtmahl, ungebeichtet, ohne Ölung;

> Und ohne Abendmahl und letzte Ölung

The line has become tamer, less charged with passion through simplification.

> And in the Morne and liquid dew of Youth, (I. iii)

> Und in der Früh und frischem Tau der Jugend

> Und in der Früh, im klaren Tau der Jugend,

Schlegel's attempt at reproducing a characteristic construction of Shakespeare's has been abandoned, because it looks strange in

German. But in English as well the construction is individual and unusual.

> A happinesse,
> That often Madnesse hits on, (II. ii)

> Dies ist ein Glück, daß die Tollheit oft hat, womit . . .

> Ein wahrer Schatz, den man oft bei der Tollheit antrifft;

Both translators fail to suggest the idea of that *curiosa felicitas* at which the playwright is aiming here.

> A foolish figure, (II. ii)

> Doch dies ist
> 'ne thörichte Figur:

> Wahr, daß es schad ist —: neckisch kleiner Scherz!

Schlegel sticks to the specific rhetorical term (figure), whereas Flatter avoids it, probably because he has no hope that a modern audience would understand it.

In other passages the translator's interpretative and normalizing tendencies take away more of the vigour and sharpness in Shakespeare's imagery:

> And keepe within the reare of your Affection;
> Out of the shot and danger of Desire. (I. iii)

> Und halte dich im Hintergrund der Neigung,
> Fern von dem Schuß und Anfall der Begier.

> Halt hinter deinen Wünschen dich zurück,
> Bleib fern dem Ziel und der Gefahr der Lust!

> Giue thy thoughts no tongue,
> Nor any vnproportion'd thought his Act: (I. iii)

> Gib den Gedanken, die du hegst, nicht Zunge,
> Noch einem ungebührlichen die That.

> Was du denkst, das zeig nicht,
> Noch zeig dein Handeln, daß du unschön denkst!

> But in a Fixion, in a dreame of Passion, (II. ii)

Bei einer bloßen Dichtung, einem Traum
Der Leidenschaft,

Durch Einbildung, durch Schmerz, den er sich vorstellt,

Th' expectansie and Rose of the faire State, (III. i)

des Staates Blum' und Hoffnung,

des Reiches Stolz und Hoffnung,

In each case the modern translator moves towards abstract speech, and pays for it by a serious loss of vitality, forgetting that much of the dramatic quality of Shakespeare's language lives in dramatically conceived metaphors. Why give up the personification in the following passage?

transforme Honestie from what it is, to a Bawd, (III. i)

die Tugend in eine Kupplerin verwandeln,

die Ehrsamkeit zur Unzucht zu verleiten,

It would be unfair to suggest that Flatter replaces figurative by conceptual speech whenever he encounters a recalcitrant image; sometimes he chooses a figurative equivalent of his own, but this is usually more conventional and tamer than the original:

A Violet in the youth of Primy Nature; (I. iii)

Ein Veilchen in der Jugend der Natur,

Ein Frühlingsveilchen an der Jugend Schwelle,

For lone oft loses both it selfe and friend:
And borrowing duls the edge of Husbandry. (I. iii)

Sich und den Freund verliert das Darlehn oft,
Und Borgen stumpft der Wirtschaft Spitze.

Darlehn verliert sich selbst, verliert den Freund —
Und Borgen frißt wie Rost den Glanz der Wirtschaft.

Whereto serues mercy,
But to confront the visage of Offence? (III. iii)
Wozu dient
Die Gnad', als vor der Sünde Stirn zu treten?

Wozu dient Gnade,
Als vor die Sünde schützend hinzutreten?

III

We next turn to one of Flatter's most inevitable and convincing aims, the revision of passages where Schlegel's reading was faulty or misleading for one reason or another. Here he is sometimes the executor of the results of modern research and sometimes the agent of his own perspicuity and taste:

He's fat, and scant of breath. (V. ii)

Er ist fett und kurz von Atem.

Er ist erhitzt und außer Atem.

Whether 'tis Nobler in the minde to suffer (III. i)

Ob's edler im Gemüt, die Pfeil und Schleudern

Ist es nun edler, im Gemüt zu dulden

Thus Conscience does make Cowards of vs all, (III. i)

So macht Gewissen Feige aus uns allen;

So macht Bewußtheit Memmen aus uns allen;

your Honesty should admit no discourse to your Beautie.
(III. i)

Eure Tugend keinen Verkehr mit Eurer Schönheit pflegen
muß.

daß Ihr Eurer Ehrsamkeit nicht erlauben sollt, Eure
Schönheit zu verhandeln!

A little more then kin, and lesse then kinde. (I. ii)

Mehr als befreundet, weniger als Freund,

Zu viel verwandt, zu wenig zugewandt —!

A courageous attempt to get closer to the original pun!

But looke, the Morne in Russet mantle clad,
Walkes o'er the dew of yon high Easterne Hill, (I. i)

Doch seht, der Morgen, angethan mit Purpur,
Betritt den Tau des hohen Hügels dort,

Doch seht, der Morgen, noch im grauen Mantel,
Beschreitet schon den Tau des Bergs im Osten.

The new version gets rid of the associations of pomp and royalty in Schlegel, and lives up to Dover Wilson's interpretation of the passage.[13] Its only weakness lies in the introduction of the non-representative words "noch" and "schon", which reduce the vividness of the image a little. The following passage, all-important in Flatter's explanation of the tragedy,[14] is translated in his most interpretative manner to make sure that "pitteous action" is understood as he — I think rightly — wants us to understand it.

Least with this pitteous action you conuert
My sterne effects: (III. iv)

Damit nicht deine klägliche Gebärde
Mein strenges Thun erweicht:

Sonst lenkt mich noch das Schauspiel deines Mitleids
Vom bittern Vorsatz ab;

Not all of Flatter's improvements of this type are equally convincing, however. Some of them might even be called decidedly wilful. In the following specimens Schlegel is the more faithful translator:

---

[13] The editor of the New Cambridge *Hamlet* says (p. XXXVI): ".. the word 'russet', used to describe the indeterminate reddish-brown or grey of the sky at daybreak, recalls the coarse homespun cloth, which is its original sense, and so gives birth to the image of Dawn as a labourer mounting the hill to his work of the day, his mantle thrown across his shoulder."

[14] Cf. *Hamlet's Father*, XV: "The Rock in the River".

With all my loue I doe commend me to you; (I. v)

Nun, liebe Herrn,
Empfehl' ich euch mit aller Liebe mich,

So, edle Herren,
Verlaß ich mich auf Euch in aller Freundschaft;

These tedious old fooles. (II. ii)

Die langweiligen alten Narren!

Diese ekligen alten Narren!

to see a robustious Pery-wig-pated Fellow, teare a Passion
to tatters, to verie ragges, (III, ii)

ein handfester haarbuschiger Geselle eine Leidenschaft in
Fetzen, in rechte Lumpen zerreißt,

wie solch ein aufgebrachter Perückenheld sich vor Leidenschaft in Stücke reißt, daß die Fetzen fliegen . . .

Though inclination be as sharpe as will:
My stronger guilt, defeats my strong intent, (III. iii)

Ist gleich die Neigung dringend wie der Wille;
Die stärkre Schuld besiegt den starken Vorsatz,

So groß mein Wunsch auch ist, heiß wie die Lustgier,
Die Schuld ist stärker als mein stärkster Drang

Here, Flatter, who has also translated Shakespeare's *Sonnets*, introduces a very special meaning of "will", which is hardly justified
by the context.

this is a benefit,
And not reuenge: (III. iii; Q₁)
Why, this is base and silly, not reuendge, (Q₂)
Oh this is hyre and Sallery, not Reuenge. (F)

Ei, das wär' Sold und Löhnung, Rache nicht.

Meuchelmord wär' das, Hinrichtung — nicht Rache!

This is Flatter's most extraordinary venture: In his appendix he explains at length that "hyre and Sallery", the reading he accepts, must be taken as a *quid pro quo* for "assassination" and "execution". To the present writer's mind this is utterly pointless. In his opinion Q1 expresses the general drift of this passage, as of many others, correctly, and Schlegel's version is sound. He cannot convince himself that the difference between assassination and revenge has anything to do with the difference between killing a victim in his prayers and killing him while he is about some profane business.

> why, it appeares no other thing to mee, then a foule and pestilent congregation of vapours. (II. ii)

> kommt es mir doch nicht anders vor, als ein fauler und verpesteter Haufe von Dünsten.

> ach, mir erscheint's als der trübe Dunsthauch faul verpesteten Auswurfs.

An opportunity for finding something better than Schlegel's "Haufe von Dünsten" has been missed here.

In reading the two German versions of the following passage we wish to point to the possibility that "his wonted way" should be translated less literally. Could it not mean "his wonted behaviour", "his normal self"?

> Will bring him to his wonted way againe, (III. i)

>   zurück ihn bringen
> Auf den gewohnten Weg,

> Wird ihn die rechte Straße wieder heimführ'n —

> To heare, and see the matter. (III. i)

> Zum Hören und zum Sehn des Dings zu laden.

> Das Zeug mit anzusehen und anzuhören.

Polonius is inviting the royal couple in Hamlet's name to witness the play. I am not sure that Delius was right in discovering a "tinge of contempt" in the word "matter"; there is certainly not more of it than could be exactly expressed by the neutral term "Sache". The following reference of King Claudius to theatrical performances seems to be less contemptuous, too, than it sounds in Flatter's rendering:

> To these delights. (III. i)
>
> zu Ergötzlichkeiten
>
> zu derlei Scherzen!

IV

In this section we are going to deal with the methods employed by Flatter as antidotes against the euphemistic and dignifying tendencies which are a minor inadequacy of Schlegel's version. He is usually careful to call a spade a spade, and does not tolerate expressions by which hard and sharp lines are rendered poetical and harmless.

> This is the very extasie of Loue, (II. i)
>
> Dies ist die wahre Schwärmerei der Liebe,
>
> Dies ist der echte Wahnsinn der Verliebtheit,

> an Anticke disposition (I. v)
>
> Ein wunderliches Wesen
>
> Ein fratzenhaftes Wesen

Perhaps some readers will think "fratzenhaft" as wide of the mark as "wunderlich", but on the opposite side. A rather striking new rendering of a piece of Hamlet's bawdy talk is as follows:

> Faith, her priuates, we.
> In the secret parts of Fortune? (II. ii)
>
> Ja, wirklich, wir sind mit ihr vertraut.
> Im Schoße des Glücks?
>
> Stimmt, manchmal gibt uns Fortuna Zutritt —
> Ins Geheimkabinett?

In the next passage Flatter is more explicit than Shakespeare, but also more abstract and, inevitably, tamer:

> why she would hang on him,
> As if encrease of Appetite had growne
> By what it fed on; (I. ii)

> Hing sie doch an ihm,
> Als stieg der Wachstum ihrer Lust mit dem,
> Was ihre Kost war.

> oh, sie hing an ihm,
> Als steigerte die Sattheit die Begierde
> Nach weiterem Genuß!

Flatter also makes use of a number of colloquial expressions, especially in the conversations of the guardsmen in the opening scene:

> Haue you had quiet Guard? (I. i)

> War Eure Wache ruhig?

> War auf der Wacht was los?

> Lookes it not like the King? (I. i)

> Sieht's nicht dem König gleich?

> Schaut's nicht dem König gleich?

> Why such impresse of Ship-wrights, (I. i)

> Warum gepreßt für Werfte,

> Warum läßt man die Schiffsbauer so schuften,

We may welcome these lively touches, but we should hesitate to applaud the following restrictive rendering of a phrase we have learnt to read as a strange first pointer to one of the dominating moods of the tragedy:

> And I am sicke at heart. (I. i)

> Und mir ist schlimm zu Mut.

> Und ich hab's herzlich satt.

Nor do we think that regional expressions, all but incomprehensible for large sections of the German reading public, should have been admitted:

> as so tis put on me; (I. iii)
> und so erzählt man mir's,
> wie man es mir versetzt hat, —

> to tarre them to Controuersie (II. ii)
> aufzuhetzen
> aufzuhussen

We do not intend to enter into Flatter's interesting discussion of the "To be or not to be" soliloquy, where he gives his reasons for his use of the phrase "Schluß zu machen" in the following passage; but we submit that this low and trivial phrase can only be introduced here through a regrettable lapse of style, whatever its justification from the point of view of meaning.

> Or to take Armes against a Sea of troubles,
> And by opposing end them: (III. i)
> Sich waffnend gegen eine See von Plagen,
> Durch Widerstand sie enden.
> Oder dem Heer von Plagen sich zu stellen
> Und kämpfend Schluß zu machen?

"Heer von Plagen" is an interesting deviation from the original, recalling 18th century scruples with respect to this and other Shakespearian metaphors. Flatter avoids the expected "Meer von Plagen" because he believes that "a Sea of" was a dormant metaphor for Shakespeare, which, stirred to life by a literal translation, does not fit into his own conception of the whole passage. Our answer to this is that it is very risky to dogmatize on the degree of life, i. e. of the power of evoking definite mental images, that Shakespeare and his audience felt in a metaphor and that neither "a Sea of troubles" nor "ein Meer von Plagen" can call up vivid and, possibly, disturbing mental pictures, because this metaphor does not lend itself to visualization. It will be taken in both languages as a strong but somewhat vague expression for "very many".

Although convinced of the superior virtues of the Folio, Flatter feels obliged to reproduce Hamlet's oaths even where they are omitted in his favourite text. He considers Schlegel's solutions as too euphemistic, and removes such slight veils as we find in the originals. The crude and unhappy effect of the expletives he gives to his Prince Hamlet is enhanced by the absence of such mitigating rust as is provided by the long and general usage of an oath.

> s'bloud there is somthing (II. ii; Q₂)
> There is something in this (F)

> Wetter, es liegt hierin

> Gott's Blut, etwas Unnatürliches liegt da verborgen;

> Gods bodykins man, better. (II. ii)

> Potz Wetter, Mann, viel besser.

> Gotts Tod, Mensch, besser![15]

If we are looking for a convincing proof that Flatter's work is not based on a theory or a set of theories, that it is the result of a struggle with the texts in which he sometimes neglected the demands of consistency, we can find it in some stylistic contradictions of his translation. We have illustrated his method of getting away from the Romantic poetic diction; we should add that there are also passages where his own style is more indirect than either Shakespeare's or Schlegel's:

> He tooke my Father grossely, full of bread,
> With all his Crimes broad blowne, as fresh as May, (III. iii)

> Er überfiel in Wüstheit meinen Vater,
> Voll Speis', in seiner Sünden Maienblüte.

> Er schlug den Vater mitten im Schmaus des Lebens,
> Den Maitag seiner Sünden ungebüßt,

> When he is fit and season'd for his passage? (III. iii)

> Bereitet und geschickt zum Übergang?

---

[15] In deference to the Q₂ — not the Folio — text, the same unfortunate expletive is used in II, ii, 603, in III, 2, 388, and in V, i, 297.

Das Herz geläutert und versehn zum Heimgang?

In these examples we find our translator falling into a comparatively vague and elevated diction that is farther away from Shakespeare's devastating directness than the renderings of Schlegel, who kept his eyes, here and elsewhere, steadily and unflinchingly on the very words of Shakespeare. "Mitten im Schmaus des Lebens" is flabby and general if we compare it with "full of bread" and "Voll Speis'". The two lines from which these words are taken are without the necessary rhythmical character, too. "Das Herz geläutert und versehn zum Heimgang" is exactly the kind of translation of which Flatter and other critics complain when it occurs in Schlegel. In our second quotation Schlegel has caught an echo at least of the cold and bitter objectivity of the original.

A word should be said here of Flatter's onomatopoeic effects, as they are objects of his constant attention. They are frequently striking, as in

Der Hahn, des Morgens fröhliche Fanfare,
Mit seinem stolzen, schmetternd hellen Ton
Weckt er den Gott des Tags; (I. i)

On rare occasions only they tend to lead too independent an existence. The following line, splendid if read by itself, fails to echo the melancholy tone of the Queen's whole tale, whereas the original and Schlegel's version are better connected with the whole by the prevalence of dark vowels and diphthongs in them:

That shewes his hore leaues in the glassie streame: (IV. vii)

Und zeigt im klaren Strom sein graues Laub,

Die Blätter, silbrig, spiegeln sich im Strom.

V

We have stated above that Flatter is usually free from the itch of finding a rendering of his own where Schlegel had already hit on a good one. There are, however, quite a number of passages where he changes the old text without being able to improve it. We quote five of them:

the Maiesty of buried Denmarke (I. i)

die Hoheit des begrabnen Dänmark

des Königs tote Majestät

> you speake like a greene Girle,
> Vnsifted in such perillous Circumstance. (I. iii)

> Ihr sprecht wie junges Blut,
> in solchen Fährlichkeiten unbewandert.

> Du redest wie ein Küchlein,
> Das die Gefahr der Sache gar nicht ahnt.

The Ayre bites shrewdly: is it very cold?
(Q₂: it is very colde.)
It is a nipping and an eager ayre. (I. iv)

Die Luft geht scharf, es ist entsetzlich kalt.
's ist eine schneidende und strenge Luft.

Die Luft geht beißend rauh; 's ist bitter kalt!
's ist eine scharfe Luft und schneidet arg.

Thou wretched, rash intruding foole, farewell, (III. iv)

Du kläglicher, vorwitz'ger Narr, fahr wohl!

Du schmählich aufdringlicher Narr, leb wohl!

Thou liu'st, report me and my causes right
To the vnsatisfied. (V. ii)

Du lebst: erkläre mich und meine Sache
Den Unbefriedigten.

Du lebst: stell mich und meinen Fall zurecht
Jenen, die dunkel sehn!

The line in our last quotation but one is disappointing both by the ineffective rendering of Shakespeare's three adjectives and by the lack of a clear rhythmical pattern. Another rhythmically disappointing passage uses the same adverb-adjective combination:

> In the dead wast and middle of the night (I. ii)

In toter Stille tiefer Mitternacht

Im tödlich stillen Graun der Mitternacht,

Both translations lack the characteristic construction and the stress concentration (in "deád wást") of the original, but the majestic gait of Schlegel's line is far more awe-inspiring than the artificial phrase "Im tödlich stillen Graun". A complete breakdown of the rhythm happens even at the supreme moment of the tragedy: How are we to speak the following line, unless we are prepared to use the impossible form "Engelschar'n"?

And flights of Angels sing thee to thy rest, (V, ii)

Und Engelscharen singen dich zur Ruh'!

Mögen dich Engelscharen zur Ruhe singen!

These faults are particularly surprising, considering that a careful reproduction of rhythms, pauses and sound configurations, with all their implications for the actor, is Flatter's most characteristic purpose. Its influence is all-pervasive in the translation; it is visible in the structure of many lines as well as in the attempt to make the most of the "theatrical" punctuation of the Folio. In the matter of pauses Flatter does not leave anything to chance or to the reader's and actor's discernment, but makes a generous use of dashes. In our next illustrations we see him as a successful imitator of Shakespearian patterns:

The Hand more Instrumentall to the Mouth, (I. ii)

Die Hand dem Munde dienstgefäll'ger nicht,

Die Hand ist nicht gefügiger dem Mund

Here the restoration of the original word-order and rhythm is a clear gain. Cf. also:

And at the sound it shrunke in hast away,
And vanisht from our sight. (I. ii)

Und bei dem Tone schlüpft' es eilig weg
Und schwand aus unserm Blick.

Und auf den Laut verlor es sich in Eile

Und schwand aus unserm Blick.

Now might I do it pat, (III. iii)

Jetzt könnt' ich's thun, bequem;

Jetzt könnt' ich's glatt vollziehn,

A striking idea, this rendering of "pat" by "glatt"! In the follow-ing verse the German actor is given the exact equivalent to the English "too — too". It contains two of Flatter's dashes; neither of them is derived from the Folio text, which contains a meaningless comma only. He drops it in agreement with all the other editors and translators. Some readers will regret Flatter's rejection of Dover Wilson's revolutionary emendation, which he could not accept as he does not share Wilson's views concerning the authority of Q2.

O that this too too sallied flesh would melt, (I. ii; Q2)
Oh that this too too solid Flesh, would melt, (F)
O, that this too too sullied flesh would melt, (Wilson)

O schmölze doch dies allzu feste Fleisch,

Oh —, schmölze doch dies zu — zu feste Fleisch,

Occasionally Flatter's delight in keeping as close as possible to the original rhythms and sound patterns leads to some Anglicizing of German:

The Bird of Dawning singeth all night long: (I. i)

singe
Die ganze Nacht durch dieser frühe Vogel;

Der Morgenvogel all die Nacht lang ruft.

A countenance more in sorrow then in anger. (I. ii)

Eine Miene, mehr
Des Leidens als des Zorns.

Er zeigte mehr von Kummer als von Zorn.

And there are even passages where an excessive attention to sensuous details does harm to the meaning and to the general result of the translation:

> Indeed my Lord, it followed hard vpon. (I. ii)

> Fürwahr, mein Prinz, sie folgte schnell darauf.

> Wahrhaftig, Prinz, sie folgte hart am Fuß.

> Your leaue and fauour to returne to France, (I. ii)

> Vergünstigung, nach Frankreich rückzukehren,

> Gunst und Gestattung, rückzukehr'n nach Frankreich:

Neither "hart am Fuß" nor "Gestattung" are current German; the price paid for the preservation of "hard" in the first line and for the alliteration in the second is too high. The same is true of the rhythmical similarity — which is apparent rather than real — of the following translation:

> Or that the Euerlasting had not fixt
> His Cannon 'gainst Selfe-slaughter. (I. ii)

> Oder hätte nicht der Ew'ge sein Gebot
> Gerichtet gegen Selbstmord!

> Oder hätt' Er, der Herr, nicht sein Gebot
> Gerichtet gegen Selbstmord!

There is no warrant in the original for the peculiar tone of "Er, der Herr", nor for the inclusion of the word "Fee" in the next passage:

> The faire *Ophelia*. (III. i)

> Die reizende Ophelia.

> Die Fee Ophelia![16]

It is a nice question whether the modification of the simile in the following quotation is justified by the cleverly caught echoes of the sound qualities.

---

[16] We cannot discover any convincing reason for reading "fairy" here and for dropping "fair" altogether in V, i, 265 ("What, the faire *Ophelia*?"), translated by "Wie — Ophelia?"

Like sweet Bels iangled out of tune, and harsh, (III. i)

Mißtönend wie verstimmte Glocken jetzt;

Geborstner Glocke gleich, tonlos und falsch;

Every translator, moving between two closely related languages like English and German, is tempted to translate according to etymology sometimes rather than according to the current meaning of words. Here are two instances where we are not sure that Flatter was well advised in giving way to this temptation:

The nights are wholsome, (I. i)

Die Nächte sind gesund,

Die Nächte sind voll Heils,

be a breeder of Sinners? (III. i)

Sünder zur Welt bringen?

Sünder ausbrüten?

We could be as critical here of his equivalents as he is of Schlegel's rendering of "questionable",[17] which he corrects rather disappointingly:

Thou com'st in such a questionable shape (I. iv)

Du kommst in so fragwürdiger Gestalt,

Du trittst einher so rätselhaften Anblicks,

VI

It is an interesting observation that the wish to produce a version in which all theatrical values in the text are fully exploited has two contradictory effects on our translation: It spurs Flatter to

---

[17] He says (*Shakespeare*, III, 212): "'questionable shape': nicht, wie bei Schlegel, 'fragwürdig' im Sinne von 'verdächtig' oder 'Argwohn erregend', sondern zu Fragen (zur Befragung) herausfordernd." But we are not to lose sight of the possibility that some speakers may be able to suggest the intended meaning by a special intonation of "fragwürdig".

the closest imitation of the physical details of Shakespeare's lines, but it can also lead him away from the original. Not infrequently can we observe changes of emphasis which serve to heighten the dramatic quality of the speeches. In the next quotation Flatter's text is more theatrical than either the Q2 or the Folio text:

> What, ha's this thing appear'd againe to night. (I. i)
> Nun, ist das Ding heut wiederum erschienen?
> Nun — heute nacht, war's wieder da, das Ding?

The word-order of the original is quite normal; in Flatter's version it is specially arranged so as to express the intensity of Marcellus' curiosity and to produce the maximum of suspense. Excellent, but does not Flatter get dangerously near to teaching Shakespeare his job here? Different types of changes of emphasis are illustrated by the following examples:

> Would I had met my dearest foe in heauen,
> Ere I had euer seene that day *Horatio*. (I. ii)

> Hätt' ich den ärgsten Feind im Himmel lieber
> Getroffen, als den Tag erlebt, Horatio!

> Im Himmel wüßt' ich lieber meinen Erzfeind
> Als daß ich das erleben mußt', Horatio!

> You would pluck out . . .; you would sound mee . . . (III. ii)
> Ihr wollt in das Herz . . . dringen, Ihr wollt mich . . . prüfen:
> ausreißen wollt Ihr . . .; aus mir herausholen wollt Ihr . . .

> Now could I drink hot blood,
> And do such bitter businesse as the day
> Would quake to looke on. (III. ii)

> Nun tränk' ich wohl heiß Blut,
> Und thäte bittre Dinge, die der Tag
> Mit Schaudern säh'.

> Rauchend Blut könnt' ich nun trinken
> Und Dinge tun, so bitter, daß der Tag
> Schauderte, sie zu sehn.

It is also his interest in the theatrical pauses that occasionally tempts Flatter to improve Shakespeare's as well as Schlegel's text. He knows of our tendency to drop the logical connecting links in passionate language, and he makes use of it in order to give vigour and immediacy to his speeches and to get rid of some of those extra syllables which are the eternal trouble of a translator of English verse into German.[18] This lends his style an exciting staccato quality:

> he hath importun'd me with loue,
> In honourable fashion. (I. iii)

> Er hat mit seiner Lieb' in mich gedrungen,
> In aller Ehr' und Sitte.

> Er setzte mir so zu mit seiner Liebe —
> In aller Form — !

Here it is a comma, found in the Folio text only, which induces Flatter to divide Ophelia's speech in this surprising fashion. She stops after "Liebe", because she is afraid of having said too much, and tries to correct the mistake in her final three words. An attractive interpretation for the actress!

---

[18] It is Flatter's policy to avoid the extra lines tolerated by Schlegel, and to accept the sacrifices demanded by such compression:

> and at last
> Vpon his will I seald my hard consent, (I, ii; Q₂)

> Daß ich zuletzt auf seinen Wunsch das Siegel
> Der schwierigen Bewilligung gedrückt.

> ja, zum Schluß
> Drückt' ich auf seinen Wunsch mein schweres Siegel.

> There on the pendant boughes, her Coronet weeds
> Clambring to hang; an enuious sliuer broke, (IV. vii)

> Dort, als sie aufklomm, um ihr Laubgewinde
> An den gesenkten Ästen aufzuhängen,
> Zerbrach ein falscher Zweig,

> Da, einen Ast mit Blumen zu bekrönen,
> Hob sie sich auf — voll Tücke brach ein Zweig —

In the same figure, like the King that's dead. (I. i)

Ganz die Gestalt wie der verstorbne König.

Genau so die Gestalt —: der tote König!

But with a crafty Madnesse keeps aloofe: (III. i)

Hielt sich vielmehr mit schlauem Wahnwitz fern,

Vielmehr — im Wahnsinn schlau — weicht er uns aus,

And now Ile doo't, and so he goes to Heauen, (III. iii)

Jetzt will ich's thun — und so geht er gen Himmel,

Und jetzt — ich tu's! — und so geht er zum Himmel

As appears from these examples Flatter's use of dashes is by no means always grounded on the Folio punctuation. They are useful instruments of a translator who, at a pinch, values conciseness and dramatic effectiveness more highly than strict fidelity. We have found evidence for the same attitude in other sections of our inquiry. It is characteristic of the method of Flatter, who is neither a poet-translator with his instinctive sense of style, nor a scholar-translator with his passion for accuracy — though he possesses a fair measure of either of their valuable gifts; he is the experienced man of the theatre who succeeds in providing the German-speaking actors of our days with a remarkably lucid and actable version of Shakespeare without sacrificing too much of what must remain difficult and mysterious about his masterpieces. His text is of interest for the Shakespearian scholar as well, as it throws light on qualities of the original that have been overlooked by many observers. If we hesitate to call his fine version of *Hamlet* a great translation after having compared it with Schlegel's text, it is mainly because we miss in it the marks of that absolute humility which seems to be a condition of the supreme achievements in the translator's exacting art. (1955)

V.

Daniel Defoe:
An Artist in the Puritan Tradition

THE BEST-KNOWN tendency of what its roughly called the Puritan movement is perhaps its uncompromising enmity to many forms of artistic activity. Critics like to assert, when they are dealing with great poets who were connected with Puritanism, that they achieved artistic success in spite of its influence, certainly not because of it. This statement is as true in the case of Defoe as in that of Milton or Marvell. We shall describe a desperate battle between Defoe's creative impulses and his Puritan views concerning art. If that were all and Puritanism merely something to be overcome in order to make artistic work possible, there would be little justification for speaking of Defoe as an artist in the Puritan tradition. But there is another fact. Even while defeating Defoe's aversion to the telling of invented stories, his creative impulses were directed towards aims conditioned by this author's Puritan frame of mind.

I do not intend to load this paper with definitions of the various meanings given to the term *Puritan;* I rather choose to replace it for the present by the name of the religious organization of which Defoe was a member, the Presbyterian Church.

The nature of the Calvinistic Presbyterian doctrine, which won its stronghold in Scotland in the second half of the 16th century, is well known. Calvinistic theology corresponded to an utterly pessimistic attitude towards all that belongs in this world. It appealed to persons and groups of persons who were struck by a sense of sin when they observed themselves, and of incompleteness when they looked at the world around them. This lower reality seemed evil to them and without value if not touched by the grace of God. The all-important question, which dominated the lives of the original Calvinists, was: Am I touched by the grace of God? Shall I dwell in the realm of the saved, or remain enslaved to this shadowy reality, a victim of senseless accident, without the power of resisting the influences of demons? The more important this question appeared to an individual, the more thoroughly did he organize his whole existence around this central point. The ultimate purpose of life was to prove that he who lived it was one of the elect. Minor purposes had to be subservient to it. Human activities were pronounced more or less useful in the pursuit of the ultimate end, and accordingly they were valued. The highest importance was given to various religious exercises; it was a duty of a neutral character to provide the means of living for oneself and one's family; but it was barely permissible to indulge in any recreation. Time, that precious opportunity for the working out of our salvation, was not to be squandered away in the pursuit of worldly enjoyment. Richard Baxter, who stood in this tradition, admonished his readers:

> You must not love the world, as your felicity, or for it self or for your fleshly lusts: But you must make use of the world, in the service of your Creator, yea and love it as a sanctified means of your Salvation, and as a wilderness way to your promised inheritance.[1]

We may call this method of evaluating earthly experiences by discovering their importance as means to an end the Calvinistic approach to reality. In spite of its unworldliness it is characterized by some definitely utilitarian traits. It is not astonishing that a man who had been taught this attitude in his youth could become a thorough utilitarian in the ordinary secular sense of the word if he replaced the transcendental end of life by ends of this world. That is what happened to a great number of Calvinists towards the end of the 17th, and in the course of the 18th, century; and among them to Defoe.

We know that he was the son of Presbyterian parents, who ranked themselves with the Dissenters in 1662, two years after Daniel's birth. During the following three decades the Dissenters suffered various forms of persecution, inflicted on them by the restored Stuart kings, who favoured the Catholic Church, and by Parliaments, the majorities of which had been disgusted by the results of religious toleration under Cromwell's rule. This persecution, at first, had the usual and proper consequences of per-

---

[1] *The Poor Man's Family Book,* London 1674, 166.

secutions: it increased the religious zeal of the persecuted. Daniel spent his childhood in an atmosphere of religious exaltation. He had the examples of men before him who sacrificed worldly advantage and security for the sake of religious convictions. When the time came, his parents decided to have their son prepare for the profession of a dissenting minister, and therefore sent him to the academy of Charles Morton at Newington Green, near London.

Why is it that his life became something completely different from what we should expect after such a beginning? We know practically nothing of the particular reasons responsible for Defoe's turning away from a theological career at the end of his education at Newington Green. But the study of his writings gives us a very clear answer to the general questions we have asked. They show that Defoe's own experience of reality had nothing in common with that of a believing Calvinist. He lacked the sense of sin, of a need for salvation, of the insignificance of things earthly, of the weakness of human reason unaided by the grace of God, even of the reality of the powerful Calvinistic God, whose will was destiny. His experience did not only differ from, but it contradicted that of an ideal Calvinist. His education at Newington Green had been of a peculiar, modernistic type. Charles Morton gave less weight to the study of the classical languages than did the authorities of the universities. He devoted much time to instruction in English, history, mathematics, and the natural sciences. It is probable that Defoe became so intensely interested in these secular subjects that he forgot the original purpose of his studies at Newington Green. It is certain that the new optimistic faith in the power of human reason to discover the laws of nature and to regulate human affairs got a strong hold on him.

The political situation of his own religious group led him to develop this first acquaintance with the movement of empiristic rationalism, of which Bacon, Hobbes, and Locke were the leaders. The English Presbyterians found themselves in a queer position since their attempt to win power over the whole of the state at the outset of the Civil War had failed.[2] Like their Scottish brethren

[2] Cf. C. E. Whiting, *Studies in English Puritanism from the Restoration to the Revolution*, New York and Toronto 1931, 46.

they held strictly orthodox views concerning the nature of the Church, which, being the Corpus Christianum, had to exist one and indivisible. Being violently opposed to any toleration of schism and heresy, they found themselves treated as schismatics by the Church of England after the Restoration. Consequently they were forced to fight *for* toleration in England. As soon as the Romanizing tendencies of Charles II and his brother became apparent the Presbyterians saw the necessity of securing toleration for Protestant Dissenters in opposition to the regal power, especially to the doctrine of the divine right of kings. The arguments they needed in their struggle were offered them by Algernon Sidney and John Locke, who developed the secular theory of the state based on the social contract. A political alliance with the Whigs could alone give hopes of preserving the Presbyterian interests. Defoe accepted these facts resolutely, and became the strange creature which is an orthodox liberal. While he was studying the writings of the great Whig thinkers his original tendency towards the new rationalism of his time gained strength. Implications, other than political, of the new doctrine made themselves felt in his thought. He often assumed the part of a prophet of the goddess of reason in his books and pamphlets published between 1700 and 1710. For example, he dedicated his long poem *Jure Divino*, in which he incorporated political theories inspired mainly by Locke,

> To the most serene, most invincible, and most illustrious Lady, Reason, first Monarch of the World; Empress of the East, West, North, and South; Hereditary Director of Mankind; Guide of the Passions; Lady of the Vast Continent of Human Understanding; Mistress of all the Islands of Science; Governess of the Fifteen Provinces of Speech; Image of, and Ambassador Extraordinary from, the Maker of all Things; the Almighty's Representative and Resident in the Souls of Men, and one of Queen Nature's Most Honourable Privy Council.[3]

A vehement believer in the possibilities of reason Defoe used this instrument in his dealings with all aspects of human life, and could not always stop this practice when he had to consider religious matters. Unless he controlled himself by exerting his will-power,

---

[3] W. Hazlitt, *The Works of Daniel De Foe* ... London 1841–43, III, *Jure Divino*, Dedication.

his reasoning inevitably carried him toward deistic views. The all-terrible God of his fathers, whose inexplicable will had been the immediate cause of everything that happened, faded away from his eyes' sight, and became a mere postulate of his reason, which needed the idea of a first mover in the universe. The will of God tended to become a mere form of speech, a poetical name for the law of nature. Only when the natural cause of a natural phenomenon had not yet been discovered, and seemed undiscoverable, was a kind of reservation established for the old-fashioned will of God. Defoe thought of these questions in unguarded moments precisely as did the deistic leaders of his time. He expressed their views quite openly in some pamphlets and so-called poems, which he manufactured in his younger years, without having the slightest suspicion that he turned deist in so doing. For, in spite of his extreme rationalism, in spite of his deistic tendencies, Defoe never considered himself anything else but a true, orthodox Presbyterian. His fight for the toleration of orthodox Protestants did not prevent him from crying out loudly against the damnable errors of deists, unitarians, sceptics, and such persons. The fact that they often appeared among his political allies, the Whigs, made him feel extremely uncomfortable. Several times, in prose and verse, he encouraged the government to use forcible means for suppressing those hated heretics. He heartily approved of the state of affairs in Scotland, where schismatics and heretics were persecuted severely.

We have before us an astonishing divergence between Defoe as he really was, and Defoe as he wished to be. It gives us the key to an understanding of his renowned duplicity. The reasons for his political wanderings from one party to the other and then back to the first, were not merely those of a poverty-stricken opportunist who seeks bread wherever he can get it.

This divergence of which we are speaking forced the task on Defoe of finding more or less satisfactory compromises between the demands of his rebellious rationalism and those of the orthodox dogmas which he did not intend to sacrifice. This task schooled him most effectively in the arts of sophistical reasoning and self-deception.

The question arises: Why did Defoe defend the orthodox dogmas so tenaciously when they were by no means supported by his experience of life? Why did he prevent his strong leanings towards deism from having their way? The shortest answer is: he could not dispense with orthodox Christianity, for he could find in no other system a solid foundation for his ethics. He tried out the new solutions that were offered him by the philosophers of his time; but he always came back to the will of God as the source of the moral law. He found that the deistic theories in particular were on this point beyond his reach. Whereas the empiristic rationalism of Locke attracted him powerfully, the idealistic rationalism of Shaftesbury remained incomprehensible to him. The first part of this statement is explained by the consideration that the Calvinist's and the empiristic rationalist's approaches to reality were very similar, though their notions of the content of reality were opposed. The purposive evaluation of worldly phenomena was common to both groups, but the purpose was different. The Calvinist wanted to use nature in his struggle to prove himself one of the elect; the empiristic rationalist wanted to use it to promote the secular aims of man.[4] This similarity between two far different views of life can help us to an understanding of the ease with which Defoe glided from Presbyterianism into empiristic rationalism. Reason, as defined in Locke's *Essay*, was the instrument of the empiristic rationalist. It was a marvellous instrument indeed for analysis, for the discovery of causes and effects, but ethically it was perfectly indifferent; it could be used from every point of view; it was able to indicate clearly what was useful for an individual or a group in a certain situation, but never what was good or bad in an absolute sense. An ethical system developed by reason, as defined by Locke, had to start with the equation of the useful and the good; in short, it had to be a utilitarian system like that sought by Bernard de Mandeville. Locke himself refrained from applying his reason to ethics, leaving this field in the care of the churches. Defoe sometimes wavered.

> And yet if all Religion was in vain,
> Did no Rewards or Punishments contain,

---

[4] This point is discussed by Ernst Cassirer in *Die platonische Renaissance in England und die Schule von Cambridge*, Leipzig und Berlin 1932, 48 f.

> Vertue's so suited to our Happiness,
> That none but Fools cou'd be in love with Vice,[5]

he reasoned. When fighting against the vices of his age he had a tendency to expose them as unreasonable and harmful, not as sinful. An amusing instance of this method occurs in his *Essay upon Projects*, where he violently attacks the custom of swearing. His Lockian reason is seriously shocked by it, for:

> 'Tis a senseless, foolish, ridiculous practice: 'tis a mean to no manner of end; 'tis words spoken which signify nothing; 'tis folly acted for the sake of folly, which is a thing even the devil himself don't practise. The devil does evil we say, but it is for some design, either to seduce others, or, as some divines say, from a principle of enmity to his Maker. Men steal for gain, and murder to gratify their avarice or revenge; whoredoms and ravishments, adulteries and sodomy, are committed to please a vicious appetite, and have always alluring objects; and generally all vices have some previous cause, and some visible tendency; but this, of all vicious practices, seems the most nonsensical and ridiculous; there is neither pleasure nor profit; no design pursued, no lust gratified, but is a mere phrensy of the tongue, a vomit of the brain, which works by putting a contrary upon the course of nature.[6]

Defoe cannot forgive the custom of swearing, because it does not take its place in a chain of cause and consequence as every decent phenomenon is obliged to do, above all, because he can discover no real purpose aimed at in swearing.

He never followed this line of argument otherwise than in a somewhat playful manner. He was dimly aware of the dangerous faculty of reason, as defined by Locke, to serve purely egoistic ends, to make palatable to an individual practices that were clearly sinful from a Christian, and antisocial from a practical point of view. He met successful and perfectly comfortable sinners in everyday life as well as good men oppressed by misery. And he concluded that virtue was safe only in a universe in which super-

---

[5] *A True Collection of the Writings of the Author of the True Born Englishman*, London 1703, 95 f.
[6] Hazlitt, op. cit., III, *An Essay upon Projects*, 37.

natural sanctions existed. He expressed this conviction in the following manner:

> ... no method can be so direct to prepare people for all sorts of wickedness as to persuade them out of a belief of any Supreme Power to restrain them. Make a man once cease to believe a God, and he has nothing left to limit his appetite but mere philosophy; if there is no supreme judicature, he must be his own judge and his own law, and will be so; ...[7]

Thus the defense of the orthodox Christian religion became a necessity for him. It was the result of pragmatical reasoning, not the effect of religious experience.

The solution of the problem offered by the deists, and especially Shaftesbury, departed from the sphere of empiristic rationalism. Under the influence of Leibniz they conceived the idea of a principle in nature itself that tended towards harmony and perfection. They believed that men had only to listen to some hidden law of their own natures if they wanted to become creatures of moral beauty. Virtue is its own reward, they insisted. Of course Defoe was acquainted with this view, and considered it. At one time he believed to have grasped the principle and said:

> I know nothing, no, not one instance in life, wherein virtue may be more truly said to be its own reward, than in this particular; .., who has length of days, who sound constitution? who has strength of body, agility of limbs, who enjoys an uninterrupted health, but the temperate, the moderate, and the virtuous?[8]

How utterly Shaftesbury's meaning was out of his reach is shown also by the following perplexed question:

> For if to future State we've no regard,
> How then can Vertue be its own Reward?[9]

Shaftesbury's doctrine was the result of an approach to reality different from that common to the Calvinist and empiristic

---

[7] G. A. Aitken, *Romances and Narratives by Daniel Defoe*, London 1895/96, III, 89.
[8] Hazlitt, *op. cit.*, III, *The Use and Abuse of the Marriage Bed*, 101.
[9] *A True Collection ...*, 116.

rationalist, an approach that did not regard the things of nature as means to ends outside of themselves, but as ends in themselves. Whereas the Calvinist severed the objects of our natural experience completely from the divine realm of truth; whereas the empiristic rationalist merely tried to know those properties of the objects, the knowledge of which gave him power over them, Shaftesbury conceived of the objects as of incomplete, yet representative, parts of the realm of truth, and as of living symbols of an ultimate reality. Even the possibility of this Platonic, and at the same time essentially poetic, approach remained unintelligible to Defoe all through his life.

A study of his attitude towards nature and the arts proves this statement conclusively. We shall first briefly describe how he looked at nature. He was perfectly capable of feeling enthusiasm at the sight of it. The study of the enormous organism, in which every part has its place and function, fascinated him. In the *Review* he glories once in nature's beauty:

> The Subserviency of the Creatures one towards another, is one of the Great, and perhaps one of the greatest Beauties of the Creation; the Earth breeds and feeds innumerable Creatures, that are of no other known Signification, than again to feed other Creatures; the Worms feed the Fowls, the Flyes the Fish, the small Birds the large, the small Fishes the Great, and all together, Nourish, Feed, Cloath, divert or serve the Worlds great Tyrant, MAN.[10]

Nature interested Defoe mainly as a field for human activity. If he saw no way of making a piece of land serve the ends of man, he had little to say about it. In *Caledonia*, a poem which he composed in 1706 in honour of Scotland and the Scottish nation, he tried to describe the landscape of the northern kingdom among other things. The sight of the coasts of Scotland inspires him:

> Fitted for Commerce and cut out for Trade;
> The Seas the Land, the Land the Seas invade.
> The Promontory Clifts with Hights embosst,
> And large deep Bays adorn thy dang'rous Coast;
> Alternately the Pilot's true Relief,

[10] *Review*, IV, 320.

These warn at Distance, those receive him safe;
The deep indented Harbours then invite,
First court by day, and then secure at night;
The wearied Sailors safe and true Recess,
A full Amends for wild Tempestuous Seas.[11]

He devotes many couplets to the sea:

Calm Tides, smooth Surface, and a shining Brow,
And gentle Gales for Wealth and Commerce blow.
These reconcile the once so dreadful Waste,
And *Art* and *Industry* supply the rest.
Hail Science, Natures *second Eye*,
Begot on Reason *by Philosophy*,
Mans Tellescope to all that's *Deep* and *High* . . .[12]

An ode to science interrupts the description. There are six lines in
Caledonia, remarkable for their delicacy, which characterize
Defoe's attitude to perfection:

Natures a Virgin *very Chast* and coy,
To Court her's nonsense, if ye will enjoy,
She must be ravish't, When she's forc't she's free,
A perfect Prostitute to Industry;
Freely she opens to th' Industrious hand
And pays them all the Tribute of the Land.[13]

Defoe's description is at its best when he is dealing with a
thickly populated, thriving region like the surroundings of London.
Beginning an account of the charms of the Thames near the capital,
he says in his *Tour through England and Wales:*

I shall sing you no songs here of the river in the first person
of a water nymph, a goddess, (and I know not what) according
to the humour of the ancient poets. I shall talk nothing of the
marriage of old Isis, the male river, with the beautiful Thame,
the female river, a whimsy as simple as the subject was empty,
but I shall speak of the river as occasion presents, as it really is
made glorious by the splendour of its shores, gilded with noble

[11] *Caledonia. A Poem in Honour of Scotland and the Scots Nation*,
Edinburgh 1706, 5.
[12] *Ibid.*, 7 f.   [13] *Ibid.*, 59.

palaces, strong fortifications, large hospitals, and publick buildings; with the greatest bridge, and the greatest city in the world, made famous by the opulence of its merchants, the encrease and extensiveness of its commerce; by its invincible navies, and by the innumerable fleets of ships sailing upon it, to and from all parts of the world.[14]

Man mastering nature was the object of Defoe's enthusiasm; if wild, untouched scenery inspired him at all, it inspired him with plans how it too could be made man's slave.

Defoe approached the arts in the same purposive, unimaginative, and antipoetic way. It is true he was less shy of books dealing with secular matters than his Presbyterian forbears had been. He was an eager reader of biographies and of books on science, history, geography and travel. But he held the strictest Puritan views concerning works of an imaginative character if they were not allegories written with the definite purpose of improving the reader. He called the production and the reading of purely artistic works, the telling of a good story for the fun of it, a deplorable waste of time. His theory was very explicit on these points. And his practice was in perfect harmony with the theory when he acted as a critic of the great imaginative works of literature. He could never forgive Homer's having made the Trojan War the subject of an evidently unreliable and fanciful poem, which he called "that Ballad-Singers Fable to get a Penny".[15] Had the Greek poet known his business he would have written the true history of the Trojan War. Defoe had more patience with the poets of later ages, which possessed historians who related the facts. He studied the historians, and left the poets alone, as they just did not interest him. There were very few books of poetry in his library.[16] Milton's major works were given an exceptional position, as this poet's professed aim, to "justify the ways of God to men", met with Defoe's approval. However, he deplored the fact that Milton fell into several serious heresies in accomplishing his plan.[17]

[14] Everyman's Library, No. 820, 173 f.
[15] *An Essay upon Literature*, London 1726, 117.
[16] Cf. G. A. Aitken, "Defoe's Library", *The Athenaeum*, June 1, 1895.
[17] Cf. Walther Fischer, "Defoe und Milton", *Engl. Studien*, LVIII (1924), 213—227.

He left this comparatively neutral attitude towards imaginative literature for an aggressive one when he came across works of an erotic nature. He preached against the "Latin Bawdy Authors Tibullus, Propertius and others"; against the poems of the Earl of Rochester, of course; and against French romances and play-books in general. He even frowned upon Chaucer's achievements, though he was ready to excuse that poet on account of "the unpoliteness of the Age he lived in".[18]

Defoe took a much firmer stand in the question of the theatre, and did his best to keep alive the Puritan tradition of antagonism to the stage. Though the Nonjurors were among the political groups he abhorred, he did not hesitate to applaud loudly Jeremy Collier's famous pamphlet levelled at the immorality of the English stage. He accused the authors of the Restoration comedies, the players, but also the audiences of taking "Prophaneness and Lewdness for Wit, Buffoonry for Humour, vicious Intrigue for Plot, Oaths and Curses and Blasphemy, for Politeness of Phrase, and a general Air of Wickedness for a Test of pleasing".[19] It is true he did not object to the existence of theatres as such. He did not follow Richard Baxter to the extreme of flatly denying the lawfulness of an actor's profession. If the stage had decided to produce what Defoe termed "sober plays" it could have won his support. We can form an idea of what his sober plays would have been like — if he had dared write them — by studying the so-called "Historical Dialogues" in the three volumes of the *Family Instructor*. They would have been lively, not without dramatic tension in individual scenes, but on the whole hopelessly given to improving the audience by showing how God reclaims or punishes the sinful, and rewards the virtuous. Though something akin to his ideal was growing up in the sentimental comedy during the first decade of the 18th century, Defoe lost all hope that the theatre would ever live up to his lofty standards. Therefore he once raised the fundamental question in the *Review:* are theatres necessary at all? He answered it in the negative, having pondered the indisputable fact

[18] William Lee, *Daniel Defoe: His Life and recently discovered Writings*, London 1869, II, 31.
[19] *Review*, III, 519.

that a besieged city will never be obliged to surrender for lack of a theatre.[20] In 1709 he proposed an utterly fantastic plan: all lovers of virtue are to contribute to a fund that will be used for ridding the country of theatres. Every actor is to get a pension for life on condition that he will never again step on a stage in England. The playhouses shall be used for other purposes; the licenses must be destroyed.

There is more to be said on Defoe's moralistic and utilitarian ideas concerning art; but this, I think, is sufficient to make us wonder how the holder of such views could ever become a notable creative writer.

Defoe published his first fully-developed story, *Robinson Crusoe*, at the age of 59. Before he did this he produced a truly overwhelming amount of journalistic writings. At first sight all these newspaper articles, essays, pamphlets, biographies, conduct books, plain descriptions of facts, as well as his efforts in verse, seem to have been written strictly within the limits that his Puritan views set up with regard to literature. They all pursued practical aims. If they tried to be entertaining they did so, according to their author's profession, in order to achieve their main purpose more successfully. Yet if we look at them more closely we discover that, in some instances, two gifts of Defoe's sought and found expression that enabled him later to become the teller of such great stories as *Robinson Crusoe, Captain Singleton, Moll Flanders*, etc.

The first of these gifts was the power of recording, in the most lively manner, observations of facts, human and extra-human, which he gathered from his own rich experience and from books. His Puritan conscience had nothing to say against the communication of experience for the purposes of information and improvement. But in the documents which belong to Defoe's earlier years there occur little realistic descriptions, reproductions of keenly observed scenes of everyday life that have nearly nothing to do with the informative or improving purpose of the whole. They stand there for their own sake, because it gave delight to the author to catch a piece of experience so perfectly. I quote such a

[20] *Review*, III, 509 ff.

passage. It is once more taken from the paragraphs on swearing in the *Essay upon Projects*. In order to make quite plain to his readers what he meant, Defoe found it necessary to introduce the following little scene:

> . . . what language is this?
> "Jack, God damn me, Jack, how do'st do, thou little dear son of a whore? How hast thou done this long time, by God?" and then they kiss; and the other, as lewd as himself, goes on: "Dear Tom, I am glad to see thee with all my heart, let me die. Come, let us go take a bottle; we must not part so; prithee, let's go and be drunk, by God!"[21]

The Puritan teachers have never minced words in their attacks upon vice. Justifying themselves by pointing out to critics the outspokenness of the Bible in such matters, they called everything by its name and an ugly thing by an ugly name. Their purpose was simple and clear. It is different in the case before us. Defoe used the opportunity for depicting a little street scene, giving a sketch of characters, a bit of an action, and a suggestion of atmosphere. It is done artlessly; yet there is something artistic about it. A new, amoral element has cropped up in the midst of the moralistic piece. Defoe's conscience noticed that something was wrong with that passage. Therefore he put the following complicated excuse into the preface of the *Essay:*

> In the chapter of academies, I have ventured to reprove the vicious custom of swearing. I shall make no apology for the fact, for no man ought to be ashamed of exposing what all men ought to be ashamed of practising. But methinks I stand corrected by my own laws a little, in forcing the reader to repeat some of the worst of our vulgar imprecations in reading my thoughts against it, to which, however, I have this to reply:
> First: I did not find it easy to express what I mean without putting down the very words, at least not so as to be very intelligible.
> Secondly: Why should words repeated only to expose the vice, taint the reader more than a sermon preached against lewdness

---

[21] Hazlitt, *op. cit.*, III, *Essay upon Projects,* 37.

should the assembly; for of necessity it leads the hearer to the thoughts of the fact, but the morality of every action lies in the end; . . . .[22]

What happened here on a small scale was to be repeated later on a much larger one. Defoe tried to cover all his long, absolutely amoral stories of low life with similar moralistic clothes. But every time he tried it, the clothing proved a little thinner, and finally, in the case of *Roxana, the Fortunate Mistress*, it was nothing more than a veil, a veil, besides, that had slid down from the incorrigible sinner it was supposed to envelop, and barely covered her feet.

We turn to the second of Defoe's gifts which contained artistic possibilities. It was his capacity for taking up parts and playing them successfully, for slipping into another man's or woman's position and acting naturally in it. We have observed that, by Locke's definition, reason is an instrument that can be used from every point of view. Defoe's reason enjoyed its full share of this capacity. Given a cause, it knew how to make a plausible case for it. Given a situation, it instructed Defoe how an ordinary human creature like himself would act in it. Disgusted at the sight of his complicated (to say the least) political life, Charles Gildon accused him once of being a modern Proteus.[23] This comparison, happy in the sense meant by Gildon, is even more apt in respect to his achievements as a story-teller. He was able to change shapes and yet to remain always the same. Robinson Crusoe, making a judicious use of the resources of his island; the terrified but nevertheless inquisitive saddler, staggering through the desolate streets of the plague-stricken capital; the Cavalier, serving in the armies of Gustavus Adolphus and Charles I; sturdy Moll Flanders, who changes husbands and lovers and steals without losing her nerve and sound judgment; Colonel Jacque, who courageously elbows his way through life in spite of a miserable start, all these attractive characters have more than a family likeness; each of them shows the traits of the hard-headed and common-sense Daniel Defoe.

[22] Hazlitt, *op. cit.*, III, *Essay upon Projects*, 5.
[23] Charles Gildon, *Robinson Crusoe examin'd and critizis'd;* ed. by Paul Dottin, London and Paris 1923, 65.

This aptness for playing parts also can be observed in Defoe's writings long before the beginning of his creative period. It led him to steps that were the contrary of practical on two early occasions. All critics of Defoe have encountered considerable difficulties in explaining the attitude taken by him in his first contribution to the violent controversy concerning the practice of Occasional Conformity.[24] This practice made it possible for Dissenters to evade the incapacities imposed upon them by the Test Act of 1673. Knowing how much he abhorred this Act, which prevented the members of his party from holding office, we might expect him to defend Occasional Conformity. But, to the astonishment of his friends and enemies and of the modern critics also, he published a pamphlet in 1698 in which he sang a melody all of his own.[25] He appears on the stage in the part of the uncompromising man of righteousness, and demonstrates by sharp reasoning that Occasional Conformity is utterly illogical. If the worship in the Church be sinful, then a Nonconformist has to avoid it always; if it be lawful, then his dissenting is sinful. There is only a clear choice possible: God or Baal. At some places in this pamphlet Defoe's pleasure in his part runs so completely away with him that his remarks contradict other passages in the same piece. Naturally his friends were ill-pleased with the stand he had taken. The aged Presbyterian minister John Howe called the pamphlet "idly sophistical",[26] and that is just what it is. Defoe tried for some time to defend the queer position he had chosen for himself, and then decided upon a barely disguised retreat.

The same pleasure in impersonating people played him a much worse trick in 1702, when he came out with his celebrated *Shortest Way with the Dissenters*. It was the object of this pamphlet to oppose the advance of Toryism that followed upon Queen Anne's accession to the throne. Defoe wanted to make a wild High-Church divine appear as ridiculous as possible by imitating his style

---

[24] Cf. W. P. Trent, *Daniel Defoe. How to know him.* Indianapolis 1916, 27 f.
[25] *An Enquiry into the Occasional Conformity of Dissenters, in Cases of Preferment.*
[26] In *Some Consideration of a Preface to an Enquiry, Concerning the Occasional Conformity of Dissenters, etc.*, London 1701.

and way of arguing in an exaggerating manner. Unfortunately for himself he did not stick closely enough to this plan. While writing long stretches of his text he forgot all about the political situation and his task of drawing a caricature, and simply enjoyed impersonating a panting, furious High-Church divine, who encourages the government resolutely to cut out of the nation the cancerous growth of Nonconformity. As a result he produced a character-sketch rather than a caricature. No wonder that many of the less discerning readers mistook the author's meaning. He was obliged to print an explanation of his pamphlet. Now the Tories, some of whom had greeted him as a valuable confederate at first, moved to prosecute him for libel, and finally brought him to Newgate.

Defoe used his Protean gift on many other practical occasions with better results. He wrote a series of pamphlets draped as a Quaker in the years after 1714. He took part in the ink-war that is known under the name of the Bangorian Controversy, in the guise of a Turkish merchant. And when Harley, his friend and erst-while protector, sat imprisoned by the triumphant Whigs after Queen Anne's death, he endeavoured to help him by faking the memoirs of M. Mesnager, the gentleman whom Louis XIV had sent to London in 1711 with the task of preparing the way for the peace-treaty of Utrecht.[27]

It is doubtful whether the two gifts of which we have been speaking would ever have found more than somewhat precarious expression in the service of practical or moralistic aims if it had not been for an undertaking engaged in by Defoe in the year 1715. The coming of George I to England meant a definite victory for all the Whigs stood for. Deistic and unitarian ideas enjoyed a growing popularity in Low-Church and Dissenter circles. Defoe discovered with amazement how little resistance his own group, the Presbyterians, put up against the influx of all kinds of heresies. He decided that the root of these evils was the disappearance of the Puritan family government, that the only way to stem the flood of religious modernism was to reform the family. He wanted to do something about the matter himself. There existed a great number

---

[27] *Minutes of the Negociations of Monsr. Mesnager, at the Court of England,… Written by Himself*, London 1717.

of reliable, systematic books on the best organization of the Christian family. They defined and classified the spiritual and secular duties of the father, the mother, the children, and the servants in a most satisfactory manner.[28] The trouble was that these works, composed by the Puritan divines of the 17th century, no longer interested even the middle-class people for whom they were intended. To write one more of these books was therefore out of the question for Defoe. He never engaged in a literary undertaking that did not promise a reasonable sale from the start. He wanted to make the good old truths palatable to the degraded taste of his contemporaries by presenting them in a new and unusual form. Inasmuch as people decline to be taught without being amused, I shall amuse them in order to teach them. That is what Defoe asserts in the preface of his *Family Instructor*. Similar slightly hypocritical remarks stand at the beginning or end of most of his later stories. Instead of composing another catalogue of Christian duties Defoe gives a paradigm of the conversion of a family in his conduct-book, a family far gone already on the road of modern worldliness.

We meet a little boy who has grown to be about five years old without having a clear notion as to the nature of his creator, the trinity, the atonement, and similar religious fundamentals. There is a girl in the family who reads French novels and play-books without shame and compunction. The eldest son and another sister indulge "in all possible Folly and Levity, such as *Plays*, *Gaming*, *Loosness* of Life, and *Irreligious* Behaviour, not immodest or dishonest . . .; but they were bred up with *Gayety* and *Gallantry*".[29] And the parents, out of an inexplicable hardness of heart, tolerate such goings-on for a long time without interfering. This desperate situation is mended in the first part of the *Family Instructor*. The father is awakened to a consciousness of his neglect by a set of rather mature religious questions which his youngest child asks him out of natural curiosity. The dreadfulness of what he had done weighs heavily upon his mind. The whole family is clearly in

[28] Cf. L. L. Schücking, *Die Familie im Puritanismus*, Leipzig und Berlin 1929.
[29] *The Family Instructor*, London 1715, 1st ed., 84.

danger of being eternally damned. He consults with his wife, and they decide to take drastic measures immediately: daily family worship is reinstituted. French novels and play-books are burnt, the whole of Sunday is reserved again for religious purposes. Three of the children are overjoyed at hearing of these innovations, as they have had a definite feeling before that something was wrong with the family. But the two elder children prove rebellious. There occur lively scenes between the saved and the lost souls. The father, hardening himself with some difficulty to be equal to his duty, finally puts the ultimatum before the two rebels: they must either comply with his demands, or leave his house at once. They go. It becomes apparent that the son is one of the damned by pre-destination. After an ignoble career in London he enters the army, is wounded, and dies alone and friendless. His sister is more lucky. A pious cousin ventures to marry her, though his future father-in-law warns him that the man who marries this girl runs more risk than a grenadier in storming a counterscarp. The initial period of his conjugal life taxes his patience to the utmost, but then grace intervenes, and everything is settled satisfactorily.

So much for the matter of the *Family Instructor*. There is little of Defoe's renowned realism in this book. The religious purpose dominates powerfully over all minor purposes. And when Defoe wanted to teach religion he could not be realistic. His characters are figures made to fit into the Calvinistic scheme, which knows only three classes of human beings: the converted, the convertible un-converted, and the unconvertible. Only the son and the daughter in the state of sin exhibit some human traits; the good people are mere puppets. The course of the action also is artificial; it is made up for moralizing purposes in the spirit of flat rationalism. Using such methods Defoe has not only produced bad literature but also one of the worst religious books imaginable, the book of an essen-tially unreligious rationalist who tries to be religious. The weak-ness of his product becomes particularly apparent if we compare it with, for example, Bunyan's *Life and Death of Mr. Badman*. Bunyan also moralizes abundantly; but he does not construct first a sham reality in order to be able afterwards to moralize about it. Mr. Badman does everything forbidden by God without trouble of conscience. When he desires the fortune of a rich and pious girl he becomes a church-goer for some time. Once her husband he takes off his mask, and makes her utterly miserable. Having fallen into a serious illness, he is caught by a fit of death-bed repentance — which later disappears when the illness leaves him. Finally he dies quite peacefully, a fat and happy sinner. Facing these unpalatable facts, Bunyan holds fast to his faith. This gives him the power of writing a sound and stirring religious book. Defoe, when he attempts to preach religion, ignores such facts. His virtuous people are blessed with success on earth. His sinners receive terrible, visible punishment. Sham conversions, death-bed repentances are unknown to him. A corollary of his religious sterility is the abundance, either ridiculous or boring, of religious sentimentality in his work. When the sense of sin overcomes his characters, and again, when they feel themselves touched by grace, there is no end of weeping and moaning. There occur about thirty scenes of tears in the first part of the *Family Instructor*. We may note here that such religious scenes are the only ones in the whole body of Defoe's works in which he emphasizes the description of violent emotions. The Calvinists trained themselves to beware of fixing their affections on wordly things. The effects of this training are still present in Defoe. Though his interest in this world is intense and absorbing, it is never emotional. Though he demands in *The Use and Abuse of the Marriage Bed* that there be something more between candidates for marriage than sexual attraction, and something more also than appreciation of one another's virtues, he is distrustful of the so-called higher forms of the passion of love. The form of love that he praises is a very sober and temperate affair. When he portrays love scenes in his stories, he gives detailed accounts of the reasoning processes in his men and women, but only short matter-of-fact sketches of their emotional reactions.[30] In theory he defends the view that strong affections must be reserved for things divine. As these things have become most unreal to him, he cannot but describe the workings of religious affections in scenes of lachrymose sentimentality, a sentimentality that tries to atone for the absence of true feeling by violent gesticulation, loud outbursts, oppressive pathos. It makes us laugh or yawn, but it re-

[30] Cf. G. A. Aitken, *op. cit.*, VII, 17, 34, 53, etc.

sponded perfectly to the needs of a public that found itself in the same religious situation as Defoe.

Still in 1715 a second edition of the book became necessary. Defoe shows himself extremely proud of his success in its preface. The apology for the new way of presenting old truths is much shorter than in the first edition. He talks with satisfaction of the beauties of his text.

Just what were these beauties? First, there were again those homely descriptions of details of everyday life, those happy imitations of the language of the common man which we have mentioned already. Secondly, there were passages of undeniable dramatic tension. Certain situations occurred in the false moralistic scheme that roused the instincts of the story-teller in Defoe. He developed them in an interesting way. The main parts in such scenes are always played by the sinners. Defoe later became acutely conscious of the fact that the fertile period of a converted sinner's life for the story-teller's purposes is the sinner's career before his conversion. As yet he took advantage of it only accidentally. Let me mention one of the situations in question. The family we have met returns from church on the Sunday on which the reform plan is put into force. All its members are supposed to spend the rest of the day in religious meditation. But the wicked eldest daughter insists on having her drive in the park. A discussion between mother and daughter ensues. At first the terms used are polite, the atmosphere cool. As the dialogue proceeds Defoe artfully makes us feel how the nerves begin to vibrate, how anger begins to boil under the surface. The sentences become shorter, the phrases more edged. We seem to hear the heavy breathing of the combatants. At last a relieving outbreak occurs, and the mother boxes the ears of her obdurate child.

We find many scenes of this type in the second volume of the *Family Instructor*, published in 1718, in which the pleasure of story-telling is indulged in more freely than in the earlier book. We omit the discussion of this strange product, half novel, half conduct-book, and turn to the first of Defoe's histories of conversions in which the natural development of the action is not distorted by the moralistic scheme: *Robinson Crusoe*. Here, evidently, the story of Robinson's adventures at sea and on his island follows its own logic. It is the primary element; the moralistic scheme is merely an interpretation of what happens; it does not influence the course of the action. It can even be cut away, and still the action remains coherent and satisfactory. The scheme of conversion is not always very carefully handled. The fact that the boy's desire to go to sea and to seek adventure is considered a sinful propensity at the beginning of the book seems strange to us. Especially as *Robinson Crusoe* was written by a man who certainly did not see anything wrong in the activity of the merchants and mariners who promoted the growth of England's sea power. Gildon's attack on Defoe's famous work shows that the author's attitude towards the boy's love of the sea shocked at least one of his contemporaries. I believe that Defoe made this point only because the scheme of conversion, which he wanted to have in his book as a justifying superstructure, demanded something of the kind. If Robinson's misfortunes had to appear as a means by which Providence punished and improved a sinner, Robinson had to be a sinner. Defoe made him one by interpreting his going to sea against the will of his parents as a sin. In doing so he applied antiquated standards, developed by the Puritan teachers of the 17th century, who definitely saw a sin in a man's wish to choose a course of life other than that which Providence has made natural for him.

Though *Robinson Crusoe* was thus made into a history of a conversion, its composition caused trouble to Defoe's conscience. Though he deceived many readers, he could not hide from himself the fact that it was not an autobiography as it purported to be. Mr. A. W. Secord's careful study of Defoe's sources shows conclusively that he did not invent many things in it.[31] He equipped himself for his task by reading as many descriptions of travels as possible. Most of the little stones he used in the composition of his mosaic were empirical facts. But the whole was fiction nevertheless, perilously near to a kind of literature he thoroughly abhorred in theory. He made many attempts to explain for his own and his readers' benefit why the kind of story he wrote was good and useful, whereas the chimney-corner romances and inventions of

---

[31] A. W. Secord, *Studies in the Narrative Method of Defoe.* University of Illinois Studies in Language and Literature, IX, 1924.

other men were deceitful and dangerous lies. How difficult the question was for him is shown by the involved sentences and ambiguous terms in which most of these explanations are couched. We shall consider one of them. Defoe asserts in the *Serious Reflections . . . . of Robinson Crusoe* that invented stories of the desirable type, "published historically" — that is, as though they were narratives of fact — "are once for all related", and, the moral being drawn, remain allusive only.[32] This is a very curious statement. In *Robinson Crusoe* the moral is certainly drawn; but we know that many of the early readers did not conceive of it as being a parable, but a history of fact. In Defoe's later works the moral is drawn more carelessly. What is the moral of *Captain Singleton*, the hero of which first amasses wealth as a pirate, then converts himself, and enjoys the fruits of his labours in peace? In the *Memoirs of a Cavalier*, the *Journal of the Plague Year*, and the travel-books no moral is drawn at all. Whether it is drawn or not, Defoe's stories are very successful attempts to make fiction appear not allusive but like a report of fact.

What does Defoe mean when he speaks of a story which is "once for all related". Does he think of the notion of poetic truth according to which a work of art has to represent something universal in the special? If he means that, he means something he could never achieve; for this type of production demands that idealistic approach to reality which was, as we have seen, utterly impossible for him. In this he remained bound by the Puritan tradition to the last. His art consisted exactly in telling a story for once only, so perfectly for once that it looked like a report of fact. The only interpretation at his hands was that of Calvinism. And this interpretation was in contradiction to his own experience of life. When he tried to force it on the natural reality, as in the *Family Instructor*, the result was something unreal and deformed. In *Robinson Crusoe* he managed to describe natural events and to give a Calvinistic interpretation at the same time without a real interaction between the two, therefore without harm to one or the other. In the later books the interpretation is given for form's sake, or not at all. It is handled so carelessly that the results are meaningless when at

[32] G. A. Aitken, *op. cit.*, III, 102 f.; cf. also I, lxvii.

their best, and farcical when at their worst. However, we are thankful that these queer little tails that hang down from such completely amoral stories as *Moll Flanders* and *Roxana* allowed Defoe to deceive himself about what he was doing, for without such self-deception he could not have written them.

The last point I want to make is this: it would be erroneous to say that Defoe faked autobiographies only because he knew that his readers wanted books of fact and despised fiction. The same state of mind that led his readers to ask for true stories led him to write tales that should seem as true as he could possibly make them. His artistic instinct aimed at reproduction, imitation, not interpretation of natural events in literature. Because he was an artist he was not satisfied with collecting observations of nature and human behaviour, but desired to become more intensely conscious of his own experiences by reproducing them in his stories, and to undergo in imagination experience from which time and space shut him off. More and more experience he wanted, not the interpretation of one experience. His art sprang from and satisfied this thirst. It may be objected that every imitation of nature is by necessity an interpretation. This is true. Defoe, however, knew how to reduce the interpretative element to a minimum, as he was mainly interested in the outward appearances of events, not in what is mysterious and doubtful about them. He told how human common sense deals with practical obstacles. He described the actions of man; the reflexes occasioned in the mind by the clash of intelligence and the outside world were important for him in so far as they resulted in further action. He used the methods of the journalist, whose task it is to abstain from interpretation as much as possible in his reports on events. This narrow approach confined him to a primitive form of literary art. At the same time it made it possible for him to tell one charming, life-like story after the other; it gave him a fertility unknown to less straight-forward writers, who aim at higher things.[33]   (1936)

---

[33] For a detailed discussion of Defoe's pseudo-Puritanism cf. the present writer's study, *Der aufgeklärte Puritanismus Daniel Defoes,* Swiss Studies in English, I, Zürich und Leipzig 1936.

VI.

The Sorrow of Love

A Poem by William Butler Yeats Revised
by Himself

WHEN WILLIAM BUTLER Yeats was in his twenties he seemed to be
the perfect period poet, so excellently well did his mentality and
his style fit into the *fin de siècle* atmosphere. He disliked his own
Victorian age as heartily as any one of the other aesthetes, and he
eagerly sought to escape into some imaginary realm of beauty. In
his later years, however, this man showed an amazing power of
renewing himself. He never gave up his tenacious search for the
reality behind the surface of things, which was at the same time a
search for a true basis of communication with his fellow men. He
pursued it when he studied mysticism and occultism, when he made
the legends of Old Ireland the source of his symbols, when he
worked for the Abbey Theatre, getting into contact, and often
conflict, with all sorts of facts and people, and when he finally
evolved the private philosophy laid down in *A Vision*. While he
was doing all this he moved from one stage of thought and being
to the next, a process that was strikingly mirrored both by his
changing style and by his changing facial expression. To penetrate
and exemplify these parallel developments is the fascinating task
of the lover and student of Yeats' poetry.

It has been undertaken several times since the poet's death. We
only mention three books, all equally worthy of their subject. Louis
Macneice, in his well documented introduction,[1] goes as far as a
lover of Yeats' poetry who is at the same time a young modernist
can go. His irrepressible consciousness of knowing almost everything, except the writing of poetry, much better than good old
Yeats is not altogether an asset for his study. Another, shorter
book was written by V. K. Narayana Menon.[2] It is charmingly
prefaced by Sir Herbert Grierson. Menon is more successful in
dealing with Yeats' earlier periods than when he approaches his

[1] *The Poetry of W. B. Yeats*, Oxford University Press 1941.
[2] *The Development of William Butler Yeats*, Edinburgh 1942.

later ones. Here he is far too much preoccupied by what he thought it necessary to call the poet's "fascism" — a fault that was perhaps inevitable in 1942. Fortunately, Peter Ure, the author of the latest study of Yeats, could write in a less oppressive atmosphere.[3] He wisely abstained from another general survey, and concentrated on one most important aspect of the poet's development: his struggle for an efficient poetical method of communication. The present writer does not think that Ure's extraordinary expansion of the meaning of the terms "mythology" and "mythological" serves a useful purpose. Ure speaks of "myths" even where the poetic symbols are derived from practical everyday experience. Having discussed the use of mythological material in the strict sense of the term, he opens a new chapter, declaring: "So far we have treated of the mythological subject in the accepted sense, of Yeats' handling of themes drawn from the race symbols common to the 'indomitable Irishry' and expressed in their ancient classical literature. This definition of mythology must now be extended to cover material which provides a like poetic stimulus, but in which the myth derives not from the experience of the race but from that of the individual poet."[4] Neither his explanation of this necessity nor his practical use of the terms in question could convince us. We should prefer to speak of Yeats' symbols throughout: the young poet drew them from his Romantic predecessors, from mystics, from the strange imaginings of the people and from the dreams of his nights and days; a little later they were mainly taken from mythology, especially Irish mythology, because this seemed to him a storehouse of symbols with an unrivalled force of communication; and when the poet had learned to face practical tasks and real people, his symbols were derived from his contact with and his memory of them. The philosophy of *A Vision* was another source of symbols for him. In this adequate account of the facts we legitimately use "symbol" in an older and wider sense than the representatives of the modern symbolist school of poetry, but the term is not strained as "myth" is in Ure's essay.

[3] *Towards a Mythology. Studies in the Poetry of W. B. Yeats*, London 1946.
[4] *op. cit.*, 28.

A study of Yeats, based on all the relevant facts, will only be possible when a complete edition of his plays and poems will be on hand. To produce it is a fine, but laborious task on account of the poet's well-known passion for revision. When he had reached a new stage of his development he often was not satisfied to write poetry of a new kind; he felt compelled to modify the creations of his former self because they had become troublesome to him. This tendency is highly characteristic of Yeats, in whose later thought the struggle of a man against himself plays so important a part,[5] and who could at times be a very severe critic of himself.[6] In revising old work Yeats grappled with manifestations of "the opposite of his true being". To friends who complained of this habit, which deprived them of stable and definite versions of the poems they liked, he answered as early as 1908:

> The friends that have it I do wrong
> When ever I remake a song,
> Should know what issue is at stake:
> It is myself that I remake.[7]

[5] In *A Vision* (edition of 1937), e.g., he says of the mysterious "instructors" that used his wife as their medium in order to communicate their wisdom to him: "It was part of their purpose to affirm that all the gains of man come from conflict with the opposite of his true being." (p. 13.)

[6] Cf. for instance the end of the letter from John Aherne (an entirely symbolical friend of the poet's) to Mr. Yeats, in which his early prose as he used it in *Rosa Alchemica* (1896), *The Tables of the Laws* (1896) and *The Adoration of the Magi* (1897) is discussed: "He is, however (...), bitter about your style in those stories and says that you substituted sound for sense and ornament for thought. ... I wrote once to remonstrate. I said that you wrote in those tales as many good writers wrote at the time over half Europe, that such prose was the equivalent of what somebody had called 'absolute poetry' and somebody else 'pure poetry'; that though it lacked speed and variety, it would have acquired both, as Elizabethan prose did after the *Arcadia*, but for the surrender everywhere to the sensational and the topical; that romance driven to its last ditch had a right to swagger. He answered that when the candle was burnt out an honest man did not pretend that grease was flame." (*A Vision*, 55.)

[7] *The Collected Works in Verse and Prose of William Butler Yeats*, Stratford-on-Avon 1908, II, epigraph.

This being so, the collation of all the editions of Yeats' poems and plays will be one of the major tasks of his editors, and it will produce material of great value if we shall know how to interpret it.[8]

This article is an attempt at such interpretation. We propose to compare in it three versions of the short poem *The Sorrow of Love*.[9]

Early Version (EV)
1892

The quarrel of the sparrows in the eaves,
    The full round moon and the star-laden sky,
And the loud song of the ever-singing leaves
    Had hid away earth's old and weary cry.

And then you came with those red mournful lips,
    And with you came the whole of the world's tears,
And all the sorrows of her labouring ships,
    And all the burden of her myriad years.

And now the sparrows warring in the eaves,
    The crumbling moon, the white stars in the sky,
And the loud chanting of the unquiet leaves
    Are shaken with earth's old and weary cry.

Revised Version (RV)
1899

7 & 8: And all the trouble.   10: The curd-pale moon.

[8] The present writer has undertaken this task in the case of a single play, *Deirdre*, and has included the results in *Three Anglo-Irish Plays (Bibliotheca Anglicana*, V), Bern 1943.

[9] We owe the early version (EV), which appeared in *The Countess Kathleen and Various Legends and Lyrics* (1892) to Louis Macneice, who quotes it *op. cit.*, 69 f.; the revised version (RV), which has three alterations only, is taken from *The Collected Works in Verse and Prose of W. B. Y.*, Stratford-on-Avon 1908, I, 157, the final text (FT) from *The Collected Poems of W. B. Y.*, New York 1934, 46. I am indebted to Mr. D. W. Foster, Cambridge, for the information that RV was printed for the first time in 1899, in the second revised edition of *Poems by W. B. Y.*, and that FT is found first in the volume *Early Poems and Stories*, published by Macmillan & Co. in 1925.

The brawling of a sparrow in the eaves,
The brilliant moon and all the milky sky,
And all that famous harmony of leaves,
Had blotted out man's image and his cry.

A girl arose that had red mournful lips
And seemed the greatness of the world in tears,
Doomed like Odysseus and the labouring ships
And proud as Priam murdered with his peers;

Arose, and on the instant clamorous eaves,
A climbing moon upon an empty sky,
And all that lamentation of the leaves,
Could but compose man's image and his cry.

Macneice has preceded us in comparing EV and FT.[10] He
offers a good appreciation of EV; his interpretation of FT, however, seems less satisfactory. Having indicated some of the more
striking formal changes, he continues:

And the poem is no longer languid.

But perhaps this poem ought to be languid. There is no law
which demands that all poems should be close-knit or vigorous
or virile. The poem is no longer languid but it no longer rings
true. Yeats, with a different poem in his mind's eye, has distorted it. It has become neither one thing nor the other. Mantegna
may be a higher kind of painter than Giorgione but Mantegna
must not tamper with Giorgione's canvases. The new version as
a whole is both ill-digested and obscure. For example, in the
last line the word "compose" appears ambiguous; at first sight it
might mean the exact opposite — i. e. might mean "lay to rest".
The introduction of Odysseus and Priam is high falutin, dis-
rupting the original simplicity. The substitution of "A girl
arose" for the second person, "And then you came", dissipates
the lyrical feeling and introduces a pompous note which is here
discordant. Considering the fate of this poem I agree with A. E.

[10] *op. cit.*, 69—72.

who wrote: "I feel a little sad sometimes that the later self-conscious artist could not let the earlier halfconscious artist be."

The following pages will show why we have ventured to cover the ground once more after Macneice. Having listened to EV we agree with him that it is attractive "in the languid, self-pitying, late Victorian manner". The poet appears in the pose of the late-born, melancholy man, who is haunted eternally by something as indefinite as "earth's old and weary cry". He is diverted from his preoccupation with that cry by the fascination of natural phenomena. Three of the four mentioned (the full round moon, the star-laden sky, the loud song of the ever-singing leaves) are traditional beautiful objects, and the poet's passive and obedient soul responds to them with great joy. "The quarrel of the sparrows in the eaves" seems a somewhat queer companion of those three. It is not mysterious, subdued, and beautiful, but loud, even shrill, certainly not a traditional thing of beauty like the others. This opening, which might be accused of being out of harmony with the rest of the stanza, betrays the possibility in Yeats to which FT owes its existence. The second stanza calls up the poet's mistress, using the image of "those red mournful lips". This is entirely in keeping with the conventional imagery of the first stanza. It is striking with its antithesis of the colour of blood, life and passion and the gloomy adjective "mournful".[11] The suffering the lady brought with her is expressed by imagery in which vagueness and definiteness of outline are strangely and not too satisfactorily mixed. The clash is harshest in "the sorrows of her labouring ships". It evidently vexed the poet at the time of the first revision when he replaced the vague, poetical "sorrows" and the conventionally poetical "burden" by "trouble", a hard and practical everyday word, which removes a suspicious note of sentimental sighing from the two lines. The last stanza shows nature changed by Ruskin's pathetic fallacy. It no longer hides "earth's old and weary cry"; it is full of it. The quarrelling of the sparrows is heightened to warring. It is no longer the full round moon that is remembered, but the crumbling, i. e. the waning moon. Yeats used "crumbling"

[11] Those "red lips" appear in other poems as part of Yeats' imagery of

in the same sense much later, in *The Phases of the Moon,* where the second part of the poem opens with the line:

> And after that the crumbling of the moon:[12]

This points to the fact that it was not dissatisfaction with the expression itself which made the poet replace it by "the curd-pale moon" in RV. The reason for this change can be guessed: it is the point of the poem that the *same* natural phenomena take on a different appearance after the poet has passed through his love experience. A crumbling moon is not the same as a full round moon; paleness, however, is an aspect of the full round moon that impresses Yeats in his new mood. The pathetic fallacy modifies both the function and the quality of his impressions. It renders them more intense (quarrel > warring; loud song > loud chanting); it also gives prominence to new features in the objects of nature (the paleness of the moon, the whiteness of the stars, the restlessness of the leaves). Whereas the first lines of this stanza are an echo with a difference, the final one ends with the powerful repetition of the phrase "earth's old and weary cry".

In turning to FT we first want to compare its metrical structure with that of EV. The fundamental metrical scheme of the two poems is the same. In both of them the stanzas are composed of four lines of five iambic feet each. This scheme is observed much more strictly in FT than in EV. Its resistance against the pressure of the poet's emotion is much stronger. In EV the scheme is extremely elastic and plastic. I find no less than ten points of height-

---

dangerous beauty: cf. the beginning of *The Wanderings of Oisin,* where the hero and his fellows meet

> A pearl-pale, high-born lady, who rode
> On a horse with bridle of findrinny;
> And like a sunset were her lips,
> A stormy sunset on doomed ships;
>> *(The Collected Works,* 1908, I, 176)

and a beautiful stanza from *The Rose of the World:*

> Who dreamed that beauty passes like a dream?
> For these red lips, with all their mournful pride,
> Mournful that no new wonder may betide,
> Troy passed away in one high funeral gleam,
> And Usna's children died. *(Ibidem,* 149)

[12] *A Vision,* 1937, 62.

ened stress in it where two or more stressed syllables stand side by side, and break through the iambic rhythm: fúll roúnd móon / lóud sóng / awáy eárth's óld / And thén yóu cáme / réd móurnful / wórld's téars / whíte stárs / loúd chánting / únquíet léaves / eárth's óld. In FT their number is reduced to three. In EV there are eight groups of unstressed syllables, producing anapaestic rhythms: ănd thĕ stár-lădĕn ský / ănd thĕ lóud / ŏf thĕ éver / ŏf thĕ wórld's / ĭn thĕ ský / ănd thĕ loúd / shakĕn wĭth eárth's. In FT I can discover only three such groups: thăt hăd réd / lĭke Odýsseus / ănd thĕ lá-bouring. In both poems there occur a number of half-stresses, which we have not counted as departures from the iambic scheme.[13]

What is the meaning of these observations? EV shows a rhythmical pattern full of movement and variation. Stress-concentration and stress-isolation give emotional emphasis to quite a series of images and ideas. The frequent use of these devices can suggest a tendency to luxuriate in emotions for their own sakes, and it decidedly does so in the second stanza of the poem before us. In other places it is not a sign of such weakness; there it is an expression of the fact that the poet was communicating three experiences that he felt to be equally important and compelling: the healing effect of nature, all the trouble of an impossible love, and the change in his impressions of nature, caused by the strain of that love. FT is less emotional, more virile and intellectual in its strict adherence to the chosen rhythmical scheme. Its sparing use of the devices of stress-concentration and stress-isolation renders them particularly effective. There are two groups of three stressed syllables; they appear connected with the central idea of the poem: óut mán's ímage / compóse mán's ímage. Besides, there are two stresses in contact in the verse:

A gírl aróse that had réd móurnful líps

Here the emphatic effect is heightened because the stressed syllables are preceded by two unstressed ones: a combination of stress-concentration and -isolation. The meaning of this particular rhythmical arrangement will appear later. The whole rhythmical pattern of FT suggests that the poet no longer surrendered

[13] Cf. Thĕ quárrĕl ŏf thĕ spárrŏws ìn thĕ eáves.

himself to all of the three experiences that had been important for him when a young man. It does so in combination with a great number of other changes which it is now our task to discuss.

The disposition of the three stanzas has remained the same in FT. The central motif, which is at first "blotted out" and then "composed" by nature, is "man's image and his cry". It is much more definite and concrete than "earth's old and weary cry"; and the verbs in inverted commas, the one colloquial and direct, the other abstract and difficult, are also good pointers to the almost metaphysical style of the whole.

In the first line "quarrel" is replaced by the picturesque, slightly contemptuous "brawling", which hints at the vulgarity and insignificance of the noise of the sparrows. The singular "a sparrow" is not only chosen because it is more specific than the plural; in the light of what follows it is also meant to increase our amusement at the tiny cause of a dreamy young poet's enthusiasm. That young man's romantic cult of nature strikes the older Yeats as a little absurd. This suspicion, aroused by the first line, is turned into a certainty by the rest of the stanza. "Brilliant", the new epithet given to the moon, is purposely "near-fetched", and avoids the poetic associations that had been so important in the early poem. The same is true of "all the milky sky": a quick, almost impatient, summary of an impression which does not fascinate the poet in the old way. And the third line with "all that famous harmony of leaves" is even tinged with something like quiet mockery at the former self that desired to be lulled by "the loud song of the ever-singing leaves".

What is Yeats' new attitude to the love experience recorded in the second stanza? He looks at it in the same detached, even slightly amused way. The personal and intimate "And then you came" is replaced by the objective and rhetorical "A girl arose", in which there may be an ironic undertone. We feel irony also in the use of all the beautiful old time imagery that follows. It plays about the "red mournful lips", given so much rhythmical prominence, about "the greatness of the world in tears", in which all the old vagueness is retained, and about the Odysseus and Priam similes, which are more definite. They all belong to the old high style. Therefore three fourths of the stanza are made dependent on the verb "seemed", which puts distance between them and the poet. The ironic imitation of the old style is made perfect by the reappearance of the anapaestic rhythm in the Odysseus line. The whole treatment stresses the illusionary nature of the love experience. This illusion, however, possessed the virtue of destroying the older nature illusion and of rendering nature capable of revealing a glimpse of reality: man's image and his cry. We should overshoot our mark if we failed to notice that the poet's rejection of two powerful illusions of his youth is full of tender respect. After all, they were creations of his imagination, for him the most important source of truth. It had helped him in his first phase to escape from a reality which he detested; it had enabled him to love in the old high way of love. And the unhappiness which sprang from his love made him face reality for the first time. Thus his love was a creative illusion. And was not the whole of the poet's life a passing from one creative illusion to the other, the philosophy of *A Vision* being the supreme example of one?

The positive effect of the love-illusion is expressed in the third stanza. It is instantaneous, as is stressed by the repetition of "arose" and the precise adverbial phrase "on the instant". The latter is not the language of immediate experience, but of a critical survey of the past. The same is true of the purposely intellectual and difficult "Could but compose", with which the poem reaches its greatest distance from the style of its predecessor. The natural phenomena which are no longer means of escape from, but symbols of reality are approached with the utmost seriousness. There is something hard and challenging in "clamorous eaves"; the contemptuous note of "brawling" has disappeared. There is only one thing visible in the sky: the climbing moon. The stars are forgotten. This stressing of the moon symbol need not astonish us, as Yeats in his maturity saw the character and fate of man connected with the changing phases of the moon. The participle "climbing", while forming an effective alliteration with "clamorous", points to the movement of the heavenly body; its most important quality for an imagination permeated by a moon philosophy. In "all that lamentation of the leaves" there is again the tense seriousness noted above. The two epithets of EV have been dropped. In the whole of the new poem Yeats has used nine epithets only, whereas there were sixteen (according to Macneice seventeen) in EV: another symptom of the change from a predominantly emotional to an intellectual attitude towards the recorded experience.

Our comparison of the two versions has shown them to be in reality two different poems on the same set of experiences: the first gives them immediate expression in a style that strives to be rich, even luxuriant, in rhythm, sound, choice of words and imagery, the style of an aesthete of the nineties; the second is a revaluation of those experiences, even a piece of severe self-criticism, in a terse and metallic style, reaching from the colloquial to the abstract, capable of subtle irony. This style places Yeats among the leaders of a much younger generation of post-war poets. There is pessimism in both poems; in the first it is largely an aesthetic pose, in the second it springs from experience and knowledge. Together the poems are an impressive illustration of Yeats' continual "conflict with the opposite of his true being". In his maturity he saw that opposite in the young man who had fled from a reality he did not really know, trying to create by his poetic imagination a world of beautiful illusions. And his true being? We are reluctant to speak of it in a few words. We catch a glimpse of it when we see him facing reality with all the terrors he discovers in it, when he speaks of the illusionary nature of his dreams and nevertheless desperately clings to them as long as he finds them creative. Yeats' own best commentary on what has happened to *The Sorrow of Love* in the course of revision is a short poem, printed in 1910 in *The Green Helmet and other Poems:*

THE COMING OF WISDOM WITH TIME

Though leaves are many, the root is one;
Through all the lying days of my youth
I swayed my leaves and flowers in the sun;
Now I may wither into the truth.[14]

At the end of our survey we must briefly return to Macneice's commentary quoted above. We believe we have refuted his adverse criticism of FT; we disagree with almost every single point in it, and think that Yeats knew very well what he was doing when

[14] *The Collected Poems of W. B. Y.*, New York 1934, 107.

he changed EV.[15] The new poem appears to us coherent, clear, a subtler and more fascinating creation than its predecessor. Nevertheless there remains one undeniable difficulty about the revision: it appears side by side with unrevised work in the later reprints of the *Rose*-poems to which it belongs, and it is no longer in harmony with such pieces as *The Pity of Love*, which precedes, and *When You Are Old*, which follows it.   (1948)

[15] Macneice's conclusion has the support of Sir Herbert Read, cf. "The Later Yeats" in *A Coat of Many Colours*, London 1945.

VII.

William Butler Yeats
and
The Ballad of Reading Gaol
by Oscar Wilde

WHEN W. B. YEATS published *The Oxford Book of Modern Verse* in the autumn of 1936, it found a rather cool reception, the critics judging it mainly as a contribution to a representative series of anthologies and finding it an unsatisfactory one. H. A. Mason[1] e. g. called the poet-editor's taste "merely eccentric", and R. Hillyer's[2] strictures upon his method of selection as well as upon the introduction to his book were almost equally severe. Without scrutinizing these and similar judgements, we claim that Yeats' achievement appears in a different light as soon as we ignore the question how he fulfilled his task in the service of the famous series of anthologies of the Clarendon Press, and consider his selection and introduction as an extensive and many-sided manifestation of the poet's taste in the final phase of his life. Viewed from this angle both of them become fascinating documents.

One of the surprises awaiting the reader of the book is the form in which *The Ballad of Reading Gaol*, the only poem by Oscar Wilde admitted to the volume, makes its appearance. Yeats printed no more than 38 of the 108 stanzas of Wilde's final version of the poem. As he placed the preposition "From" before the title we are tempted to neglect his text as just a selection from a poem too long to be reproduced in its complete form: a frequent, though regrettable feature in most anthologies. However, if we turn to the introduction and read the poet's explanation of the operation he performed upon Wilde's poem we find that he intended the stanzas he printed to be much more than merely a collection of striking passages; it was his ambition to print the poem in the form in which it can face the criticism of posterity. We quote the passage concerning Wilde from Yeats' introduction. The first sentence in it refers to a hypothetical young man looking for methods of poetic expression in the eighteen-nineties:

[1] *Scrutiny*, V, 1937, 449—451.
[2] *Modern Language Notes*, LII, 1937, 618—619.

Nor would that young man have felt anything but contempt for the poetry of Oscar Wilde, considering it an exaggeration of every Victorian fault, nor except in the case of one poem not then written, has time corrected the verdict. Wilde, a man of action, a born dramatist, finding himself overshadowed by old famous men he could not attack, for he was of their time and shared its admirations, tricked and clowned to draw attention to himself. Even when disaster struck him down it could not wholly clear his soul. Now that I have plucked from the *Ballad of Reading Gaol* its foreign feathers it shows a stark realism akin to that of Thomas Hardy, the contrary to all its author deliberately sought. I plucked out even famous lines because, effective in themselves, put into the Ballad they become artifical, trivial, arbitrary; a work of art can have but one subject.

> Yet each man kills the thing he loves,
>   By each let this be heard,
> Some do it with a bitter look,
>   Some with a flattering word.
> The coward does it with a kiss,
> The brave man with a sword!
>
> Some kill their love when they are young,
>   And some when they are old;
> Some strangle with the hands of Lust,
>   Some with the hands of Gold:
> The kindest use a knife, because
>   The dead so soon grow cold.

I have stood in judgement upon Wilde, bringing into the light a great, or almost great poem, as he himself had done had he lived; my work gave me that privilege.

Yeats proudly invokes his own achievement as a poet in order to justify his extraordinary enterprise. He could have added that he had often sat in judgment upon his own poems in a way not very different from his present attitude towards Wilde's *Ballad* and that he had frequently re-written the works of his own early periods. Now, when he was trying to give a new and better shape to another man's work, he refrained from any kind of re-writing, but relied entirely upon a daring method of drastic excision. The following paragraphs are an attempt to understand and evaluate his procedure.

The key-passage we have quoted contains a number of hints from which we can start. There is the remark about the foreign feathers Yeats plucked out and about the famous lines he sacrificed because they struck him as artificial, trivial, and arbitrary in the *Ballad*. The final sentence after the semicolon explains why lines "effective in themselves" can become bad as parts of a poetic organism: They suggest that Wilde pursued several inconsistent, even contradictory aims in his poem, that he was unable to isolate a single subject and devote himself whole-heartedly to its development. Yeats believed that he could not do this because even intense suffering had not completely absorbed his love of ostentation and pose. It was his aim to transform the *Ballad* into "a great, or almost great poem". With that bold nonchalance which came naturally to him in his old age and should not be mistaken for arrogance, Yeats claimed to have done something for the poem which Wilde would have done for it himself, had he been granted further growth as a man and an artist.

In order to come to a better understanding of Yeats' diagnosis and its results it is necessary to find out what exactly he meant by the words "foreign feathers". At first sight we tend to think that they were aimed at Wilde's well-known habit of culling images and phrases from the works of other poets and of transmuting them — not always successfully — into poetry of his own. However, Yeats' omissions from the ballad show clearly that he was far from attempting anything as pedantic as the consistent removal of borrowed phrases and images.[3] When he decided to omit stanza I, 5,[4] he was perhaps influenced by the knowledge that the most impressive image in it came from Coleridge, but similar borrowings

---

[3] Bernhard Fehr has shown in his *Studien zu Oscar Wildes Gedichten* (*Palaestra*, C, Berlin 1918) that the *Ballad* contains fewer borrowings than Wilde's earlier poems.

[4] Dear Christ! the very prison walls
    Suddenly seemed to reel,

did not disturb him in other places.[5] Indeed, the somewhat ambiguous expression "foreign feathers" was meant to cover everything in the *Ballad* that, to Yeats' mind, is foreign to its true subject. He defined his idea of what it should be by his two remarks on its style (stark realism) and its subject (but one subject). Both of them help him to rationalize his intuitive conviction that Wilde was unable to remain true to the primary impulse to which the poem owed its existence, either because that impulse had been weak and impure or because Wilde, in developing his theme, had yielded to the temptation of secondary purposes and interests. Yeats evidently preferred the second of these explanations, otherwise he could not have hoped to recover the true form of the poem by the simple method of excision.

Which were the secondary interests responsible for the stanzas eliminated by Yeats? Preeminent among them was Wilde's desire to give, with the help of a great number of personifications, a general meaning to his experience of prison life and even to draw a moral from it. This tendency is particularly strong in part V, which contains the following lines:

> The vilest deeds like poison weeds,
>   Bloom well in prison-air;
> It is only what is good in Man
>   That wastes and withers there:
> Pale Anguish keeps the heavy gate,
>   And the Warder is Despair.

They are, among other things, a striking plea for prison reform, but Yeats evidently was of opinion that this was a case of good

---

> And the sky above my head became
>   Like a casque of scorching steel;
> And, though I was a soul in pain,
>   My pain I could not feel.

[5] The two stanzas which, according to Fehr (*op. cit.*, 205), unmistakably echo Fitzgerald's *Omar Khayyàm* are e. g. retained by Yeats; the second of them is even given an important position at the end of his version.

intentions taking the place of good poetry. He omitted the whole of part V.

The propagandistic tendency is only part of the evidence betraying the fact that Wilde, in elaborating his poem, attempted to give a meaning and an application to an experience that had depressed him so horribly because it had been a routine sequence of utterly futile events. Beside it, there is Wilde's strange desire to force the identification with the doomed murderer upon the reader and to possess him with the idea that he is perhaps an even worse criminal than this victim of justice although he has gone scot-free so far. Stanza I, 7:

> Yet each man kills the thing he loves,
> By each let this be heard,
> Some do it with a bitter look,
> Some with a flattering word,
> The coward does it with a kiss,
> The brave man with a sword,

which is found again, with slight variations, at the very end of Wilde's poem, is by no means the only one inspired by that desire. Together with similar stanzas it gives the reader to understand that he is a mean scoundrel and, at the same time, surrounds the condemned man with a glamour of heroism. Recognizing how forced and dubious all this is, Yeats took to his scissors, convinced that here the older poet had lost the hard and bare ground of his primary experience from under his feet and indulged in one of his sentimental fancy flights. Wherever Wilde's tendency to step back from his experience, to comment upon it, to drag all sorts of higher significances into it, makes itself felt, and wherever he becomes a spectator of his own fate, Yeats interfered. Stanza III, 16 may serve as an example of the commenting and sympathy-seeking kind rejected by the poet-editor:

> Alas! it is a fearful thing
> To feel another's guilt!
> For, right within, the sword of Sin
> Pierced to its poisoned hilt,
> And as molten lead were the tears we shed
> For the blood we had not spilt.

In III, 7 Wilde appears to be the spectator of a prison scene:

> With slouch and swing around the ring
>   We trod the Fool's Parade!
> We did not care: we knew we were
>   The Devil's Own Brigade:
> And shaven head and feet of lead
>   Make a merry masquerade.[6]

One of the most important omissions concerns the execution itself, not only the introductory stanzas I, 10—16, describing the horrors which remain unknown to the contemporary who — by accident or from cowardice — has not physically killed:

> He does not die a death of shame
>   On a day of dark disgrace,
> Nor have a noose about his neck,
>   Nor a cloth upon his face,
> Nor drop feet foremost through the floor
>   Into an empty space,

but also stanzas III, 26—37, expressing the prisoners' consciousness of the progress of the execution from which they are separated by walls. What is the justification of this radical sacrifice of much that is certainly extremely effective? We find it in the impression that the double development of the macabre motif is executed with too much cleverness, calculation, and with a pseudo-refinement bordering upon the vulgar. Yeats' distrust of Wilde's craving for effective elaboration and sheer virtuosity was consistent. It demanded the sacrifice of many more famous stanzas. The weird dance of the shapes of Terror, harrassing the prisoners during their condemned fellow's last night (III, 19—25), disappeared although, or rather because, the author, making a generous use of self-quotations,[7] had spent on it the whole arsenal of his striking, but super-

---

[6] Cf. also three more eliminated stanzas: III, 17 (where the poet sees with the eyes of the warders), IV, 7 and IV, 8.

[7] Concerning this point cf. Robert Merle, *Oscar Wilde. Appréciation d'une Œuvre et d'une Destinée*, Rennes 1948, 447 ff.

ficial art of onomatopoeia and of sound and rhythm control. And in part IV we look in vain for the stanzas developing the theme of the pitiful burial in the prison yard.

We turn to the question of what is left in Yeats' version after the elimination of the generalizations, personifications and of the purple-patch poetry. We find the stanzas that speak simply and directly of Wilde's prison experience, stanzas composed in the true ballad style, which demands rapidity, the skipping of details, however decorative, and connecting links, however ingenious, without being afraid of repetition, stanzas containing terse, realistic, and idiomatic lines. Such lines occur in the opening stanzas, in the description of Wilde's unhappiest fellow prisoner:

> He walked amongst the Trial Men
> In a suit of shabby grey;
> A cricket cap was on his head, . . .,

in the first allusion to this man's doom:

> When a voice behind me whispered low,
> *"That fellow's got to swing"*,

and in the presentation of the prisoners under the mental pressure of the approaching execution:

> We sewed the sacks, we broke the stones,
> We turned the dusty drill:
> We banged the tins, and bawled the hymns,
> And sweated on the mill:
> But in the heart of every man
> Terror was lying still.

In Yeats' version the masterful lines of this type predominate and determine the character of the whole poem. The growing terror in the souls of the prisoners and the horrors of the hanging scene are expressed through allusion and suggestion rather than through elaboration. The glaring, sensational colours have given way to the appropriate dun and grey, and the horror is no longer made unreal by tricks of virtuosity. A particularly fine and brotherly action done by the experienced poet for one who had died before he achieved an entirely mature and reliable taste is his choice of the final stanza of his version. Suppressing most of the lines on the grave in the prison yard, which had proliferated without check under Wilde's hands, as well as the whole of part V and part VI, he found this simple and moving end for the *Ballad:*

> For where a grave had opened wide,
>   There was no grave at all:
> Only a stretch of mud and sand
>   By the hideous prison-wall,
> And a little heap of burning lime,
>   That the man should have his pall.
>
> For three long years they will not sow
>   Or root or seedling there:
> For three long years the unblessed spot
>   Will sterile be and bare,
> And look upon the wondering sky
>   With unreproachful stare.
>
> They think a murderer's heart would taint
>   Each simple seed they sow.
> It is not true! God's kindly earth
>   Is kindlier than men know,
> And the red rose would but blow more red,
>   The white rose whiter blow.

An interesting question remains: Is there a relation between the text prepared by Yeats and the version published by Robert Ross in 1911[8] and described by him as a "shorter version based on the original draft of the poem"? That original draft composed at Berneval was doubtless rather close to Yeats' idea of what the poem should be, and the expansions which Wilde added in Italy,[9] because he wished to enhance the weight and importance of a composition that was to rehabilitate him in the eyes of the world, introduced many of the elements rejected by the editor of *The Oxford Book of Modern Verse.* There is nothing to prove that Yeats knew of this version and considered the possibility of including it in his

[8] In *Selected Poems of Oscar Wilde, including The Ballad of Reading Gaol*, Methuen, London 1911.
[9] Cf. Robert Merle, *op. cit.*, 444 ff., on these romantic expansions of the realistic original draft.

anthology instead of risking the adventure of creating a text of his own. Nor is it possible to pretend that Yeats intuitively discovered and cut out Wilde's Italian expansions and reconstructed the Ross-version[10] in this way. He came close to it, when he omitted the nocturnal dance of the shapes of Terror as well as the whole of parts V and VI. In editing the rest of the *Ballad*, however, he went his own way, sacrificing 33 stanzas that appear in the Ross-text and accepting 9 that cannot be found there. Most of the rejected ones show traces of that generalizing tendency which Yeats considered an artistic fault, and many of the Italian stanzas admitted by him are without the taint of sentimental or sensational elaboration. This cannot be said with conviction of II, 7—9, stanzas in which the author plays a daring game with the auspicious and the ominous meanings given to the images of the tree, the high position, and the dance. Fortunately, Yeats could not resist the fascination of these ambiguous lines:

> For oak and elm have pleasant leaves
> That in the spring-time shoot:
> But grim to see is the gallows-tree,
> With its adder-bitten root,
> And, green or dry, a man must die
> Before it bears its fruit!
>
> The loftiest place is that seat of grace
> For which all worldlings try:
> But who would stand in hempen band
> Upon a scaffold high,
> And through a murderer's collar take
> His last look at the sky?
>
> It is sweet to dance to violins
> When Love and Life are fair:
> To dance to flutes, to dance to lutes

---

[10] Bernhard Fehr (*op. cit.*, 198), when he took stock of the stanzas contained in the final version only and missing in Ross' text, overlooked four of them, and Merle (*op. cit.*, 444 f.) repeated his result, adding a new error of his own: He prints IV, 13 instead of IV, 18. The corrected list is as follows: I, 11; II, 2, 3, 6—9; III, 3, 6, 11, 14, 18—25, 27, 31, 32; IV, 12, 18, 20, 21; the whole of parts V and VI.

> Is delicate and rare:
> But it is not sweet with nimble feet
> To dance upon the air!

Our observations permit the conclusion that Yeats brought the *Ballad* in line with stylistic ideals dear to him, and to many younger poets as well, in the nineteen-thirties. We suspect that his violent reaction against some of Wilde's stylistic vices was rooted in the consciousness that they had been his own temptations in his early period. Is it enough to say that he transformed a late Victorian poem into a modern one — no mean achievement, considering that omission was the only instrument he used? We do not think so. Yeats did more than that. His claim that he made a better poem of it by purging it of its impurities is justified. The reason why it will not supersede the full text is not an aesthetic, but the simple historical and biographical one that this is *The Ballad of Reading Gaol* published by Oscar Wilde himself. (1957)

VIII.

The Orestes Theme

in Three Plays by Eugene O'Neill, T. S. Eliot
and Jean-Paul Sartre

MODERN DRAMATISTS with the most divergent convictions and artistic aims agree in their interest in the time-honoured mythological themes because they find human types and situations in them that they want to re-create in terms of their own experience or to analyse according to one of the latest psychological theories. In the following pages we propose to compare three plays connected by their dependence upon the story of Orestes, the inheritor of the curse of the Atrides, who, in order to revenge the murder of his father Agamemnon, incurs the guilt of killing his mother as well as her new husband Aegisthus, and is pursued for this crime by the Eumenides until the gods permit his purification. This great theme, perfected in the prototypical European drama, the *Oresteia* of Aeschylus, treated again by Sophocles and Euripides, touched upon by the author of *Hamlet,* and nobly revived in Goethe's *Iphigenie auf Tauris,* is also the background of O'Neill's *Mourning Becomes Electra* (1931), of T. S. Eliot's *The Family Reunion* (1939), and of Jean-Paul Sartre's *Les Mouches* (1943). What use have these three contemporaries made of it? What are their reasons for connecting their works with it? In order to answer these questions we are going to outline the plots of the modern plays, investigate their relation to the myth and its Greek dramatizations as well as the motivation of the dramatic events and their meaning.[1]

Mourning Becomes Electra is the tragedy of the Mannons, an aristocratic New England family, which is destroyed in 1865/66, at the end of the Civil War, by a series of private catastrophes.

---

[1] The following texts are referred to: *Mourning Becomes Electra* in vol. II of *The Plays of Eugene O'Neill,* Random House, n. d.; *The Family Reunion,* a play by T. S. Eliot, Faber and Faber, 1939; Jean-Paul Sartre, *Théâtre,* Gallimard, 1947.

Brigadier-General Ezra Mannon is poisoned by his wife Christine in the night after his homecoming. She has hated her husband since the first night of her marriage, and wants to be free for her lover, Captain Adam Brant. Brant is the son of Marie Brantôme, formerly a nurse in the family, and of Ezra's uncle David Mannon, who had got her with child and had therefore been expelled from his home and from the family's firm by Ezra's father Abe, his less enterprising rival for Marie's love. Brant helps Christine in her crime under the influence of her stronger will, and because he hates the son of Abe Mannon, who has conscientiously carried on the family tradition of leaving Marie Brantôme a prey to starvation. Although the cowardly murder is excellently planned, its execution miscarries in one point. Lavinia, the daughter of the unhappy couple, who is passionately devoted to her father and suspicious of her mother, discovers what is going on, and becomes, by her stony presence, a source of terror for Christine. As soon as Christine's darling son Orin returns from the war Lavinia tries to set him free from his exaggerated attachment to his mother and to win him for her plans of revenge. He has hated his father so much that he would be ready to hush up his murder, but he cannot forgive his mother's *liaison* with Brant. When Lavinia takes him to witness a secret meeting of the murderous couple on the captain's ship at Boston, he kills Brant cold-bloodedly, and then informs his mother of her lover's death in the most brutal manner. For Christine the possibility of living on is gone; she ends by suicide. Lavinia and Orin cannot escape the effects of their deed although they seek oblivion on a trip to the South Seas, all through the play a symbol of innocent natural life. When they return Lavinia has her mother's full forms and beauty; she wants to forget her part in the Mannon tragedy, and is possessed by a wild desire to enjoy life. She disgusts her old suitor Peter by pressing immediate marriage on him, but she discovers in the end that she has lost her chance of a normal life. She gives him up, and decides, a true Mannon again, to punish herself by living alone in the company of her dead. This final change, however, comes over her only after Orin has also left her. He develops the Mannon conscience on their trip; he rebels against her domination, and cruelly torments her, until she wishes him dead, and thus repeats her mother's crime, in intention at least. In a fit of exasperation she tells her brother what she thinks, and starts him on his way to suicide.

O'Neill's debts to Greek drama are numerous. He has given his material the form of a trilogy, and arranged it in Aeschylus' way: The first part *(Homecoming)* shows the murder of Ezra, the second *(The Hunted)* Lavinia's and Orin's revenge and Christine's suicide, the third *(The Haunted)* the fate of the revengers. There is also the concentration of Greek drama: The evil that has slowly grown in time is represented at the moment when it ripens towards catastrophe. The unities of time and place are carefully, but not slavishly, observed: The action of the first two plays passes within a fortnight in the spring of 1865; the third play covers a little more than a month in the summer of 1866. With the exception of a single one (the murder of Brant) all the scenes occur in front of or inside the sinister Mannon house. Moreover, O'Neill makes his own use of the convention of the chorus. It is rather a modest one, as Seth Beckwith and the various representatives of the townspeople who comment with him upon the strange aloof ways and the terrible fate of the aristocratic Mannons are treated in a strictly realistic style, a characteristic trait of which is the introduction of dialect. There is hardly any profundity or wider vision in these comments: they are the superficial gossip of average people. The Greek example can also be discovered in the fact that the dramatist found it hard to keep masks out of his play. Again and again he stresses the mask-like expression on his protagonists' faces. Each one of these mask-like faces is stamped by one of the overpowering passions impelling the Mannons to destroy one another and themselves. Most appropriately the Mannon house itself wears its white Grecian temple portico — a symbol of harmony and poise — like a delusive mask.

But the most striking of O'Neill's borrowings is the story itself, of course. He has not appropriated more than the mere story, however, and perhaps part of its effect. He motivates the events in his own way, using the theories of modern psychology and biology. Christine Mannon's hatred of her husband has its origin in the psychological make-up of the two partners and not in any particular deed of Ezra's. Only her anger at Ezra's forcing Orin into a military career might be considered an echo of Clytemnestra's fury after the loss of Iphigenia. In Ezra and the others who share with him the Mannon blood O'Neill offers a study of the psychological plight of those late-born Puritans who have inherited from their ancestors a moral code without the religious faith originally bound' up with it. Thus he connects his trilogy with such treatments of a great American theme as Hawthorne's novels and tales and George Santayana's *Last Puritan*. Cut off from its religious roots, the Puritan moral code retains its power over the Mannons because it is the basis of their self-respect and aristocratic family pride. Having lost all relation to their vital and expansive impulses, it becomes a power for death. In the Mannons the *frein vital* and the *élan vital* are not only antagonistic; they tend to destroy each other. Christine is as different from the Mannon type as possible: a person made to give herself wholeheartedly to life and passion. Therefore she has attracted Ezra just as Marie Brantôme had fascinated both David and Abe Mannon. But he cannot respond to her love in her way. One part of his being rejects his passion for her as low and sinful, and the beginning of their sexual relationship breeds disgust and contempt in both of them. The children of the unhappy couple inherit a double nature. They are still under the Mannon code, but they know also the desire for their mother's strong impulsive life. All their actions are ambiguous. At first Orin resists the Mannon inheritance, and becomes a prey to the Oedipus complex. He loves his mother with an exaggerated passion, and is nerved by it to kill her lover. Lavinia's devotion to her father is similarly exaggerated, and yet, when she urges her brother to revenge him, she does not act from pure motives either. Adam Brant, by his Brantôme blood, has stirred up her passionate nature, too, and deep down in her heart there is jealousy of her mother. After the destruction of Brant and Christine Orin is hopelessly at war with himself. He allows his Mannon nature with its sense of guilt and sin and its desire for punishment to dominate him in order to torture himself and his sister, who tries in vain to suppress the same element in herself.

We need not enumerate the many further psychological subtleties of the play. Those we have discussed suffice to show what O'Neill set out to do. In his version of the Orestes myth he attempted to replace the curse of the Atreus family by a complicated psychological mechanism and to create the impression that this mechanism controls human existence more inexorably than any *fatum* or curse known to the ancients. He used all the resources of his remarkable artistry to hide the fact that the dice in his hands were loaded, that his characters and his situations corresponded to theories rather than to life itself. The whole work is, like many another one of O'Neill's, a magnificent *tour de force*. This is inevitable as he wanted to compose it in accordance with strictly deterministic principles and to give it the appearance of life. *Mourning Becomes Electra* is the drama of determinism: Human existence in it is a closed circle, in which there is no escape, no freedom possible from the working of natural and psychological laws of a mechanistic type. Orin struggles in vain in the web of a malevolent spider. The possibility of expiation and purification, known to the Greeks and to Goethe, is gone. Thus O'Neill evokes in his spectators a terror that is colder and more hopeless than that excited by any classical tragedy. His drama has grown in a philosophical mood characteristic of many of the best American minds of the early twentieth century; the mood of the rebels against the Puritan tradition, whose minds were formed by the experience of the tremendous physical growth of the United States in the nineteenth century and by the scientific discoveries and the pseudo-scientific hypotheses of the same age.

T. S. Eliot, who was born in the same year as O'Neill (1888), had felt the impact of the same experiences and theories in his American youth. For him they had been accompanied by a devastating sense of futility and unreality, against which he set out to struggle. Our motto in studying *The Family Reunion* shall be a remark of Eliot's on Shakespeare's ability to appeal to different types of spectators, which is found on p. 153 in *The Use of Poetry and the Use of Criticism* (1933): "For the simplest auditors there is the plot, for the more thoughtful the character and conflict of character, for the more literary the words and phrasing, for the more musically sensitive the rhythm, and for auditors of greater sensitiveness and understanding a meaning which reveals itself gradually." The poet adds that he has tried himself in "a couple of scenes, of a verse play" to construct a drama with several layers of meaning. Doubtless, he is thinking of the two *Sweeney Agonistes* scenes of the years 1926 and 1927. When Eliot composed *The Family Reunion* he succeeded in doing what he had merely attempted in those scenes.

If the play has failed to impress the general public, the reason must be looked for in its uppermost layer of meaning. The dramatist has been somewhat stingy in giving "the simplest auditors" their food. He introduces them to an aristocratic family of northern England, who assemble at Wishwood, the family seat, to celebrate the birthday of Amy, Dowager Lady Monchensey, their senior and head, in the traditional way. Her sisters and brothers-in-law have arrived for the party, but she is still expecting her three sons. Only Harry, the eldest, comes; the two others are kept away by motorcar accidents they have suffered or caused. Harry is in a strange state of perturbation. He has been abroad since his marriage eight years ago, and has recently lost his wife under unusual circumstances. On their way home from New York she has fallen overboard. Now he shocks his relations by accusing himself of having pushed her into the sea. With satisfaction the simple auditor smells a crime interest in the story, but he is badly disappointed by what follows. Harry has long talks with his cousin Mary, with the family doctor Warburton, and with his aunt Agatha, and he sees ghosts in the windows. The question whether he is really a murderer, or not, is left open. He leaves the party prematurely to face an unknown future, and his mother dies from shock shortly after his departure. Agatha and Mary perform a strange funeral ceremony, walking round the birthday cake and muttering verses of a runic type.

For the "more thoughtful" auditors, however, there is almost as much interesting psychology in the play as in *Mourning Becomes Electra*. Amy, her sister Agatha, and Harry are the most striking characters. As a young wife Amy was tied to a husband who did not love her and for whom her sister Agatha became the great passion of his life. In spite of their estrangement she stayed with him, and bore him the children whom she educated in a spirit of jealous and possessive love. Especially after her husband had left her and had died she gave rein to this tendency. Harry, her eldest and ablest son, as well as his cousin Mary, who was brought up with him, reacted to this type of love by a strong desire for independence. As early as possible Harry married a woman whom his mother disliked. Amy resisted the fact of his marriage with her whole tenacious will, and tried to preserve Wishwood in precisely the same state in which Harry had left it. (When he actually comes home and finds everything unchanged, this makes him only the more acutely conscious of the fact that he is an entirely changed person.) She received the news of his wife's death with undisguised satisfaction, and hoped that her son's marriage would prove merely an unhappy episode in his life. When Harry's brief visit destroys this illusion her weak heart gives way, and she collapses. Agatha has suffered no less than her sister. The passion of her brother-in-law for her was so overwhelming that he conceived the plan of murdering his wife at the very time when Harry's birth was approaching. Agatha prevented this crime because she cared for the child that was going to be born rather than from love of her sister. She learned to love Harry with a mother's love. That is why she is now able to help him in the great crisis of his life. But the most fascinating case for the psychologist is Harry himself. We have pointed out that he married early to get away from his mother. His marriage proved no less unhappy than that of his parents, partly because it was an escape marriage, partly because Harry transferred his antipathy from his mother to his wife. He suppressed his growing hatred of her, but after her death he was haunted by a sense of guilt, and thought, at times, that he was her murderer. Immediately after his arrival at home he even sees the threatening shapes of the Eumenides. His guilt-complex is healed in a way while he discovers the facts about the unhappy married life of his parents, and realizes that his father had wished before him to murder his wife. This is a satisfactory explanation of the chief events of the play for the thoughtful auditor who cannot grasp its real meaning.

That meaning is in no way hidden by the author. On the contrary, he does his best to express it as clearly as he possibly can. Nevertheless, it can only be understood by those who have ears to hear it. For those acquainted with Eliot's poetry there are numerous signs telling them where to look for his intention. The play does not take place in "depraved May" or in April, "the cruellest month", but only a very little earlier: late in March. It is the season

of birth and growth in nature, when the lack of both in the spiritual sphere can become torture. The spectator is invited to witness a birthday party, but the birthday cake becomes the centre of a
funeral ceremony. It is one of Eliot's recurrent motifs that life may
be death and death life, that being born may be a kind of dying and
dying a way of being born.[2] The distance between O'Neill and
Eliot may be measured if we remember the sneering way in which
Ezra Mannon refers to this very idea as to an outworn Puritan
obsession: "That's always been the Mannons' way of thinking.
They went to the white meeting-house on Sabbaths and meditated
on death. Life was a dying. Being born was starting to die. Death
was being born." (p. 54.) What is the essence of a dead convention
for the one dramatist is the most exciting and important new discovery for the other. There are other pointers in Eliot's play, e. g.
the numerous short or long remarks by which the figures gifted
with a more than average awareness of spiritual things interrupt
the futile conversation of the normal people in a shocking way.
Besides, Mary, Agatha, and Harry are allowed moments of abstraction when they can speak their most secret intuitions. There
are the key passages, none of which is simpler and more straightforward than Agatha's two lines:

What we have written is not a story of detection,
Of crime and punishment, but of sin and expiation. (p. 104.)

As we have seen it is Harry who is haunted by an intense sense of
sin. It sets him apart from all the other figures of the play, and
makes him cry out at the sight of the Eumenides:

No, no, not there. Look there!
Can't you see them? *You* don't see them, but I see them,
And they see me. (p. 25.)

These lines contain a quotation from Aeschylus' *Choephoroe*,
which was also used by Eliot as one of the mottos of *Sweeney
Agonistes*.[3] Harry's sense of sin is connected with the murder of

---

[2] Cf. the last line of *Animula:* "Pray for us now and at the hour of our
birth." (*Collected Poems* 1909—1935, London 1936, 112.)

[3] *Choephoroe*, 1509: "ὑμεῖς μὲν οὐχ ὁρᾶτε τασδ', ἐγὼ δ'ὁρῶ." (*The
Oresteia of Aeschylus*, edited by George Thomson, Cambridge 1938,
vol. I, 280).

his wife, which he has perhaps not commited, and it is modified when his aunt tells him of a similar deed contemplated by his father.

> What might have been and what has been
> Point to one end, which is always present.[4]

Besides, the sphere of Christian responsibility does not include deeds alone, but wishes, dreams, and thoughts as well. Nor is his sense of sin restricted to his real or intentional murder. It springs from the whole of the psychological situation in which the murderous plan could grow. Here we reach an important link between O'Neill's and Eliot's plays. Harry's situation is that of the latecomer, who lives, or rather, vegetates, imprisoned in O'Neill's closed circle, on the relics of a lost spiritual tradition, without a religious faith, a knowledge of values, and a sense of reality. It is perhaps one of Eliot's profoundest insights that men, as well as nations, are excited by this situation to deeds of violence, by which they try to win back their lost sense of being real. Harry's consciousness of sin has a further dimension, which we have not mentioned yet: It leads to the discovery of the reality of original sin in the Christian sense. The climax of Eliot's play comes when Harry, helped by Agatha's disclosures, but for no logically explainable reason, is touched by the intuition that his sense of sin is no curse at all, but a terrible privilege, the pulley capable of raising him out of the closed circle, the experience that renders his salvation possible. At this moment of intense happiness he decides to face the Eumenides instead of running away from them and to seek expiation of his guilt. Agatha and Mary have a degree of understanding of what is going on in him, but not Amy and the other more normal members of the family. Agatha even hints at the possibility that Harry's experience may be decisive not only for him alone, but, through the efficacy of vicarious suffering, for all his unhappy family.

What are the connections of this play with the Orestes myth? The most important one is found in the figure of Harry, of course. He is a modern Orestes, pursued by the Eumenides. What attract-

---

[4] T. S. Eliot, *Four Quartets*, London 1944, 7.

ed Eliot most in the story of the descendant of the Pelops family was the fact that his fate and his guilt were determined by the crimes of his parents and their forbears and that the curse from which his sufferings sprang was brought to an end by the intervention of the gods. He made it the background of his play because he found analogies in it to the modern creed of determinism as well as to the Christian ideas of original sin and expiation. It enabled him to represent the closed circle of the moderns as impressively as O'Neill and, besides, the way of breaking through it that exists according to the Christian faith. We do not think it useful to elaborate occasional parallel traits in the other figures of Eliot's play and those of the Greek myth.[5] The poet has developed his characters freely according to his own complex plan. But he followed the example of Greek tragedy in many points of form. He observed the unities more strictly than O'Neill. There is a chorus in the play. It is formed by Ivy, Violet, Gerald, and Charles, four of the normal unperceptive members of the family. These are allowed an awareness of the plight of the average modern unbeliever when they speak as The Chorus, an awareness they lack when each of them takes part singly in the drawing-room conversations of the play. Thus, in Eliot's as well as in O'Neill's drama, the deeper insight is with the protagonists, the members of the chorus being average people with average reactions. But these reactions, as rendered by Eliot, have a wider application; they do not belong to our time only, but to all ages. This is partly due to the fact that his chorus speaks in verse. *The Family Reunion* is a verse play. It is not our task to discuss the qualities of Eliot's dramatic verse, whose importance can hardly be exaggerated, as it is based on the rhythms and idioms of modern speech, and reaches high degrees of intensity, although it resists the dangerous fascination exerted by the great Elizabethan plays on many generations of dramatic aspirants.

In 1943 Jean-Paul Sartre took up the Orestes theme in *Les Mouches*, certainly one of the most discussed plays of the war years. The French dramatist does not remove the story from its

---

[5] An attempt to do this will be found in H. W. Häusermann's essay on T. S. Eliot in *Neue Schweizer Rundschau*, Mai 1945.

Greek setting. His scenes are laid in the city of Argos, where the customs of the people are rather primitive; the city itself, however, is placed in a Greece of a much more advanced civilization. In characterizing his figures Sartre is no more hampered by historical scruples than O'Neill and Eliot.

Hiding his identity under the name of Philèbe, Oreste returns to the city of his fathers in the company of his pedagogue as a highly civilized young man, who has gathered the most approved knowledge of his time on his extensive travels. He is proudly described by his teacher as "jeune, riche et beau, avisé comme un vieillard, affranchi de toutes les servitudes et de toutes les croyances, sans famille, sans patrie, sans religion, sans métier, libre pour tous les engagements et sachant qu'il ne faut jamais s'engager, un homme supérieur enfin..." (p. 23 f.) This young man is made acquainted with the secrets of Argos in a series of scenes. No less a personage than Jupiter himself tries to disgust him by a depressing description of the plight of the fly-infested town and its inhabitants. Since the murder of Agamemnon they all labour under a guilt complex. They voluptuously deplore their great sin, overwhelm every casual listener with confessions of their guilt, and undergo imaginary torments every year on the Day of the Dead. This state of things is agreeable to the eyes of Jupiter: "Ils ont mauvaise conscience, ils ont peur — et la peur, la mauvaise conscience ont un fumet délectable pour les narines des Dieux." (p. 20.) There is a reason for the bad conscience of the people: They secretly enjoyed the killing of Agamemnon. They sought an act of violence for a reason that sounds quite familiar to a student of Eliot: "Les gens d'ici n'ont rien dit, parce qu'ils s'ennuyaient et qu'ils voulaient voir une mort violente." (p. 16.) Oreste wants to leave the town, but he is kept back by the spectacle of Electre, who comes to insult the statue of Jupiter. She burns with hatred against the protector of her mother and her stepfather, who force her to do menial services in the palace, and she dreams of revenge. Oreste is fascinated by his conversation with her and Clytemnestre, in which the similarity of mother and daughter becomes as evident as their antagonism. His next impression of the people of Argos is got while he is taking part in the death rites celebrated by the royal couple and the High Priest near the temple in the mountain. The insane spell keeping the people in fear and subjection is almost broken by Electre, who appears in a white robe and dances a sacrilegious dance of joy, but Jupiter intervenes, and restores the rule of superstition by one of his petty miracles. Electre must expect the worst from the enraged king. In the crucial scene of the play Oreste offers to flee with his sister, and when she refuses, saying that she must wait for her brother at Argos, he makes himself known to her. Now she pities him, and tries to send him away, believing that the weight of his task as Agamemnon's son will be too much for him. But he decides to stay and to shoulder his task. Jupiter, foreseeing what is to follow, does his best to change the course of events. He warns Egisthe of his danger, but the king is tired of the role his past crimes force him to play at Argos, and does not take any action. Oreste kills him and Clytemnestre. The rest of the play analyses the different reactions of Electre and Oreste to their crime. Electre behaves exactly like her mother after the murder of Agamemnon. She is overwhelmed by the enormity of a deed that she has passionately desired for many years. She feels repentance, and seeks expiation, and thus becomes a willing, though terrified, victim of the Erinnyes, who make an old woman of her in one night. In short, she behaves as Jupiter wants a human being under his rule to behave. Not so Oreste. He is also under the strain of having performed a deed of the utmost gravity. But he has planned and executed it as an act of justice: "J'ai fait *mon* acte, Electre, et cet acte était bon. Je le porterai sur mes épaules comme un passeur d'eau porte les voyageurs, je le ferai passer sur l'autre rive et j'en rendrai compte." (p. 84.) He does not permit Jupiter to rouse any sense of guilt in him: "Je ne suis pas un coupable, et tu ne saurais me faire expier ce que je ne reconnais pas pour un crime." (p. 94.) And he asseverates: "Le plus lâche des assassins, c'est celui qui a des remords." (p. 98.) This rebellion against Jupiter is given the widest significance. Oreste has discovered the god's carefully hidden secret: Man is created for freedom and therefore destined to turn against the gods themselves. Oreste wants to be the first creature that risks the necessary rebellion, and thus sees a Promethean task before him. He tells Jupiter: "Mais, tout à coup, la liberté a fondu sur moi et m'a transi, la nature a sauté en arrière, et je n'ai plus eu d'âge, et je me suis senti tout seul, au milieu de ton petit monde bénin, comme quelqu'un qui a perdu son ombre; et il n'y a plus rien eu au ciel, ni Bien, ni Mal, ni personne pour me donner des ordres." (p.101.) And a little later: "Car je suis un homme, Jupiter, et chaque homme doit inventer son chemin. La nature a horreur de l'homme, et toi, toi, souverain des Dieux, toi aussi tu as les hommes en horreur."[6] As soon as Oreste has made his decision he is filled by missionary zeal. He wants to give his people the freedom he is enjoying himself. Jupiter warns him:

> JUPITER: Pauvres gens! Tu vas leur fair cadeau de la solitude et de la honte, tu vas arracher les étoffes dont je les avais couverts, et tu leur montreras soudain leur existence, leur obscène et fade existence, qui leur est donnée pour rien.
>
> ORESTE: Pourquoi leur refuserais-je le désespoir qui est en moi, puisque c'est leur lot?
>
> JUPITER: Qu'en feront-ils?
>
> ORESTE: Ce qu'ils voudront: ils sont libres, et la vie humaine commence de l'autre côté du désespoir. (p. 102.)

In his farewell speech to his people Oreste promises to carry away with him all the weights of the past and to leave them free to begin a new life: "Vos fautes et vos remords, vos angoisses nocturnes, le crime d'Egisthe, tout est à moi, je prends tout sur moi. Ne craignez plus vos morts, ce sont *mes* morts. Et voyez: vos mouches fidèles vous ont quittés pour moi. Mais n'ayez crainte, gens d'Argos: je ne m'assiérai pas, tout sanglant, sur le trône de ma victime: un Dieu me l'a offert et j'ai dit non. Je veux être un roi sans terre et sans sujets. Adieu, mes hommes, tentez de vivre: tout est neuf ici, tout est à commencer. Pour moi aussi la vie commence. Une étrange vie. . . ." (p. 108.) That is all we hear of the life on the other side

---

[6] Cf. the end of the first act of Goethe's *Iphigenie auf Tauris:*
> Denn die Unsterblichen lieben der Menschen
> Weit verbreitete gute Geschlechter,
> Und sie fristen das flüchtige Leben
> Gerne dem Sterblichen, wollen ihm gerne
> Ihres eigenen, ewigen Himmels
> Mitgenießendes fröhliches Anschaun
> Eine Weile gönnen und lassen.

of despair: It will be new, strange, and utterly different from anything that was in the past.

Despite his revolutionary tendencies Sartre is supported in the organization of his play by the example of Greek tragedy. His place economy is only a little less strict than his time economy. There is an impressive *Choeur des Erinnyes*. Otherwise, the chorus is disintegrated in the manner of O'Neill to make room for the representation of various types of citizens of Argos. The medium of the play is a prose grounded on the cultured speech of modern France and capable of imagery and rhythms of great force and beauty.

Like his two predecessors, Sartre introduces a considerable amount of modern psychology into his treatment of the myth. But it is no more the *raison d'être* of his play than of *The Family Reunion*. Like the other dramatists, he was attracted by the story because he found it a striking symbol of the bondage imposed on mankind by fate according to the ancients and by the many determining factors discovered by science according to the moderns. He did not follow O'Neill, who had no use for the fact that the myth is also one of purification and liberation. For him, as for Eliot, the possibility of liberation was its most important feature. Therefore such terms as guilt, remorse, repentance, and expiation are found almost as frequently in his play as in Eliot's. For both authors Orestes' crime, committed under the sway of the family curse, turns out to be a blessing in disguise, as it becomes one of the causes of his liberation. But how different is Sartre's way of liberation! He does not restore their full original meaning to the terms we have mentioned, but allows their value to sink below zero. They belong to the old order, which Orestes is to bring to its end. They are symbolized by the disgusting flies that have given the play its name. They are defended by Jupiter, a capricious tyrant, a low magician, and altogether a shabby caricature of a god. Sartre sells them very cheaply, indeed, in order to make Oreste his own master and sovereign judge of the justice of his acts. It may be admitted that there is a sordid kind of self-accusation and repentance as well as a sordid cult of the past and its dead, and that Sartre is hitting at them when he describes the state of the people of Argos before Oreste's coming. But he does not seem to know anything of the validity of true repentance and expiation and of an existence in a living tradition. A key to what has happened to him may be found, we believe, in his short introduction to the German translation of *Les Mouches* published by the Oprecht Verlag this year. There he states that the play was written to strengthen the spirit of resistance in the French when their country was occupied. At that time a man of the *résistance* was depressed by the way the Vichy-minded Frenchmen, traditionalists of a peculiar stamp, wanted to play the part of the defeated according to ancient rules. He tried to make his compatriots forget their brooding over the errors of the past and their self-accusations and to encourage them to act in a new way in an unheard-of situation. In *Les Mouches* we find truth for one definite situation represented as general truth. Sartre would probably reject this accusation of jugglery on the plea that there are only truths for definite situations. But he has certainly not resisted the temptation to generalize. Moreover, we cannot suppress the suspicion that he allowed his thought to be contaminated by the sophisms of the criminal victors of the moment. The Hitlerites bragged of the entirely new start they had made; they chose their own acts in utter freedom from any ethical tradition, and defended their justice *à outrance;* they found enough supporters to convince them in their own minds that their acts were not only personally, but also socially just. Must not sentences like the following have sounded pleasant in their ears? "Quand une fois la liberté a explosé dans une âme d'homme, les Dieux ne peuvent plus rien contre cet homme-là. Car c'est une affaire d'hommes, et c'est aux autres hommes — à eux seuls — qu'il appartient de le laisser courir ou de l'étrangler." (p. 79.)

However, we have got to admit that *Les Mouches* is not alone the play of a situation; it has grown in a definite philosophical mood, representing a reaction against the pressure of determinism no less violent than Eliot's, and springing from a diagnosis of the present plight of western civilization no less devastating than his. It leads Sartre to the proclamation of a new type of superman, who enjoys a kind of freedom impossible to man, an attempt that recalls the example of Nietzsche. This superman and his race are to build a new life in the blank sphere on the other side of despair.

What will he do there but murder and enslave, unless he can make the discoveries that have enabled Eliot to give new life and meaning to some of the oldest ideas and facts of our civilization, discoveries that would force him to give up his claim to absolute freedom? (1949)

IX.

The Achievement of Eugene O'Neill

1. The Dramatic Experiments

I DO NOT THINK that anybody familiar with the facts will oppose the view that O'Neill is the foremost in a group of writers who have begun a new era in the history of the American drama. The change occurring in the years between 1915 and 1925 is more remarkable than the one that followed as important an event as the War of Independence. A few words on the earlier periods are indispensable for an understanding of O'Neills achievement. Whatever its effects on other spheres of life the War of Independence failed to liberate the theatrical life of the former colonies from its traditional dependence upon the example of London. It is true, the American theatres of the late 18th and the 19th century could boast of American actors, but these very often did not interest the public as much as the star actors of London who found frequent tours through the growing United States profitable undertakings. There were American dramatists as well but they found it hard to compete with their European colleagues, and frequently restricted their endeavours to the clever rehandling of French, German, English and other foreign plays. When the dramatists tried to be original they were so in their matter rather than in their manner. They filled the approved patterns of the European theatre with American material. An early example is William Dunlap's sentimental tragedy *André* (1798), treating an episode in the War of Independence in a style that reminds us of Addison's classicism although it pays tribute to the 18th century delight in tear-compelling thrills. A melodrama without classicist self-restraint is James Nelson Barker's *Tragedy of Superstition* (1824) taking the spectator back to the days of the Puritan theocracy in New England and showing the dreadful consequences of Puritan superstition. The simple, crude psychology, the delight in sensational stage events, such as the fighting off of an Indian attack on a village, are traits of melodrama. It is worth noticing that plays of this sort did not necessarily require a happy ending in the period under discussion. Later in the century audiences would have boggled at the cruel end of Barker's hero and heroine. Such historical plays were accompanied by dramatic versions of beloved American legends like the one of the beautiful Indian princess Pocahontas and of Rip van Winkle, e. g. *Pocahontas or the Settlers of Virginia*, composed by George Washington Custis in 1830. In the hands of this author the story loses much of its point because he is prevented from depicting the enemies of the white settlers in appropriately sinister colours by his interest in the romantic dream of the noble savage. Cooper's most idealized Red Indians appear realistic compared to his stage-figures. Of course, the American dramatists never restricted themselves completely to American subjects. The nostalgic delight in things European, so prevalent among the cultured class in the last century, led many writers to the treatment of the great romantic themes of the old world. They were no more afraid of the fate of the imitator than the architects who filled the growing towns and cities in the Middle and the Far West with buildings illustrating the styles of all ages and countries but lacking an organic connection with their surroundings and even with their purpose. A high place among the numerous imitative dramas of the age is rightfully accorded to George Henry Boker's *Francesca da Rimini* (1855), an amazingly successful attempt to out-Shakespeare Shakespeare in the middle of the 19th century.

The production of romantic plays of this sort never stopped, but in the second part of the century melodramas and comedies mildly reflected the mild tendency of the contemporary English plays towards factual and psychological realism and the treatment of one of the pressing problems of the day. In 1859, a short time before the outbreak of the Civil War, Dion Boucicault's *Octoroon* was produced in New York. In it this versatile purveyor of melodrama to the theatres of Great Britain and the United States gave a lively idea of the conditions on a plantation in Louisiana at the moment when the northern and western form of life began to oust the southern one. We are invited to weep over the impossible love and heroic death of beautiful Zoe, who is classed as a negress although only one of her eight great-grandparents was black. The surface of the play is realistic, especially in the scenes depicting the manners and the language of the southern negroes. As soon as we study it more closely we discover a number of conventional melodramatic types and situations under the realistic veneer. Also the wealth of sensational, partly quite impossible, incidents reveals the true nature of this play. Among them there is the hunt of the Indian boy Wahnotee after Jacob M'Closky, the conventional stage villain cleverly disguised as a Yankee sharper. The series of short cinematographic scenes that show M'Closky running for his life anticipate some of the cruder effects of the death race of O'Neill's Emperor Jones.

The formula of this play was consciously or unconsciously repeated by the most successful dramatists of the following decades. Time and again the stock types of melodrama and farce were given new settings, and pressing problems were touched in a manner that did not hurt anybody. About the turn of the century several dramatists were clever and conscientious enough to reduce the conventional element to a minimum and to introduce observations, questions and interpretations of their own into their plays. However, they never went as far in this as to endanger the success of their productions; the taste of the New York audiences remained their ultimate point of reference. Such respectable and accomplished dramatists as David Belasco, Bronson Howard, Clyde Fitch and Augustus Thomas did not find it too difficult to accept the laws laid down by that authority as they were in sympathy with them in most of their moods. An admirable illustration of this is Bronson Howard's *Autobiography of a Play*, a lecture delivered at Harvard University in 1886 on the development of his drama *The Banker's Daughter*. The most revealing pages of this document are quoted in Arthur Hobson Quinn's *History of the American Drama* (I. 44 ff.). We reproduce a few characteristic sentences in it: "A dramatist should deal, so far as possible, with subjects of universal interest, instead of with such as appeal strongly to a part of the public only. I do not mean that he may not appeal to certain classes of people, and depend upon those classes for success; but, just so far as he does this, he limits the possibilities of that success. ... Furthermore — and here comes in another law of dramatic construction — a play must be, in one way or another, 'satisfactory' to the audience. This word has a meaning which varies in different countries, and even in different parts of the same country; but whatever audience you are writing for, your work must be 'satisfactory' to it. In England and America, the death of a pure woman on the stage is not 'satisfactory', except when the play rises to the dignity of tragedy. The death, in an ordinary play, of a woman who is not pure, as in the case of *Frou-Frou*, is perfectly satisfactory, for the reason that it is inevitable. Human nature always bows gracefully to the inevitable. ... The wife who has once taken the step from purity to impurity can never reinstate herself in the world of art on this side of the grave; and so an audience looks with complacent tears on the death of an erring woman." All this is queer doctrine for modern ears, but it was the doctrine of a serious dramatist, who had made his peace with the commercial theatres of the late 19th and the early 20th century.

Those theatres, for a time in the hands of a powerful trust, worked for financial gain in the first place, and therefore did not dream of producing plays that were not entirely "satisfactory" to the paying audiences. Of course, there were men who did not accept Bronson Howard's worldly wisdom, and they were punished by lack of success. Excellent dramas like James A. Herne's realistic problem play *Margaret Fleming* (1890) and William Vaughn Moody's *Faith Healer* (1909), a study in the religious psychology of the simple farmers in the west, had to be content with the applause of a few discerning critics.

The experiments necessary for the development of a free and sincere American drama could not take place in the old and new commercial houses. In this state of affairs it was a happy accident that an unheard-of concentration of the theatrical life in New York took place in the first decades of our century. The rather extensive American "province" found itself deprived of its usual theatrical fare because various economic factors made it unprofitable for the New York companies to tour the country in the traditional way. Thus the ground was prepared for the growth of the *Little Theatres*, which sprang up all over the country in large and small places.[1] They owed their origin to the enthusiasm of simple and

[1] Cf. Jean Carter and Jess Ogden, *Everyman's Drama. A Study of the Non-Commercial Theatre in the United States*, New York 1938.

of sophisticated theatre lovers. Their aim was not financial gain, but good productions of the great old and the most interesting modern plays. Many of them reached a fair, some an excellent standard of production. The whole movement was supported by the parallel development of the university and college theatres. In many of the best academic institutions the students were encouraged to study the history of the drama and theatre as well as the practical questions connected with the writing and the production of plays, and to experiment on well equipped special stages. The most famous dramatic department of all was the one created by Professor George Pierce Baker: O'Neill followed his courses in 1914/15. These academic institutions did not intend to serve the needs of future professionals only; they hoped to train better amateur producers and actors, better critics, and better audiences as well.

The Little Theatres that did most for the new American drama were the Art Theatres, run by young intellectuals and artists, highbrows, who were thoroughly disgusted by the methods of the commercial stages. It is not necessary to repeat the often told tale of those ambitious undertakings, which thrived particularly well in the suburbs of the big cities. We only mention the Provincetown Players, who began modestly enough in Provincetown (Mass.) in the summer of 1915, but won success and recognition as worthy interpreters of modern plays of literary merit after they had settled down in Greenwich Village, New York. Many other Art Theatres specialized in the production of the European drama since Ibsen; the Provincetown Players, however, presented mainly American plays. The most important author for whom they won recognition and a public was Eugene O'Neill. This ambitious and hard-working young author was thirty years old in 1918 when he approached the end of his dramatic apprenticeship. His youth had been adventurous. Haunted by an invincible thirst for experience he had passed through various modes of life in his own country, on the sea, and abroad.[2] As his father was a well-known actor in a

[2] For a short account of his life and work cf. Richard Kühnemund, "Das Drama Eugene O'Neills", *Anglia*, LII, 1928, 244 ff., and also A. H. Quinn, *History of the American Drama*, II, 165 ff.

touring company O'Neill was in touch with the theatre from his earliest days. As a child and as a young man he had every opportunity to observe the theatrical conditions against which he decided to rebel when he became a playwright. He arrived at this decision while he was spending six months in a sanatorium in 1913 on account of a touch of pulmonary tuberculosis. Then there followed a period of intense productivity from 1914 to 1934. While it lasted O'Neill composed a remarkable number of plays, many of which he rejected later as unworthy of preservation. If we do not count the rejected ones his contribution to dramatic literature comprises about a dozen short and twenty long works. It was important for him, as it was for many another dramatic aspirant in America and elsewhere, that he was given the chance of trying his hand at one-act plays first.[3] When he had mastered this form he moved on to the longer plays which brought him national and international fame.

It cannot be our task to give another chronological survey of O'Neill's dramas. This has been done by many writers on the American drama and on O'Neill.[4] What we propose to do, is to correlate the philosophy in the most important plays, to discover the reasons for O'Neills moving from one dramatic form to another, to approach the questions whether his changing methods spring from the whim of a writer who covers the fact that he has nothing to say by his technical skill, whether they are the inevitable outcome of his unstable view of man and the world, whether they have a personal significance only or symbolize the mental condition of one of the world's leading nations.

We can begin our interpretation by pointing out that O'Neill has hardly ever given up his opposition against the conventional

[3] Gustav L. Plessow has tried to bring the peculiarities of the modern American one-act play into a system in *Das amerikanische Kurzschauspiel zwischen 1910 und 1930*, Halle 1933 (Studien zur englischen Philologie, Heft LXXXIII).

[4] For a bibliography cf. R. Sanborn and B. H. Clark, *A Bibliography of the Works of Eugene O'Neill*, New York 1931, and Fred B. Millett, *Contemporary American Authors*, New York 1943, 517 ff. Comprehensive studies of the dramatist have been attempted by B. H. Clark (New York 1929), by S. K. Winther (New York 1934), by R. D. Skinner (New York 1935), and by O. Koischwitz (Berlin 1938).

theatre, against the play that is "satisfactory" in the sense of Bronson Howard. Like many lesser men of the Little Theatre Movement he absolutely refused to show a picture of life on the stage that was distorted by conventions dear to the paying majority. It is true, once, in a mood of relaxation, he followed the beaten path. This happened when he composed the charming comedy *Ah, Wilderness!* (1933), the only one of his plays in which we find humour. Nevertheless, it is his outstanding characteristic that he carefully avoided the conventions cherished by the customers of the commercial theatres, and tried to introduce old and new conventions from other countries or even to invent new ones. Moreover, he was quite ready to face life in its American form. Not because he thought it perfect. He felt no desire to glorify the United States in his art, nor did he wish to escape from them. The American form of life was the one he knew best; therefore he made it his main subject. Like Sinclair Lewis, H. L. Mencken and other intellectual leaders of his generation he looked at his countrymen and their problems in a detached and critical way. And the young people who were going through the experience of the war and the post-war era shared this attitude; they read and admired Lewis and Mencken, and they proclaimed O'Neill the first dramatist of America. O'Neill's freedom from any escapist love of Europe and its tradition by no means prevented him from a close study of European literature, especially of the modern dramatists. Signs of his knowledge of Ibsen, Strindberg, Shaw and Synge are frequently met with in his plays.[5]

The strongest impression we get in surveying O'Neill's plots and figures is the deterministic mood that pervades them. If one of his human beings appears to be a free agent this is the result of an abbreviation necessitated by dramatic economy. It is manifestly impossible to unfold in a play all the influences and conditions that

[5] The structure of O'Neill's *Ile, Where the Cross is Made* and *The Rope* reminds us of Ibsen's technique. His attempts to stage his figures' illusions for us point to Strindberg, his projection of modern problems into the history of Marco Polo to Shaw, his frequent use of the Anglo-Irish idiom to Synge. On this last point cf. Andrew E. Malone, "The Plays of Eugene O'Neill", *The Contemporary Review*, CXXIX, January – June 1926, 363 ff.

have made the behaviour of a person what it is according to the deterministic creed. As a dramatist O'Neill can only relate characteristic actions to the most decisive of their causes. In many of his plays the milieu in the widest sense of the term appears as a force shaping character and destiny. In the early one-act plays the sea and its atmosphere function in this way. The half-witted hero of *"The Hairy Ape"* (1922)[6] is a creature of the stokehole on an ocean liner. The atmosphere of a New England home is a powerful agent in the Puritan plays *Desire under the Elms* (1925) and *Mourning Becomes Electra* (1931). Another shaping power that dominates the will is race. In O'Neill's negro plays *The Emperor Jones* (1921) and *All God's Chillun Got Wings* (1924) the racial characteristics of the main figures have a decisive effect on their behaviour and fate. A further determining factor is heredity. Its influence is shown incidentally in all the plays where parents and children appear: in the Puritan plays we have mentioned and in *Dynamo* (1929) it is powerful. These conditioning forces have an ally in the psychological make-up of many of O'Neill's figures. Their author has created them according to the notions of the modern psychology of the conscious and the subconscious. Not only in *Strange Interlude* (1928), where human beings are used as guinea-pigs in a long series of experiments on Freudian lines, can we observe the subtle, but nevertheless mechanical effects of youthful frustrations, suppressed sexual desires, of fixations and compensations on the behaviour of man.

These hints must suffice to show how strongly O'Neill is affected by the desire for an entirely naturalistic conception of man, so typical of the United States in the period between the two world wars. If we wish to understand why this desire and the corresponding mood could become so wide-spread we have to remember the experiences of four generations of Americans since the beginning of the great expansion. They had witnessed a gigantic struggle for the winning of the empty space in the west. Economic problems had been foremost in their minds. They had seen the most diverse types of European immigrants develop into rather uniform

[6] The date of their first publication is added to the titles of O'Neill's plays when they are first mentioned in this essay.

Americans in their new surroundings, under the pressure of one and the same huge economic task. All this prepared them for a philosophy of the naturalistic type like the one offered them by John Dewey and the radical empiricists. Heinrich Straumann, in his article "The Philosophical Background of the Modern American Drama" (*English Studies*, XXVI, 1944, 65 ff.), has worked out the affinities between this school of thought and the modern plays more in detail. He has also pointed out that the naturalistic tendency is counteracted by a metaphysical one, which he relates to the older Christian and idealistic trends of American thought. His diagnosis of a clashing of the two tendencies in O'Neill is a most valuable result of his inquiry.

We turn once more to the plays to discover signs of O'Neill's rebellion against that same naturalistic interpretation of man by which he was fascinated so much. In his earlier and his later plays an irrational element makes its appearance which pierces through the net of conditioning influences in which his figures are caught. It takes the form of a longing for another life. This dream may be of a simple materialistic type, if a primitive man is the dreamer; it can take a metaphysical, or even a clearly religious aspect in people with finer minds. In *The Moon of the Caribees* (1919) it is the young Englishman Smitty who cannot join in the drunken pleasures of his fellow-sailors because he is tormented by sentimental memories and longings. In *The Long Voyage Home* (1919) the heavy, somewhat stupid Swede Olson tries in vain to realize his dream of a new existence in his native country far from the sea and the monotony and brutality of his present life. The title of O'Neill's first long play *Beyond the Horizon* (1920) indicates that longing is a central motive in it. The reaching out of a dissatisfied soul after a life that is different, better, fuller of love, nearer to God is important also in *"The Hairy Ape"*, *All God's Chillun Got Wings*, *The Fountain* (1926), in *The Great God Brown* (1926) and *Days without End* (1934).

A striking consequence of this metaphysical thirst in O'Neill is the number and the quality of the death scenes he has created. It is true, there are deaths in his play that appear final; the author is interested in them merely as the ends of an individual's career: such are the deaths of the Emperor Jones and of the miserable protagonists of *Diff'rent* (1921). Or O'Neill may introduce a person's death in order to study its effect on other figures. The deaths of Sam Evans in *Strange Interlude* and of Ezra Mannon in *Mourning Becomes Electra* are of this type. More characteristic are scenes of death in which the dying person turns from this life full of an intense longing for something else and something better. In *Bound East for Cardiff* (1916) the American sailor Yank meets death without struggling very hard against it because he is sick of a seaman's life, and his last minutes are illumined by his dream of another existence on a farm.

A highly characteristic end is that of Robert in *Beyond the Horizon*. When he comes to die after a life that was unhappy because a dreamer and a poet was fettered to a farm, he says: "You mustn't feel sorry for me. Don't you see I'm happy at last — free — free! — freed from the farm — free to wander on and on — eternally! (He raises himself on his elbow, his face radiant, and points to the horizon) Look! Isn't it beautiful beyond the hills? I can hear the old voices calling me to come — (Exultantly) And this time I'm going! It isn't the end. It's a free beginning — the start of my voyage! I've won to my trip — the right of release — beyond the horizon! ..."

A strange happy-unhappy scene closes *The Straw* (1921) when poor young Eileen is about to die of tuberculosis in a sanatorium. The man who has helped to sap her vitality by not responding to her love is deeply moved when he realizes what has happened. He makes her believe that he loves and wants to marry her, and her joy is so overwhelming that they both begin to believe in the possibility of a happy future for them at the moment when death is approaching.

O'Neill's final remark in *"The Hairy Ape"* is worth considering in this connection. Yank, the creature of the stokehole who is the hero of this play, has lost his primitive self-confidence, his sense of "belonging" somewhere, in the course of a humiliating confrontation with a rich and elegant young lady. It is like a "fall", a loss of the brutish innocence of this half-brother of Caliban. It fills him with a mad craving to destroy the world to which he does not belong. It makes him envy the unbroken animal nature of the gorilla in the zoo. He opens the cage to win a brother wrecker in the beast, and is suddenly hugged to death by it. And the author's laconic comment runs: "And, perhaps, the Hairy Ape at last belongs."

A stronger light shines at the end of *Desire under the Elms*, when the child-murderer Abbie and her guilty lover go to face justice, as well as at the deaths of Dion Anthony in *The Great God Brown*, of Juan Ponce de Leon in *The Fountain*, and of Queen Kukachin in *"Marco Millions"* (1927). In the extremely audacious play *Lazarus Laughed* (1927), which is entirely dominated by the life-death question, death is mystically absorbed into life. It retains no reality whatsoever except as a condition of the renewal of life. Lazarus, returned from the dead, fills the villages and cities of the empire with his irresistible laughter and his paean of the eternal power and glory of life. The play betrays the fact that O'Neill was not immune against one of the major temptations of the modern artist: he appears in the part of the prophet of some sort of new religion. His doctrine is a rather crude vitalistic creed, disguised by fine mystic words. Woe to the actor that tries to cope with the innumerable volleys of sublime laughter required of Lazarus in the course of this play!

We could define the philosophy of O'Neill's plays as determinism experienced as something that is not enough, that provokes an insatiable metaphysical thirst. Usually he is satisfied to express this inner condition in dramatic form, sometimes, however, he gropes for some mystic medicine to allay his thirst.

We now turn to a consideration of the methods by which O'Neill turned his philosophy into drama. It will be our chief care to observe where he saw the necessity of conflict in a world of beings so closely bound by the law of cause and effect, and to see how he managed to write drama, once his interest had become concentrated in the struggles within the individual souls.

In his first phase, when he composed his short plays, the last-mentioned problem did not trouble him yet. If we look at the Glencairn one-act plays, dealing with the life on a British tramp steamer, we find the young author mainly interested in the effect of milieu on behaviour. The plots are of the slightest: the last minutes of a sailor who has got injured in a commonplace accident; the talking, drinking, love-making and brawling of the crew while the ship is at anchor off an island in the West Indies at night. The strongest point of these plays is their atmosphere. They cannot therefore be called naturalistic in the strict sense of the term. Although many minute details are recorded in the stage-directions O'Neill does not attempt mere photographic reproduction: all his details are calculated to create a dramatic illusion. In *Bound East for Cardiff* the irregular form of the seamen's forecastle and the sleeping bunks ranged one above the other effectively suggest a life within narrow limits, devoid of a personal sphere. Acoustic effects are carefully introduced: the steamer's whistle is heard at regular intervals, one of the sailors is playing on the accordion. Besides, the smoke of poor tobacco is hanging in the air. No means of making the spectator conscious of the quality of the place is neglected, and the sailors that come and go become the creatures of this place for him. Although they represent different national types their reactions have become similar by their common work and life on the sea. The author is interested in group psychology rather than in individual psychology in this play and its companion pieces.

The Glencairn plays are accompanied by a group of other short works — *Ile* (1919), *Where the Cross is Made* (1919) and *The Rope* (1919) — in which an unusual personality is shown in conflict with his milieu. The milieu element is no longer the dominating feature. In *Ile* the iron will of Captain Keeney overcomes the wish of his mutinous crew to return home although his wife, who cannot stand the monotony of a protracted whaling expedition any longer, implores him, too, to give up his crazy plan of remaining at sea until he has got all the oil his vessel can carry. The captain's imperviousness approaches a kind of mania and causes his wife's nervous break-down. O'Neill's interest in abnormal mental conditions makes itself felt for the first time. The central figures in the other two plays we have mentioned are real maniacs. Captain Bartlett is possessed by the idea that he must get hold of a treasure-chest hidden on a far-off island. Although there are hints as to the origin of his illusion — to be developed in *Gold* (1920), a three-act version of the same story — O'Neill concentrates on its effects on the captain himself and on his children, his son, who is weak enough to inherit his mania, and his strong, resisting daughter. Also in *The Rope* Old Bentley's mad avarice is taken for granted, and its effects are shown on the stage, or rather the last phase of its effects. In all the three plays the motifs are clearly subservient to the author's desire to write gripping drama. We do not get this impression when we turn to the works of O'Neill's maturity.

When he composed *Beyond the Horizon* he took the step towards a new dramatic form that was to allow him the study of his figures at various moments of their career. He frequently returned to its time plan, the outcome of the fact that his characters lost their stability, and became ever changing entities that could only be comprehended by being observed at various periods of their development. Quite a series of conflicts springs from the error of a minute in this play. Robert Mayo chooses the wrong kind of wife and the wrong kind of life for himself. A born dreamer and wanderer he becomes a peasant, and soon proves unable to keep his farm going. All this happens because he loves Ruth, a girl that is of the dreaming kind also, and therefore cannot compensate his failings. They are ill-matched because they are too similar. Had Ruth married Robert's brother Andrew, also an admirer of hers, things would probably have gone well with the three of them. The consequences of their error are developed in acts II and III, which take place three and eight years later. Although the couple are full of good-will, and struggle bravely, they cannot escape a cruel process of mental and physical deterioration. They begin to scold and to quarrel; Ruth comes to despise and hate her husband for his inefficiency, and she keeps hankering after Andrew, who was also started on a wrong course of life after she made her choice. Robert even loses his love for his wife and his work, but he drudges on conscientiously. His unhappiness saps his vitality; he becomes a victim of tuberculosis. This is not the only effect of the spiritual on the physical. The faces of Ruth and Robert undergo fearful changes and mirror their plight most impressively. O'Neill has stressed this relation between mind and body in many of his later plays, in none more strikingly than in *Mourning Becomes Electra*.[7] The central motifs of the play, the clash between milieu and man, between a man and a woman that do not fit together, are the

[7] Cf. also *The Straw*, "*Marco Millions*", *Strange Interlude* and *Dynamo*.

source of drama in other plays as well. Eileen in *The Straw* gets no comfort from her brutal father and her worthless fiancé in her sickness. She falls in love with a fellow-patient in the sanatorium, the journalist Stephen Murray. While she is dreaming of her love he is merely kind to her. He uses her as his secretary, and is dreaming of his professional future and of literary fame. We have already discussed the strange end that O'Neill has tacked on to this story. It spoils the proportion of the play. We find this fault frequently enough in the biographical plays, i. e. in the plays containing various important phases of a person's life. Also *All God's Chillun Got Wings* and "*Marco Millions*" are singularly ill-constructed. Both are at the same time good examples of O'Neill's further use of the motif of the ill-matched couple. The first of them deals with the psychological consequences of a mixed marriage, the second contains a most cruel scene, in which Marco, the prosaic admirer of money and success, takes the beautiful princess Kukachin on his ship to Persia without noticing, without even having the faculty of noticing, that she loves him and hovers on the brink of insanity because he utterly fails to respond.

But the exterior disproportions we have discussed so far did not remain the chief interest of O'Neill. He was more and more fascinated by the drama going on within a single soul, if this old-fashioned word can still be used in connection with his modernistic psychological studies. He accepted the view according to which the mind is a complicated mechanism whose nature, not discernible as long as it is functioning normally, is disclosed if a crisis comes on or if a mal-formation has taken place. A striking example of what he set out to do is *The Emperor Jones*, performed by the Provincetown Players in November 1920. The powerfully built and energetic negro Jones is shown in the crisis that ends his profitable tyranny over the primitive and superstitious negro population on an island in the West Indies and also his life. The play begins when his exploited subjects rebel against him, and declare their intention to kill him by beating the tomtom in the fashion of their African ancestors. Jones believes that he can easily escape across the sea, and starts on his way through the wood to the coast. Night overtakes him. Under the influence of excitement, physical exertion and the threatening sound of the tomtom he loses his head. The veneer of half-civilization falls from him; he becomes a frightened primitive creature again that runs towards its doom instead of away from it. O'Neill uncovers the negro's subconscious being layer by layer so to speak. In doing this he employs the methods of expressionistic staging to which he has frequently returned.[8] The illusions of the fugitive become real on the stage, and appear in a series of short scenes. They do not only spring from his own past existence but also from a racial memory of the sort postulated by C. G. Jung. At first the negro, and with him the spectator, sees the two murders that have forced him to leave the United States. Then he lives once more through the sale of his own person on a slave market. There is a vision of a herd of negroes packed together on the ship that takes them from Africa to America, and another one of a witch-doctor intending to sacrifice Jones to a crocodile deity in the African forest. Jones' terror and exhaustion increase from scene to scene until he becomes an easy victim of his enemies. O'Neill has solved the difficult problem of splitting up the mind of a half-civilized creature in a series of truly dramatic scenes. At the same time he has successfully avoided the danger of giving merely an interesting case-study. The figure and fate of Jones have a symbolic value. Jones stands for the black peoples that barter away their traditions and their style of life for the technical side of the white man's civilization. Besides he represents a psychological type; the kind of person that suppresses and betrays vital elements of his being for the sake of success, and is destroyed in the end by the revolt of what he has suppressed.

The Emperor Jones is almost a mono-drama. In the longer works that followed it O'Neill attempted to combine the two chief motifs we have noticed so far. He showed the conflicts between an individual and his surroundings as well as those occurring within the individual soul, and he studied the interaction of the two. Several of these plays are no more than dramatized case-histories without the symbolic value of great drama. This is the impression we get from the reading of *Diff'rent*, a play in which a Puritan maiden fails to marry because she hears immediately before her

[8] e. g. in *"The Hairy Ape"* and in *All God's Chillun Got Wings*.

wedding that her fiancé does not come up to her ideal of absolute sexual purity. The second part of the play contains a gruesome picture of her fate as an old maid doting on a worthless young fellow by whom she is fooled and dishonoured.

The most ambitious play of this sort is *Strange Interlude*, a veritable psycho-analytical *Odyssey*. It cannot be said that the transmutation of a theory into a work of art has been quite successful in the case of this nine-act play, which shows the emotional life of a woman loving six men: her father, her youthful fiancé, her fatherly friend, her husband, her lover, and her son. The story of Nina Leeds reveals the fact that the psycho-analytical interpretation of a person's behaviour makes her a poor centre of a drama. It deprives her of her personality, and turns her into a rather formidable automaton the intricacy of whose reactions is interesting until their monotony becomes apparent. All the artistry of O'Neill cannot hide the faults inherent in the plan of this play. The most striking technical innovation in *Strange Interlude* is the development of the old "aside" into an instrument that permits the dramatist to show a person's real thoughts and his social mask side by side. The price he has to pay for this advantage is a rather dangerous slowing down of the speed of his scenes. The same device was used in *Dynamo*, a study of the religious perversion of a Puritan parson's son. O'Neill rejected it, however, when he composed his trilogy *Mourning Becomes Electra*. This drama has much more power over our feelings than *Strange Interlude*. The psycho-analytical dissolution of the characters is less complete than in the case of Nina Leeds; they do not so much give the impression of being puppets going through movements dictated by a complicated machinery of inhibitions, fixations, compensations, etc. It is the definite historical setting that lends them reality and also the spectator's recollection of their Greek prototypes.

It is not astonishing that O'Neill's psychological interest led him on to the phenomenon of the split personality. He evolved methods of making split personalities capable of dramatic representation. He used one of them in *The Great God Brown*, one of his most difficult and most revealing plays. It is full of criticism of modern American life, a trait which connects it with "*Marco*

Millions". Dion Anthony cannot and does not want to adjust himself to the standards of the successful business men, a feat performed without difficulty by his commonplace friend William A. Brown. Dion is a sensitive artist, a dreamer, in love with life or with God — he does not exactly know which. But he meets the world in the mask of a sneering contemptuous cynic, who takes pleasure in tormenting harmless souls like his wife Margaret and Brown, the successful one, who becomes his employer as well as his friend. The actor who plays the part needs a real mask which he can put on and take off, or rather several masks, because his mask ages and changes its expression as his face does. When Dion, after his wild life, dies of heart failure he leaves his mask to Brown, who becomes a double personality in consequence of that dangerous gift. The enmity between the Brown-part and the Dion-part in him grows; the mask of Dion sucks Brown's life-blood, and becomes more real and alive than he is himself, until Brown, in an incredibly daring and grotesque scene, accuses himself of having killed Dion and dies himself hit by a policeman's bullet, tormented by Dion's desire to pray and blaspheme in turns. The author of this play is suffering from the lack of coherence in modern life, from the disparity between its technical efficiency and its spiritual sterility. As is his wont he expresses his problem in psychological terms. Brown, the successful one, is a spiritual cripple, cut off from the creative life, from love, and from God, and he does not even know it before he becomes Dion's heir. Dion is different, tormented by the desire for another life, but as he must live in the world as it is, his personality is split up.

Not only Dion but all the main figures of the play wear masks at one time or another. The masks have various functions: in harmless cases they simply show different sides of a personality, but they may also make visible his fundamental inner disharmony, even his total disruption. They may protect the wearer, but they can also become an enemy that preys upon him. In the earlier scenes they are used with striking success; later on their use becomes so complicated as to be hardly intelligible if witnessed by an unprepared spectator on the stage.[9]

[9] In *Lazarus Laughed* O'Neill has found an entirely different employ-

In his miracle play, *Days without End*, O'Neill once more treated the story of a split personality. It is simpler than the one discussed above. Its hero, John Loving, appears all through the play as a double figure. John is always accompanied by Loving, whose part must be taken by a second actor of the same stature, wearing the same kind of clothes and a mask. John Loving has lost both his parents in his youth in the course of an epidemic. The shock has cost him his religious faith. This is the cause of the disruption of his personality. The relation of the John-part to the Loving-part closely resembles the relation between the two souls in Dion Anthony's breast. John is seeking a way back to God and to love, but he is constantly opposed by Loving, a cold sneering demon, an advocate of nihilism and death. The predominance of Loving comes to an end when John Loving marries Elsa, a woman who has suffered no less than he has. For both husband and wife their love is the only positive experience justifying existence in this world. Consequently the Loving-part plots to destroy their union, and succeeds in inducing John Loving to commit adultery. Once this has happened, Loving is again in the ascendant. Elsa senses that he wishes her death, and, in her desperation, gives up her resistance against a casual illness. When she is on the point of dying from pneumonia John finds the way to church and is able to overcome Loving definitely at the foot of the crucifix. The whole is called a modern miracle play. The personification of the good and the evil propensities of the soul remind us of the allegorical methods of the mediaeval and the Puritan moralists. O'Neill has used this traditional method to reveal the struggle in a modern soul in a striking manner. John and Loving always appear together; one or the other can take the lead in a conversation or merely throw in a remark now and then. They can also address one another, of course. In this way we get an amazingly vivid picture of the struggle between the two tendencies in John Loving as well as of their effects on and reactions to other people's words and actions. A final verdict on the success of this method can only be given after the play has been seen on the stage.

ment for masks. Here they have their traditional function of characterizing various types of people.

In spite of the catholic spirit of *Days without End* O'Neill remains for us the restless seeker, the man of many creeds and many forms. His great dramatic power appears in the skill with which he develops drama out of themes that are hardly promising in themselves. His intense interest in psycho-analysis is not an asset in a dramatist. Some of his plays remain interesting case studies. The more completely he analyses his figures for us the less is there of the mystery of life in them. But O'Neill undertook the task of interpreting his figures in the terms in which many of his contemporaries interpreted their own reactions and conflicts. It cannot be said that this interpretation always sprang from his immediate experience. Often he was fascinated by a theory. This, I think, is the reason why his plays — except perhaps *The Emperor Jones* and *Desire under the Elms* — remain admirable experiments. We respond to them intellectually and with part of our emotions, but there is not that complete and unreserved response exacted by the masterpieces of dramatic art. Even so, he has drawn unforgettable pictures of modern man, haunted by many clashing beliefs, superstitions and longings, often his own worst enemy, entirely unable to save himself. (1947)

2. *The Iceman Cometh*

O'NEILL's new play, published after twelve years of silence in the autumn of 1946, is not really a post-war work, the date of composition as given in the edition of the Random House,[1] New York, being 1939. The play does not differ in essentials from its predecessors; it continues the series recently published in three volumes by the same publishers. It is remarkable for the depth of its gloom, its forbidding atmosphere, plot and characters as well as for the detached, objective way in which the dramatist creates his underworld, and peoples it with a crowd of drunkards and outcasts from society. All this cannot surprise us in a play by O'Neill. Also the central theme is one that could not but appeal to the dramatist who had been a close student of the imaginative faculty in man since the beginning of his career. In his earlier works we

[1] Quotations are taken from this edition.

have frequently found such motifs as a simple man's dream of a different and better life, the hope cherished by the dying, the transmuting power of love, the illusions of the insane and the faith of those believing in the revelation of God. Thus O'Neill was fascinated by all the activities of the imagination, whether high or low, sane or abnormal, whether productive of mania or truth. In *Days without End,* the last play of the earlier series, John Loving was allowed to conquer the powers of evil under the crucifix and to save his wife, hovering on the brink of death, by his faith.

We look in vain for anything like the spirit of that ending in *The Iceman Cometh.* The function of the imagination treated in this play is dubious and problematical. The scene is "a cheap gin-mill of the five-cent whiskey, last-resort variety" situated on the downtown West Side of New York, and the time is the year 1912. All through the four acts we see parts of the bar and the back room of this establishment, both of them much the worse for lack of cleanliness and upkeep. As gray as these localities with their dirty walls are the wrecks of human beings that come and go in front of them. Harry Hope, the owner of the place, is a most accommodating personality. His employees and the company of parasites that have assembled around him are all very fond of him, certain that his lack of energy and his good-nature will prevent him from taking effective measures against fraudulent helpers and rarely paying guests. The two loud and lively waiters Rocky Pioggi and Chuck Morello, whose names indicate their origin, are careful not to exaggerate while they are abusing their master's laziness. But Rocky has found rooms in the house for Pearl and Margie, and Chuck for his Cora: three prostitutes, who help to increase the income of the two gentlemen. On the other hand the night barman as well as the day barman see to it that the indigent guests do not drink too much whiskey without paying for it. All of Harry's queer friends have a past, but no future. Therefore they have settled down in this No Chance Saloon, in Bedrock Bar, The End of the Line Café, The Bottom of the Sea Rathskeller, as Larry Slade, the most intelligent of its inmates, christens the sorry place. (p. 25.)

Ed Mosher, Hope's brother-in-law, is here, in his better days a circus man, and beside him Pat McGloin, kicked out of the police force in consequence of the discovery of his corrupt practices. We also meet the dark-skinned Joe Mott, one-time proprietor of a Negro gambling house, Piet Wetjoen, one-time leader of a Boer commando, and his enemy Cecil Lewis, a dismissed British officer. They and their fellows have all lost their positions through weakness and misfortune, but they manage to get some comfort out of their present miserable way of life. They avoid thinking too clearly about themselves by drinking considerable quantities of horrible liquor and by covering their past, present and future existences with pink-coloured webs of fancy. This is Larry Slade's conscious account of their instinctive policy: "To hell with the truth! As the history of the world proves, the truth has no bearing on anything. It's irrelevant and immaterial, as the lawyers say. The lie of a pipe dream is what gives life to the whole misbegotten mad lot of us, drunk or sober." (p. 9 f.) Whoever has the time and the patience to listen to Larry's companions can admire the glorious scenes of their past which they like to conjure up. Willie Oban, a Harvard Law School alumnus, lives through the successes of his student days again; the two enemies of the Boer War exchange endless reminiscences and protest with much chuckling and laughter that they will eternally regret having missed all the wartime opportunities for killing each other. Harry Hope's own mind works in precisely the same manner. If any one of his parasites contemplates an attack on his bottles or purse and therefore wants him to become nicely soft and tearful he mentions the name of his dear wife Bessie, deceased twenty years ago. She walks through his memories as a gentle angel of love and goodwill. Her death explains for him why his political career was a failure, why he lost all his business ambitions, why he does not even leave his house any more, but is spending his days in drunken apathy. Fortunately Bessie's brother Ned is present, from whose uncivil remarks we can gather that in reality she was as shrewish and intolerable a wife as ever plagued husband. And later on, when Harry becomes a temporary convert to truthfulness, he calls her himself a "nagging old hag". (p. 204.) Even Rocky and Chuck and their girls cherish illusions, which permit them to feel comparatively respectable and to talk contemptuously of other representatives of their trade. It is amusing to see Rocky deeply shocked if anybody is sufficiently ill-mannered to call him a "pimp", and to hear Pearl and her friends proclaim themselves "tarts", a special and higher species of streetwalker, which must not be confused with that of the common whores.

In this connection we may mention how much of the life and impressiveness of O'Neill's scenes springs from his splendid hand-ling of the various types of slang spoken by Harry and his family. Already at the outset of his career, when he wrote the short sea plays, he knew excellently well how to use the dialects spoken in London, New York, Scotland and Ireland as well as the kinds of English uttered by Americans born in Germany, Scandinavia, Russia and other foreign countries, and to produce striking effects by their juxtaposition. The same technique is used in his latest play. The harsh idioms that strike our ears do not only betray the speaker's first and second country but also his former occupation and social position; moreover, they have certain elegances in com-mon that belong to their present station. All these facts place the play among the texts that cannot be satisfactorily translated. The number of rough, but racy metaphors and similes bandied about in Harry's hotel is overwhelming, especially when the speakers supply their formidable demand for friendly, neutral and furious abuse. Here are some of their stronger terms of address: *bastard, boob, bum, cuckoo, dope, dummy, dinge, grifter, grouch, nut, punk, sap, scum, simp, slob, sucker*. The girls in the house may be called *broads, hookers, hustlers, pigs, tarts*, or *tramps*. By drinking too much *booze, rat-poison, rot-gut* or simply *stuff* in the *dive, dump, ginmill* or *joint* one gets *cockeyed, pieeyed, plastered, soused* or *stinko*. Picturesque expressions for drinking are *to lap up a starter, to grab a ball, to kill a pint, to get slugs under one's belt* or *mud in one's eye*, and for sleeping *to hit the hay, to catch a coupla winks* and *to grab a snooze*. In drab monotony both *to kill* and *to die* are replaced by *to croak*.

Even more important than the illusions enveloping the past and the present are the dreams of the future for the well-being of Harry's household. Almost every single one of his guests is con-vinced that in the near future a relative of his, or an official, or an employer, or even he himself is going to do something that will take him back to his rightful place in society. Harry plans a walk through the district for the next day to see old friends and restore long neglected important connections. While he is talking about it, his fellows exchange amused and knowing glances: he is indulging in one of his "pipe dreams"; it makes him feel comfortable although nothing of what he says will ever happen. But when their own dreams are concerned they are all just as blind as Harry. Chuck and Cora want to turn a new leaf before long; they intend to give up their sordid jobs, to marry and to buy a farm in New Jersey. Jimmy Tomorrow, one-time Boer War correspondent, believes that he can easily get back his lost position if he calls on his former employers in a sober and decent condition. He must only get his clothes mended, cleaned and pressed, and then he will start. Wetjoen and Lewis discuss their always impending voyage to England and South-Africa; Joe sees himself starting a new gambling establishment, and Willie enjoys his first successes as a brilliant young attorney.

The impression created by this account that O'Neill has given ample scope to his exposition in this play is correct. However, one after the other of his human wrecks is presented so skilfully for our inspection that our interest never flags. And very soon the suspense which has kept Harry's company out of their beds during a whole night seizes the reader, and probably also the spectator of the play. They expect a common friend of theirs: Hickey, the hardware salesman, who visits the house with great regularity twice a year to indulge his dipsomania in congenial surroundings. He is praised as a fine sociable being, an admirable drinker and giver of drinks. With infinite glee one of his favourite jokes is recalled: he will pass around a photograph of his wife in sentimental enthusiasm; and then, all of a sudden, his mood will change while he is telling how he surprised her in the hay with the iceman at his homecoming. But this time the great man has kept the company waiting far too long. They are sadly depressed by want of sleep and of alcohol. Moreover, when Hickey finally arrives, he is no longer the comfortable man they knew and expected, though he does not hesitate to pay for all the drinks they want to have. He even prepares a birthday party for Harry as only a devoted friend can do it, and graces it with the most beautiful bottles of champagne. But he accompanies his gifts with words that deprive the whiskey and the wine of all their flavour and render them positively incapable of producing a satisfactory state of intoxication. He has not become an ordinary apostle of prohibition. His aim is much more ambitious. He wants to drag his friends out of the clutches of their illusions, their "pipe dreams". He forces them to give up their swaggering talk, to realize and admit that they always were, and still are, weak and good-for-nothing cowards, and completely lack the energy necessary for a new start. Hickey's power over their minds is considerable. He can draw upon an almost unlimited fund of prestige. As a successful travelling salesman he has developed his gift of persuasion to the utmost, a gift inherited from his father, who, being a preacher, understood the fine art of selling "nothing for something", as Hickey puts it. (p. 232.) He has the jovial, hail-fellow-well-met manner affected by many Americans when they wish to convert the common man to something or other, but he does not exaggerate it. He tries very hard to radiate a catching optimism: having performed the most difficult of all operations on himself by killing his own illusions and dreams, he enjoys a kind of feverish happiness and a heady sense of freedom, and has even forgotten his craving for liquor. He praises his new condition enthusiastically, but in words that could be applied to death: "You can let go of yourself at last. Let yourself sink down to the bottom of the sea. Rest in peace. There's no farther you have to go. Not a single damned hope or dream left to nag you—." (p. 86.) And later on he promises: "You'll be in a today where there is no yesterday or tomorrow to worry you. You won't give a damn what you are any more." (p. 147 f.) The drunkards upon whom he wants to bestow these blessings are terribly disappointed; they listen reluctantly to his exhortations, and curse him as soon as he turns his back. In grotesque and in terrible scenes we witness the effect of the Gorgon face of truth on Harry's miserable crew. They get nervous and quarrelsome; they want to fly at one another's throats because they cannot bear to hear Hickey's unpalatable diagnoses repeated by their fellows. Nevertheless he succeeds in mesmerizing them into a temporary fit of activity. He asks them to really do the things they keep harping on. He is certain that all their futile attempts will fail, but this is just the medicine he wants them to swallow because it will give them his own sense of freedom and happiness. It is in the third act that he brings enough moral pressure to bear on them that they start on their much discussed errands from which they expect a turn in their affairs. One after the other hands back the key of his room with an elegant gesture, the casualness of which must hide the trembling of his hand. But very soon they are all back again, depressed by their failures, furious, or furiously drunk. Harry himself is the first to return from his famous birthday excursion; he did not get farther than the middle of the street in front of his house; there an approaching motorcar, seen by nobody but himself, frightened him so much that he rushed back to the safety of his bar. When the company is complete again in the fourth act Hickey's influence on them is rapidly waning, especially as he is himself deeply shocked by the negative result of his experiment.

In spite of Hickey's bonhomie and confidence only the most insensitive among his cronies have failed to notice something uncanny about him. He seems impelled by an intoxication that is profounder and stranger than any one produced by liquor. Larry Slade, his most perspicacious observer, hints quite early in the play that Hickey is hard pressed by some terrible secret that he would like to confess. He makes his confession gradually and in fragments. At the end of the second act we all know that he has lost his wife, at the end of the third that she has been murdered, and towards the close of the fourth and last act he confesses that he is himself her murderer. Evelyn is a figure of light, hovering beyond the horizon of the nightmarish underworld in which we move in the play. From Hickey's detailed account we learn that she fell in love with him when he was still a wild and none too promising youngster. He responded to her love, and kept exchanging letters with her after he had become a travelling salesman, although by that time he had begun to give way to his passion for liquor and cheap love affairs. Again and again Evelyn's letters brought him back to his senses, and restored his belief in a decent future. When the two finally decided to marry Hickey was certain that the worse part of his life had come to its end. But his willpower proved weak; periodically he lapsed into his old sordid habits, and came home in an unspeakable condition. Every time Evelyn received him like a modern Griselda, nursed him, and convinced him that the thing would not happen again. But he dragged her through humiliation after humiliation, and felt the worst of cads when he discovered that her love and faith could not be shaken. And this time, when he grew restless again, and felt another betrayal approaching, he went up to her bedroom, and shot her through the head in her sleep. He mentions several contradictory reasons for his horrible deed: he wanted to get rid of the woman who, by her goodness and long-suffering, had made him a continual reproach to himself; he wanted to protect the woman he loved from further ill-treatment; he wanted to kill the deceptive belief that he could ever be anything else but his present miserable self. He tried to escape from the sphere of good and evil into a moral vacuum. We have described the strange intoxication that rewarded his crime and the stranger crusade by which he tried to win companions enjoying the same existence without responsibility and without illusions. The drunkards shrink back from him, terrified by the glimpse of the void they have caught under his direction, and return with renewed zest to their comfortable dreams and their whiskey, in which they joyfully discover the old "kick" again, while they welcome the possibility of pitying Hickey as a murderous crank. For him there exists no such way of escape. He is lonely, marked by an invisible brand, in a state that is neither life nor death. It is the main enigma of the play that he does not simply commit suicide in this crisis, but chooses a long and complicated way to death. He quietly sends for the police, and when the detectives arrive they are just in time to listen to Hickey's confession. It is a great relief for him to tell the story of his life and crime although his audience, except the detectives and Larry Slade, are quite unwilling to listen, and hasten to befog themselves completely with Harry's whiskey.

What are we to make of Hickey's wish to confess what he has done and to die in the electric chair according to the law? He does not really understand his motives himself. He wants to convince everybody that there was love in his heart, when he killed Evelyn, not hate. (p. 227.) And his experiment in Harry's hotel was inspired by love as well. (p. 226.) The negative reaction of his friends depresses him: "I've had about all I can stand — That's why I phoned" — (p. 224). A little later he says: "Don't worry about the

Chair, Larry. I know it's still hard for you not to be terrified by death, but when you've made peace with yourself, like I have, you won't give a damn." (p. 228.) Does this man seek confession and expiation, or does he merely follow atavistic impulses, which have as much or as little importance for the nihilist as anything else? Is O'Neill studying psychological peculiarities, one of which permits him to end his analytically constructed play by a fascinating self-revelation? Such explanations as these cannot be lightly dismissed. But they are hardly satisfactory when Hickey's voice fades away with this helpless asseveration: "Why, Evelyn was the only thing on God's earth I ever loved! I'd have killed myself before I'd ever have hurt her!" (p. 246.) Perhaps the effect of his murder was entirely different from what he expected. Instead of killing Evelyn's faith and love he may have made them more active and powerful for his own good than before. Instead of being turned off into the void he may have been precipitated into the metaphysical sphere where such terms as love, faith, guilt, sin, confession and atonement are related to definite realities, a sphere that makes Harry's guests appear quite unreal, no matter whether they indulge their desire for booze and illusions or not. Were Evelyn's faith and love, the causes of so much acute distress for Hickey in his depraved condition, fundamentally different from the "pipe dreams" and alcoholic illusions, making the shadowy existences of Harry's drunkards bearable and, sometimes, even comfortable? O'Neill does not ask such questions, nor does he answer them. But they will trouble many students of this work, which, at first sight, appears to be wholly devoted to the exploration of a human condition where life is only to be had at the price of illusions, and where self-knowledge kills.

Hickey is not the only victim of that power in Harry's house. Very early in the play we meet the eighteen years old Don Parritt, whose mother, an active member of a group of terrorists, has just been caught by the police, and must expect to spend the rest of her life in prison. Don was the only one of her gang to escape. He has come to find Larry Slade, one of his mother's former helpers and lovers. Larry retired from the group and its activities long ago because he lost faith in the human qualities of its members, and was disgusted by the way Don's mother put her belief in promiscuous marriage into practice. Now he is as true an inmate of Harry's hotel as anybody else, his illusion being the conviction that he has ceased to care for anything, except perhaps death. The two would-be-nihilists Hickey and Larry are frequently at odds; Don and Larry, however, are drawn into a fearful struggle, which is not less terrible for being often mute. It accompanies all the Hickey episodes, and reaches its catastrophe only after the disappearance of the protagonist. It is one of those painful psychological processes that have always fascinated O'Neill, great expert at describing the reactions of infected human guinea-pigs. Don demands the older man's interest, help, and judgment. But he can only pierce his armour of cynicism and coldness by telling him the truth about himself: he accuses himself of having sold his mother and her friends to the police, a deed which he calls worse than murder, once he has made up his mind to face it squarely. He cannot find any decent excuse for what he has done; indeed, he followed a welter of confused and thoroughly ignoble impulses. He is not satisfied before Larry knows the worst, who, giving vent to his disgust and hatred, pronounces the death sentence which the desperate youth wants to hear. Don puts an end to his life by a fall from the fire escape.

Thus we find in this play O'Neill's old passion for the most accurate description of a milieu and its creatures, the old absorption by psychological processes, ruthlessly followed up to their bitter end. But he knows how to give more than case studies. We get the impression that the figures before us and their doings are poetic expressions of the dramatist's sufferings in a half crazy world. There are symbolical traits, such as the name of the play, which gives a new sense to the iceman in Hickey's vulgar joke about his wife. Harry Hope's name is no more accidental than the description of Hickey as a hardware salesman. This strange personality is most successfully enveloped by an atmosphere of mystery and terror. Death talk and death imagery are frequent throughout the play, and they are stimulated by the protagonist. Larry keeps talking of his longing for death, a habit that provokes a standing joke among his fellows:

ROCKY: "—— Jees, somebody'll have to take an axe to croak you!"
       (p. 10.)

CORA: "——Yuh'll have to hire someone to croak yuh wid an axe." (p. 70.)

Long before Hickey's arrival Willie happens to cry impatiently: "Would that Hickey or Death would come!" (p. 39.) When Hickey, tired by his trip, feels that he will fall asleep before his astonished friends, he admits: "Hell of a trick to go dead on you like this." (p. 85.) The iceman joke is alluded to again and again in the course of the play, and grows more peculiar at every mention until Larry, the speaker of the key-words, finds himself saying: "Set 'em up, Rocky. I swore I'd have no more drinks on Hickey, if I died of drought, but I've changed my mind! Be God, he owes it to me, and I'd get blind to the world now if it was the Iceman of Death himself treating! *(He stops, startledly, a superstitious awe coming into his face)* What made me say that, I wonder. *(With a sardonic laugh)* Well, be God, it fits, for Death was the Iceman Hickey called to his home!" (p. 182 f.) Another strange phenomenon is the instinct by which Hickey detects another doomed man in Don Parritt almost as soon as he sees him. These traits, together with a grotesque quality permeating everything we see and hear, give the work the unity of a grim modern Dance of Death. However, in using his symbolical devices the author is careful to respect the demands of his psychological and milieu realism. Such expressionist distortions as we find e. g. in *The Emperor Jones*, *All God's Chillun Got Wings* and *The Great God Brown* are carefully avoided. Not only in this respect does the play recall O'Neill's early style when he wrote *Where the Cross is Made* and *The Rope*, experimenting with the analytical method of Ibsen. He has never used that method more successfully than in the work before us. The coherence and solidity of its dramatic structure contrast favourably with such loose series of biographical scenes as *Beyond the Horizon*, *All God's Chillun Got Wings*, and *Strange Interlude*. Even O'Neill's thesis may be called a particularly ferocious development of what we find in *The Wild Duck*. The paradoxes of the deadly effect of truth and the life-giving power of illusion are driven home relentlessly, and our attempted speculations on the efficacy of Evelyn's virtues are not encouraged. With *The Iceman Cometh* O'Neill has returned to one of his early modes, but he has made a master craftsman's use of it: artistically the play is among his few impeccable creations. (1948)

3. *"Faithful Realism": The Problem of Style*

IF WE SURVEY the impressive series of plays from *Beyond the Horizon* (1920) to *Days without End* (1934), by which Eugene O'Neill became the first of American dramatists, we are struck by his extraordinary versatility, permitting him to move from one unexplored subject and from one dramatic style to another. Sooner or later, however, we are forced to face the question whether the artist who experimented with so many different styles ever reached complete mastery of any particular style. We are also bound to come up against the complaint, formulated succinctly by Joseph Wood Krutch in the following sentences: "Both as an intellectual and as an emotional conception *Mourning Becomes Electra* at least is in the true grand manner. To find in it any lack one must compare it with the very greatest works of dramatic literature, and to do that is to realize that the one thing conspicuously missing is language — words as thrilling as the action which accompanies them."[1]

We do not think that these strictures can be refuted as long as we base our judgment on the plays of O'Neill's great experimental period only. They are hardly justified if we take his whole achievement, including the plays written and published after 1934, into account. In these last plays the dramatist perfected a style that can properly be called his own, and he found a valid solution of his language problem. Therefore they should be considered as the culmination of his work. The present article attempts some steps towards the revaluation of O'Neill rendered necessary by the publication of *The Iceman Cometh*,[2] *Long Day's Journey into Night*,[3] *A Moon for the Misbegotten*[4] and *A Touch of the Poet*.[5] It is known that these four plays do not represent the whole of his

[1] *The American Drama since 1918*, London 1957, 119.
[2] Completed 1939, published 1946.   [3] Completed 1941, published 1956.
[4] Completed 1943, published 1953.   [5] Completed 1943, published 1957.

late production. In 1958 the still unpublished one-act play *Hughie* was produced at Stockholm, and another play of extraordinary length, *More Stately Mansions*, is still awaiting production, though even Karl Ragnar Gierow, the Swedish expert producer of O'Neill, doubts its adaptability to the stage. The two last mentioned works are fragments of one or, possibly, even two comprehensive cycles of plays the dramatist tried to write in the last phase of his creative life. The fascination exerted on him by the idea of composing in terms of a vast cycle is one of the basic facts for the student of his late work, since it seems to betray an affinity between his conception of man and an epical rather than a dramatic representation of his fate. Thus, the four published plays were written as by-products while O'Neill was obsessed by his cycle idea. But they were to become more important than the cycles. Their author considered *The Iceman Cometh* and *Long Day's Journey into Night* the best plays he had ever composed.[6]

If we inquire into the differences between O'Neill's experimental and his final period, we notice a change in his attitude towards the performance and the publication of his plays. As a glance at our list of composition and publication dates shows, he was no longer as eager to test his plays before his readers (or spectators) as he had formerly been. The main reason for this new

---

[6] On March 27, 1941, he wrote to Barrett H. Clark: "Regarding work, I've finished two plays outside the Cycle in the past two years, and I'm enthusiastic about them. Both will rank among the few very best things I've ever done, I know." (Barrett H. Clark, *Eugene O'Neill: The Man and His Plays*, New York 1947, 145.) Cf. also *op. cit.* 147, where Clark quotes from a letter written "in early September of 1943": "Although I have done no writing lately, my record since Pearl Harbor is not as poor as it might be. I have finished, except for a final cutting, another non-Cycle play — *A Moon for the Misbegotten* — and rewritten the 1928 (*sic*) Cycle play — *A Touch of the Poet*, done some work off and on on another non-Cycle — *The Last Conquest* — ... When, in addition, I consider *The Iceman Cometh*, most of which was written after war started in '39, and *Long Day's Journey into Night*, written the following year — (these two plays give me greater satisfaction than any other two I've ever done) — and a one-act play, *Hughie*, one of a series of eight I want to do under the general title, *By Way of Obit*, I feel I've done pretty well in the four war years."

attitude was not failing health, and most certainly not declining power, but rather a new quality and direction in his creative activity itself. It made itself felt in the cycle idea, which prevented him from ever feeling that he had completed his most important plan. It also appeared in his new interest in autobiographical material. In his middle period, he had usually invented his plots, or based them on facts not directly connected with his own life; plays like *The Straw* and *Ah, Wilderness!*, that harmless forerunner of *Long Day's Journey into Night*, were exceptions. In fact, Barrett H. Clark reports that O'Neill told him (a few years before 1936): "All the most dramatic episodes of my life I have so far kept out of my plays, and most of the things I have seen happen to other people. I've hardly begun to work up all this material, but I'm saving up a lot of it for one thing in particular, a cycle of plays I hope to do some day. There'll be nine separate plays, to be acted on nine successive nights; together they will form a sort of dramatic autobiography, something in the style of *War and Peace* or *Jean-Christophe*."[7] O'Neill was disappointed when, in 1926, he read the biographical sketch that opened the first version of Clark's book on him. He informed its author: "When all is said and done — and this is, naturally, no conceivable fault of yours — the result of this first part is legend. It isn't really true. It isn't I. And the truth would make such a much more interesting — and incredible! — legend. That is what makes me melancholy. But I see no hope for this except some day to shame the devil myself, if I ever can muster the requisite interest—and nerve—simultaneously!"[8] In his final plays he did muster the requisite interest and nerve, and yielded up the secrets he had so carefully hidden for many years. Both *The Iceman Cometh* and *Long Day's Journey into Night* take place in the year 1912, the most critical year in O'Neill's own life, when he almost lost himself in the aimless and dissolute ways into

[7] *op. cit.*, 162.
[8] *op. cit.*, 7. One reason why O'Neill remained so reticent where his own earlier career was concerned appears in the following statement of his wife, Mrs. Carlotta Monterey O'Neill: "He will never tell the truth about himself, because in so doing he would have to tell the truth about others close to him ... and that would involve others!" (*op. cit.*, 8.)

which he had slipped because, among other reasons, he was disgusted by his father's easy and enervating career in the commercial theatre. Harry Hope's cheap ginmill closely resembles a place frequented by O'Neill in New York at that time. This is how he referred to it later on: "In New York I lived at 'Jimmy the Priest's', a waterfront dive, with a back room where you could sleep with your head on the table if you bought a schooner of beer."[9] Harry Hope's customers and friends owe much to the companions of O'Neill's despair in 1912. In *Long Day's Journey into Night* we get even closer to his own most personal and most painful experience. Here, his parents, his brother, and his own former self are the prototypes of the four main characters, whose complicated relationship, constantly vacillating between love and hatred, are depicted with a fanatical passion for truth.[10] No wonder that O'Neill hesitated before he made these plays known to the public, and even wished *Long Day's Journey into Night* to remain unpublished until twenty-five years after his death.

In spite of all the differences between his middle and late period, his main attitudes and subjects remained the same. He always was a rebel against his father's commercial theatre and everything it stood for, and also against the cheap official idealism and optimism as well as the underlying materialism and pragmatism he found far too influential in his country. He required different values: truth on the one hand, love, faith, beauty through artistic creation on the other. These fundamental desires proved to be hopelessly antagonistic. His passion for truth forced him to reject the traditional Catholic religion of his family; in fact, it made him suspect that love, faith, perhaps even beauty, perhaps

---

[9] *op. cit.*, 16.
[10] Cf. the first part of the dedication to Carlotta, prefixed to the printed text of this play, which runs: "DEAREST: *I give you the original script of this play of old sorrow, written in tears and blood. A sadly inappropriate gift, it would seem, for a day celebrating happiness. But you will understand. I mean it as a tribute to your love and tenderness which gave me the faith in love that enabled me to face my dead at last and write this play — write it with deep pity and understanding and forgiveness for all the four haunted Tyrones."* The day alluded to was their twelfth wedding anniversary.

all the creations of the imagination, were illusions, invented by man in order to render a miserable existence tolerable. Man in the closed circle of determining circumstances was, and remained, O'Neill's great theme. He became a leader of modern drama because, as his experiments developed, the fascination of the inner, psychological mechanisms as inexorable forces ruling human fate grew on him.

If he did not change his characteristic attitudes and subjects on the threshold of his last period, where, then, is the source of the new intensity in his art? Why do we feel that now, at last, the playwright stopped experimenting, that he reached the sure touch and the finished style of a master? The main reason for this is that he realizes in a new, overwhelming way what human life is like if his purely "scientific" conception of man is true: he shows, in *The Iceman Cometh*, in *Long Day's Journey into Night* and in *A Moon for the Misbegotten*, an inferno as full of monotonous tortures as Dante's, a waste land as desolate and hopeless as Eliot's. Its inhabitants protect themselves against the deadly touch of the truth by drugs and illusions, or steel themselves by cynicism and brutality if they are strong enough to live face to face with it. This world of horror is no longer the result of abstract thought and speculation; it is an ever-present shocking obsession, threatening to stifle the playwright's breath, becoming fearfully real in the nightmare catastrophes of the Second World War. And, strangely enough, the experience of a kind of life that is in reality death or worse than death — a notion formerly derided by O'Neill as a typical Puritan delusion — is now as basic in his own art as it is in T. S. Eliot's.

And the corresponding belief that there may be life in death? Are there no signs, however hidden, of the life-giving water in O'Neill's waste land? There certainly are. One such sign is the frequent recurrence of the motif of confession in the last plays. The climax of *The Iceman Cometh* is Hickey's confession, breaking out of him in a torrent of words in the last act of the play. The author does not tell us what good the confession and the acceptance of his punishment according to the law do to Hickey beyond releasing him from an intolerable inner tension. Also in *Long Day's Journey into Night* we witness numerous confessions by the main characters, and here they help to mitigate the feelings of hatred that divide the male members of the family in spite of everything they have in common. In *A Moon for the Misbegotten* all the consolation Josie Hogan can offer to James Tyrone, Jr., whom she loves although he is a lost soul beyond all human help, is the listening to the story of his guilty life and the certainty of her forgiveness and love. These gifts cannot save him from himself and from his guilt; their whole efficacy consists in rendering him capable of a few hours of dreamless sleep in Josie's arms. In this way her love becomes "a moon for the misbegotten". Although O'Neill carefully avoids giving the motif of confession its original religious significance, his extensive use of it is an important link with Eliot, the contemporary dramatist whose fascination by the same motif has a religious basis.

O'Neill's infernal world is mainly a world of men. Some of the female characters shine with a light that seems to emanate from the Catholic faith in the Virgin Mary as well as from the playwright's own happy life with his third wife Carlotta, remembered by him in his touching dedication of *Long Day's Journey into Night*, the final section of which is as follows: "*These twelve years, Beloved One, have been a Journey into Light — into love. You know my gratitude. And my love!*" This light is in Hickey's wife Evelyn, that inexplicable and isolated figure and victim of love in the ghastly realm of *The Iceman Cometh*. We discern its flickerings in Mary Tyrone, the mother in *Long Day's Journey into Night*, even while she is sinking back into her fatal drug addiction, losing contact with her husband and sons, who can hardly live without her love. It is strong again in Josie Hogan and also in Nora Melody and, showing a different colour, in her daughter Sara.

These characters prove that O'Neill has a knowledge of a kind of love that cannot be explained as a life-giving illusion, but they show, too, that his faith in the efficacy of this love, in its power to change the world, is rudimentary.

There are also signs that he has his moments of faith in the other creations of the imagination, besides love. They appear in *Long Day's Journey into Night*, when Mary Tyrone remembers the Catholic faith of her youth, when her husband deplores the waste of the great artistic powers he possessed as a young actor, and when Edmund Tyrone confesses what his relations to the art of poetry have been. He, the representative of O'Neill's former self, does so in an impressive scene near the end of the play, when he is in his cups, of course. He has known a kind of mystical experience, for which he would like to find the perfect poetical equivalent. As T. S. Eliot knows of

> the moment in the rose garden,
> The moment in the arbour where the rain beat,
> The moment in the draughty church at smokefall . . .,

Edmund has his own moments of intuition, all of them connected with his past life on or at the sea. "Here's one. When I was on the Squarehead square rigger, bound for Buenos Aires. Full moon in the Trades. The old hooker driving fourteen knots. I lay on the bowsprit, facing astern, with the water foaming into spume under me, the masts with every sail white in the moonlight, towering high above me. I became drunk with the beauty and singing rhythm of it, and for a moment I lost myself — actually lost my life. I was set free! I dissolved in the sea, became white sails and flying spray, became beauty and rhythm, became moonlight and the ship and the high dim-starred sky! I belonged, without past or future, within peace and unity and a wild joy, within something greater than my own life, or the life of Man, to Life itself! To God, if you want to put it that way." Having recalled another similar event, he struggles hard to express its peculiar qualities: "Then the moment of ecstatic freedom came. The peace, the end of the quest, the last harbour, the joy of belonging to a fulfilment beyond men's lousy, pitiful, greedy fears and hopes and dreams! And several other times in my life, when I was swimming far out, or lying alone on a beach, I have had the same experience. Became the sun, the hot sand, green seaweed anchored to a rock, swaying in the tide. Like a saint's vision of beatitude. Like the veil of things as they seem drawn back by an unseen hand. For a second you see — and seeing the secret, are the secret. For a second there is meaning! Then the hand lets the veil fall and you are alone, lost in the fog again, and you stumble on toward nowhere, for no good reason! (*He grins wryly.*) It was a great mistake, my being born a man, I would have been much more successful as a sea-gull or a fish. As it is, I will always be a stranger who never feels at home, who does not really want and is not really wanted, who can never belong, who must always be a little in love with death!"[11]

If we remember that the longing for a "home", for a "belonging", both of them not of this earth, is an ever-present motif in many of O'Neill's early, middle, and late plays, we recognize these sentences as an invaluable key to the understanding of his work. Because he passes as an exile through his existence on earth, full of longing for a home he has almost completely forgotten, there is so much despair in his best plays, and therefore the light in them is so uncertain and devoid of warmth.

Father Tyrone, no less drunk than his son, is deeply impressed by his confession. He exclaims: "Yes, there's the makings of a poet in you all right." With bitter self-mockery Edmund repeats the words: "The *makings* of a poet", and continues: "No, I'm afraid I'm like the guy who is always panhandling for a smoke. He hasn't even got the makings. He's got only the habit. I couldn't touch what I tried to tell you just now. I just stammered. That's the best I'll ever do. I mean, if I live. Well, it will be faithful realism, at least. Stammering is the native eloquence of us fog people."

The speaker begins with a pun on "makings", giving it the secondary, specifically American meaning of "paper and tobacco for making a cigarette".[12] And he goes on comparing his attitude towards poetry with the behaviour of a fellow who is always begging for a cigarette, because he has only the habit of smoking without the paper and tobacco necessary for making one. Evidently, Edmund strives here to say something which he finds very difficult to express. Smoking is a surprising and somewhat disappointing, because ill-fitting, simile for enjoying poetry, perhaps an instance of that kind of stammering to which Edmund finds himself condemned. It seems to imply that he loves to indulge in poetic moods, but lacks the gifts necessary for their transmutation into poetry. Here, we cannot help remembering O'Neill's own frequent use of quotations from Shakespeare, Byron, Keats, Baudelaire, Rossetti, Swinburne, Wilde, Dowson and Kipling, especially

[11] *Long Day's Journey into Night*, London 1956, 134 f.
[12] *A Dictionary of Americanisms*, ed. by M. M. Mathews, 1951, 1020 f.

in his last plays. They never occur without a certain dramatic propriety; but they appear to be, at the same time, borrowings, by an author whose powers over language are limited, from happier writers. The sentence "I couldn't touch what I tried to tell you just now" shows that Edmund does not confuse the "poetic" outbreak of a moment ago with poetry. "I just stammered. That's the best I'll ever do." The following short remark: "I mean, if I live" has a certain importance. Although it is not unmotivated in the dialogue before us, it indicates that O'Neill consciously avoided the danger of losing sight of Edmund's situation in the play in his endeavour to say something important concerning the whole of his own artistic achievement. What follows is, in fact, a commentary on the style of his work: "Well, it will be faithful realism, at least. Stammering is the native eloquence of us fog people." In the second of these weighty sentences the image of the fog, one of the leading symbols in *Long Day's Journey into Night*, is used. It helps to suggest that the poetic inability of which the dramatist is clearly conscious here is identical with the incapacity of deriving more from his moments of intuition than a feeling of estrangement from the world of men, an indefinite longing for another home, and an invincible hankering after death.

And the first sentence concerning "faithful realism"? This appears to be an important piece of self-criticism. It offers a label for the style with which O'Neill began his dramatic career in the Glencairn and other one-act plays, to which he returned when he wrote some of the best works of his long and fertile experimental period, and which became definitely his own style in the years of his maturity and mastery. At first sight, it is no more than a conscientiously realistic prose style, depicting man through, and together with, his milieu. Of course, there is much more to it than this only. O'Neill indulges in a characteristic understatement because he longs for the power of transmutation and the intenser symbolical language of the great poets of the past. Evidently, he was aware of the difference between their poetic genius and the artistic intelligence and power of dramatic construction that had gone into the making of the allegorical, symbolistic, and expressionistic plays of his middle period.

We do not think that O'Neill's fame will mainly rest on those plays, but on the opposite kind, the style of which may loosely be termed "faithful realism". In the presence of his last plays it would be sheer perversity to follow him on his ways of self-criticism, and deplore that certain styles were beyond his reach. They prove convincingly that a master can change into creative possibilities the limitations imposed upon him by his inner condition and by his environment. The realism of these works leads to a full artistic triumph. It produces convincing characters, replete with life, nor does it oppose any resistance to the demands of the dramatic form. In fact, the playwright overcomes his leanings towards an epical presentation with complete success. Through his mature and subtle art of dialogue he transforms the description of characters and their environment into dramatic events. His figures come alive in a few simple situations and actions. The numerous backward glances into the past become part of the present action, because they culminate in those confessions which are among the most essential events in the plays.

Besides, his realism permits the strict economy of classical tragedy. We have pointed out the simplicity of O'Neill's plots. Each of the four plays strictly observes the unity of place, and does so without any loss to the playwright's imaginative freedom. He knows how to accompany the visible scenes by numerous reported scenes with their own different places. His contrapuntal arrangement of events that are seen in the theatre and of reported events, which become real in the theatre of the mind only, makes his realism a free and spacious style. The importance of this method appears most strikingly in the fact that two of the main characters in *The Iceman Cometh* and *A Touch of the Poet* — Evelyn and Simon — are never seen on the stage. It also permits him to observe the unity of time with perfect ease. *The Iceman Cometh* is the only one among the four plays to present a span of time longer than twenty-four hours, but it exceeds this limit by a few hours only. The time when O'Neill wrote straggling biographical plays like *"Marco Millions"* is definitely past.

Another relation with poetic tragedy appears in the surprising transparency for symbolical meanings that we discover in O'Neill's realism. The titles themselves have a symbolical quality — except *A Touch of the Poet* perhaps. The tiniest details in *The Iceman*

Cometh are permeated by death imagery, and the fog and foghorn appear not only in the speeches in *Long Day's Journey into Night:* they are also seen, or heard, by the spectators. *A Touch of the Poet* could bear the title *The Thoroughbred Mare*, and would, then, betray its affinity with Ibsen's *Wild Duck* at once, thus pointing to the fact that O'Neill's late style is indebted to the Norwegian dramatist more than to Strindberg, whose influence was stronger on his earlier work.

Another proof that the playwright found home to his own style in the last plays, the only one he could make a great style, is in their language. He found a valid solution of the problem stressed by W. B. Yeats, when he wrote in praise of Douglas Hyde's Anglo-Irish idiom: "It is the only good English spoken by any large number of Irish people to-day, and we must found good literature on a living speech."[13] He turned away for good from that problematical literary American language which had refused to come alive in some of his earlier works, and based his dialogue exclusively on the colloquial language of middle and low-class people, whose speech was frequently coloured by their European origin, and on the different forms of broken English used by the more recent immigrants. Here he found the directness, the vitality, the picturesque terms of abuse, the grotesque imagery he required in order to create speeches powerful enough to make us stop arguing about the question whether it was poetic or realistic drama he wrote. He now knew to give his characters the exactly right, the only possible words. He was never more successful in this than in depicting people of his own Irish origin. When he wrote speeches for them, he could draw on the inexhaustible source of language that had fed the works of John Millington Synge, Lady Gregory, Sean O'Casey and many another writer of the dramatic revival in Ireland. O'Neill was one of the Tyrones himself, and he was connected in a special way with Larry Slade and Pat McGloin, with the Hogans and the Melodys. Among them, there existed no linguistic perplexities for him. The fact that he so clearly preferred Irish characters and the Anglo-Irish dialect

[13] "The Irish Dramatic Movement", 1902, in *Plays and Controversies*, 1924, 29.

when he came to write the plays of his maturity, is worth pondering, because its implications concern his own inner situation as well as that of his country in the first half of our century.

We cannot close this brief account of O'Neill's "faithful realism" without remembering that he was, from the beginning of his career, an "absolute" dramatist, i. e. one who does not merely create speeches, which producers and actors are then called upon to interpret in terms of the theatre, but complete situations, visualized as stage events, characters with their unmistakable gait, their gestures, their speeches, and their changing facial expression.[14] This gift, so important in a playwright, stood him in good stead when he composed the final plays. The economical use of situations and actions we have stressed is possible because every element of this kind is highly charged with multiple meanings. The language is supplemented by impressive visual symbols: Hickey, being led away, helplessly asserting that he has never loved anything or anybody except Evelyn, the Evelyn he has murdered; Mary Tyrone, in her skyblue dressing-gown, gliding into the room where her husband and sons, reeking of whiskey, are quarrelling, making confessions, getting reconciled, and quarrelling again; Cornelius Melody, sitting on the floor with the head of the mare he has shot in his lap "sobbing like a soul in hell" — a picture not seen on the stage, but impressed on the mind's eye by Cregan's report —; and Josie Hogan, in the cold moonlight and night air, protecting her lost friend from the furies during a few hours of dreamless sleep, "a virgin who bears a dead child in the night, and at dawn is found still a virgin": these images we cannot easily forget, for they are compact symbols of everything developed in the actions and speeches of O'Neill's characters. We remember them as passionate visions of man in our time, as warning visions, demanding pity of us, but, above all, a decision.   (1959)

---

14 His being an "absolute" dramatist may be one reason for the dissatisfaction with the actual theatre that came over O'Neill in his later years. Clark reports the following impatient outbreak: "The play, as written, is the thing, and not the way actors garble it with their almost-always-alien personalities (even when the acting is fine work in itself)." (op. cit., 144.)

X.

Christopher Fry
and the Revolt against Realism
in Modern English Drama

THE TERM "poetic drama" was purposely omitted in the title of this paper because it lands one in serious difficulties of definition.[1] It is much easier to agree about what we mean by "realistic drama". It is the kind of play that reproduces the manners and the conversation of modern life or of an earlier period on the stage in order to criticize them seriously or in the spirit of satire and comedy. For several decades such plays have abounded on theatrical programmes all over the western world, and nowhere have they been more popular than in the English-speaking countries. It is even doubtful whether we are justified in believing in a revolt against them at the present moment. There is certainly no more reason for doing so now than there was ten or twenty or even fifty years ago. A visit to the main theatres of London in the autumn of 1952 was not encouraging for a prophet of the end of realism on the stage. Realistic plays dealing with psychological problems were more numerous than the representatives of any other type, and excellent actors, carefully trained for this sort of work, helped the spectator to be more than mildly interested in

---

[1] The "poetic drama" has been investigated by Moody E. Prior (in "Poetic Drama: an Analysis and a Suggestion", *English Institute Essays 1949*, New York 1950, 3—32), who studies the history of the isolation of this genre and seeks a method of overcoming it, and by Arthur Mizener (in "Poetic Drama and the Well-Made Play", *English Institute Essays 1949*, New York 1950, 33—54), who is unable to recognize it as a legitimate kind. Other useful contributions are contained in *Modern Poetic Drama*, Oxford 1934, by Priscilla Thouless, in *The Irish Dramatic Movement*, London 1939, by Una Ellis-Fermor, in *The Poet in the Theatre*, London 1946, by Ronald Peacock, and in *The Playwright as Thinker: a Study of Drama in Modern Times*, New York 1946, by Eric Bentley, whose book was reissued two years later in London, with the title: *The Modern Theatre: a Study of Dramatists and the Drama.*

the neurotic case histories contained in many of them. Fortunately there was also a beautiful performance of *Romeo and Juliet* at the Old Vic, after which most of the modern plays at the other theatres seemed partial things, almost trivial, so that the spectator felt with great force that particular dissatisfaction which is the root of all the long and repeated discussions and experiments aiming at the revival of poetry in the modern theatre. He suspected that we speak of realistic and poetic drama because something that was complete and whole in the seventeenth century disintegrated in the nineteenth.

That disastrous disintegration had its origin in an earlier loss of contact between the theatre and the traditional dramatic forms of comedy and tragedy. These were driven out of the early nineteenth century theatres by farce and melodrama, written in great numbers by clever authors, who accepted the popular stage conventions of their day, and knew how to tickle the nerves of their audiences. The serious authors continued to write the traditional types of drama, but they lacked the contact with an intelligent audience, and found the tradition too heavy to achieve a style of their own. The partial recovery that began about the middle of the last century was the work of the theatrical authors, not of the writers of closet drama. Those authors began to correct the stage conventions they had inherited by comparing them with empirical fact, with the behaviour of real people. They were no poets; therefore they permitted the scientific spirit of their age to concentrate their attention on everything that was factual and objective. Jones and Pinero were first of all men of the theatre, but they also struggled to have serious thought exercise itself upon the facts of experience. What they attempted came to fruition in the work of Shaw. He had a stronger sense of fact, a more penetrating intelligence and more of the moulding power of the imagination. He was capable of creating characters that really come to life, of writing a dialogue with an unmistakable style of its own. But he was never satisfied to present experience completely and for its own sake. He had a meddling intellect, which led him to isolate certain aspects of experience, to formulate problems about them and to think those problems to their end, and there was an unceasing war in him between this intellect and his imagination. He wrote neither realistic nor poetic plays. Shaw is a fascinating phenomenon in its own right, defying classification.[2]

The recovery of the drama in the nineteenth and early twentieth century was a partial success at best for those who knew and loved the drama of the great periods of our theatrical history. This implies that it was also a partial failure. The theorists of the realistic drama, especially Shaw's friend William Archer, were not of this opinion, of course. Archer was full of a sense of achievement and triumph when he surveyed what Wilde and Galsworthy and all the others had done. They had purified the drama that, to his mind, had been an awkward mixture of realism and poetry in the hands of the Elizabethans. He congratulated them on the expulsion of the lyrical element. This line of argument sprang from that cutting up of our total experience into departments without which realistic drama would be an impossible form. It recalls Shaw's unconvincing way of separating form from contents in some of his criticism of Shakespeare and of calling the one miraculous and the other all but idiotic.

The challenge in William Archer's views has been taken up time and again. William Butler Yeats reacted early and vehemently, accepting, however, Archer's notion of the impurity of the Elizabethan drama. His intervention accelerated the falling apart of drama into a realistic and a poetic type. He wanted to expel from tragedy, the highest form of drama, everything that, for Archer, formed the whole province of drama: the description of manners and the delineation of character. These he consigned to comedy, and concentrated in tragedy on the expression of the great, eternal passions only. His theory did justice neither to comedy nor to tragedy, but it permitted the creation of a very special kind of play, requiring a special kind of audience and stage representation. The second great writer of the Abbey Theatre, John Millington Synge, helped the cause of the drama more effectively, perhaps, than Yeats. He rejected in his practice the dichotomy of realistic

[2] Shaw's sins against the realistic code were severely castigated by William Archer in *The Old Drama and the New*, London 1923. In his above-mentioned article Arthur Mizener praises him as one of the few true dramatists of modern times, who wrote better plays than the merely realistic or the merely poetic playwrights.

and poetic plays. He trusted his imagination to transmute his complete experience into drama, thus following the way of the old masters, and he was eminently successful.

The numerous authors that rebelled against the predominance of the realistic manner in Scotland and England did not follow Synge's method. They tried to develop the poetic play as a special kind, and often merely continued the tradition of the closet drama of the nineteenth century or they introduced elements of fancy and poetry into otherwise realistic plays: this was the hardly satisfactory line followed by the Scotsmen Barrie and Bridie. All this led only to individual and temporary solutions of the problem of poetry in the theatre. Meanwhile theatrical people of artistic temperament began to get so tired of the circumstantial realism and the well-meaning discussion in the plays of leading authors that they despaired of the drama. They turned to the producer, the actor, the scene-designer and the choreographer in the hope that these would create an imaginative theatrical art, if necessary without the help of the dramatist. What men like Gordon Craig, Alexander Tairoff and Max Reinhardt did for the theatre was, in fact, part of the revolt against the tyranny of fact and discussion.

Another part of the revolt was the so-called expressionistic writing and staging. In it, the objective facts, the healthful ideas of the leading dramatists were brutalized, and the most private and irresponsible parts of experience were made the stuff of art. All the traditional methods of overcoming realistic presentation were made use of: personification, allegory, masks, the chorus, and the producers and other theatrical artists were given important and fascinating tasks. The trouble with many of these productions, which were more frequent on the Continent and in America than in England, was that they often looked like caricatures of the play hoped for by those who wanted to see poetry back in the theatre.

The most important opponent of William Archer and his school among the dramatists in England is T. S. Eliot. Like Yeats he accepted, at first, the terms proposed by Archer for the discussion. He, too, wanted to find ways of escaping from the mixture of poetry and realism he discerned in the Elizabethan plays. He found them in accepting part of the discipline imposed by the conventions of Greek tragedy. Part of their discipline only. He introduced

Greek elements into his first plays, but also a mixture of verse and prose that looks quite Elizabethan. It seems significant that Eliot, who started as a passionate defender of the poetic play against the claims of the prose play, mixed the two elements in the first drama of his own. His endeavours as a critic and a playwright have since tended to overcome the dichotomy of the realistic and the poetic play, of prose and verse. This is the true and very cogent reason why *The Cocktail Party* is a verse play looking very much like a prose play. More important even than his formal experiments is Eliot's refusal to restrict his dramatic material in the way of the realists, of Yeats or of the expressionists. He tries to respect the facts and the emotions, the objective and the subjective world. Man, for him, is not only a social and a psychological, but also a metaphysical phenomenon. He wants to seize and present it in its totality, the way Shakespeare and the other great dramatists have presented it. Here, again, he is on the way towards the necessary re-integration that will render the terms "realistic" and "poetic" drama meaningless. We cannot show here how he works out the problems of this re-integration in theory and in practice; he does it consciously, energetically and without tiring. He observes how Shakespeare does justice to the total human experience by having various layers of meaning in his works, which reveal themselves gradually to the spectator according to his sensibility, understanding, and range of experience. This is an undeniable and miraculous achievement of Shakespeare's imagination, which Eliot tries to reach in his own rather conscious manner. If we study the layer-of-meaning-technique in his plays, we cannot help suspecting that thought has sometimes been too assertive in him for the ways of the imagination.

Eliot has stated himself that, so far, his work as a dramatist has consisted in preparing the field for a new type of play. It seems that Christopher Fry is the first to gather in the harvest. For him, the problem of verse play versus prose play does not exist. The poetic play seems to have gobbled up the realistic and to have thriven on the diet. He has no scruples whatsoever about introducing poetry into the theatre. But many of the things he does are possible only because of the preparatory work of Eliot. Christopher Fry began his dramatic career very much in the way Eliot had begun his: as a writer of plays for special religious occasions. Then he decided to continue work on the assumption that audiences were as sick of the eternal discussions, the reproduction or their everyday world and troubles on the stage as T. S. Eliot and the admirers of his art. While the master laboured to disguise the difference between his plays and the average West End production, the pupil decided to be different with a vengeance. In choosing his own tactics he asserted his individuality, and revealed a dramatic talent quite different from Eliot's.

Success has justified Fry's method. He has found audiences that turned with relief to his unrestrained eloquence, and thought his trust in the power of language fascinating. Some of the ablest players and producers of England have worked for his plays and have made two of them West End successes. He has found critics who noticed with astonishment that such linguistic vitality had not appeared on the English-speaking stage since Synge gave his plays to the Abbey Theatre, perhaps even since the days of Shakespeare and his companions; some of them were reminded of Donne and the metaphysicals in listening to this new dramatist's fireworks of puns, paradoxes and strange, ingenious metaphors. The Oxford University Press has accepted his works for publication. In fact, he established himself in the short period between 1948 and 1952 as a dramatist of proven worth and greater promise. Although his language is of a kind that ought to deter the most courageous of translators, his plays have been translated and performed before interested or puzzled audiences on the continent. There is already a tentative critical evaluation of Fry's achievement by Derek Stanford, a fellow writer and friend of his, who is also ready to satisfy, within limits, the public's curiosity about the new dramatic star's life and habits.[3] In a recent survey of present-day literature the Munich literary critic Hans Egon Holthusen could not find anything respectable on the continent that was not a voice of despair, but he discerned the growth of a new positive force in Eliot, and saluted with enthusiasm its reaching maturity in Christopher Fry.[4]

[3] *Christopher Fry, an Appreciation*, London 1951, and *Christopher Fry Album*, London 1952. Vgl. auch Hilde Spiel, "Der frühe Christopher Fry" in *Der Park und die Wildnis*, München 1953, 105—118.

This splendid reception is too good not to call forth the grave doubts of the sceptics. So sudden a rise to fame, so immediate a recognition by academic and popular critics may be due to the fad of a passing hour. It seems too simple and easy, too devoid of the tragic war we have learned to expect as the price of achievement. Appearances, however, may be deceptive. Christopher Fry was born at Bristol in 1907. He has replaced his father's name (Harris) by the surname of his mother (Fry), through whom he is connected with the well known Quaker family of Bristol.[5] Before he could write his successful plays he passed through a long period of experimentation and waiting. He spent a great part of his waiting time as an actor or producer in various repertory companies, thus acquiring the necessary knowledge of his future medium. Though he wrote several pageant plays before the war, only *The Boy with a Cart* (BC) was printed.[6] It treats the legends concerning Cuthman, the Saint of Sussex, in the manner of Eliot's pageant-play *The Rock*. The war interrupted Fry's activity as a dramatist, but after it he was capable of writing the six plays that have won him general recognition. *The Firstborn* (FB), performed at the Edinburgh Festival of 1948, is a tragedy, into which many of Fry's wartime questionings have gone.[7] Moses is shown, striving to liberate the children of Israel from the Egyptian yoke and discovering, when he is near the moment of triumph, that he has also brought about the death of his young and idealistic admirer Prince Ramases, the Pharaoh's firstborn son. There followed *A Phoenix*

---

[4] Vgl. "Die Situation des Menschen in der modernen Literatur", *Die neue Weltschau*, Zweite internationale Aussprache in St. Gallen, Stuttgart 1953, 7—41.

[5] *Christopher Fry Album*, 6.

[6] "THE BOY WITH A CART was first performed in the village of Colman's Hatch, Sussex. It was later played at Canterbury, and had its first commercial production at the *Lyric* Theatre, Hammersmith, where it was directed by John Gielgud, on the 19th January, 1950." *(ibidem, 46)* The play was printed by the Oxford University Press in 1939; a second edition by Frederick Muller Ltd. was published in 1945.

[7] First published by the Cambridge University Press in 1946; reissued as quoted here by the Oxford University Press in 1949; second, revised edition 1952.

too Frequent (PF), Petronius' astonishing story of the widow of
Ephesus, who was not able to execute her plan of dying in her
husband's tomb, turned into a brilliant one-act play,[8] and the full-
length comedy *The Lady's not for Burning* (LB), which brought
success for good.[9] The outlines of this fairy-tale get somewhat lost
under an unusually luxurious growth of language. It deals with a
beautiful young witch, who does not want to be burnt and who
convinces a terribly melancholical young man, bent on being
hanged, that he is a fool and that something might be said for love.
There is the other three-act comedy *Venus Observed* (VO) with
rather more plot and character-drawing to it.[10] It is about a
middle-aged duke of irresistible charm, who invites three of his
erstwhile loves to watch an eclipse of the sun, and asks his twenty
years old son to hand an apple to the one he wants to become his
mother. The shorter play *Thor, with Angels* (TA) presents the
strange and tragic events connected with the first dawn of
Christianity over a Jutish farmstead in Kent[11], and *A Sleep of
Prisoners* (SP) the dream-life of four prisoners of war.[12]

Although they are by no means the most interesting features of
the plays a few remarks on Fry's plots seem desirable. Almost all

[8] First produced at the *Mercury Theatre*, London, on April 25th, 1946,
directed by E. Martin Browne, and revived at the *Arts Theatre*,
London, on November 20th, 1946, directed by Noël Willman. First
published by Hollis & Carter in 1946 and reissued by the Oxford
University Press in 1949.

[9] First produced at the *Arts Theatre*, London, on March 10th, 1948,
directed by Jack Hawkins, and revived at the *Globe Theatre*, London,
on May 11th, 1949, directed by John Gielgud and Esme Percy. First
published by the Oxford University Press in 1949.

[10] First produced at *St. James's Theatre*, London, on January 18th, 1950,
directed by Sir Laurence Olivier and Gilbert Miller. First published
by the Oxford University Press in 1950.

[11] First performed at the Canterbury Festival in June 1948. In an Acting
Edition published by H. J. Goulden Ltd. for the Friends of Canterbury Cathedral the text of the play was first issued in 1948. Second
Impression (Oxford University Press) 1949. Third Impression (reset)
1949.

[12] First performed in Oxford at the University Church on April 23th,
1951, and in London at St. Thomas's Church, Regent Street, on
May 15th, 1951, directed by Michael MacOwan.

of them are simple, not to say, slight, if we abstract them from the plays themselves. He has a way of picking them up here and there almost casually: from the Bible, from Jeremy Taylor's *Holy Living and Dying* (where, of all places, he found the story of the widow of Ephesus),[13] from a book of fairy-tales. He is certainly no great inventor and planner of complicated plots; we might even complain of a certain dearth of action in his plays: a serious draw-back in drama, which is compensated by the vitality of the language. A common feature of all his plots is the presence of what is unusual, startling, irrational, and even miraculous. We meet a boy, dragging his mother about in a cart; he is intent on nothing in particular, at first, then he discovers what he wants to do: build a church. And he does it, helped by a series of miracles. Or the widow, who instead of dying, falls in love with a Roman corporal, and in the end proposes to save her negligent new lover's life by hanging the body of her husband on the gallows. Fry's version of her utter change of mind is an unforgettable *tour de force*, reminiscent of the famous question of Richard III:

Was ever woman in this humour woo'd?

What happens to Fry's couple has nothing to do with the assertion of will-power or with cunning; it is simply the beautiful growth of love between two young people in very unusual circumstances. It is nature, recovering after the strain of loss and unhappiness and overcoming an unnatural decision.

When Fry introduces his unusual, even grotesque motifs, he does not simply try to be sensational. He wants to rouse the spectator's sense of wonder, and this sense is cleverly and un-ceasingly exploited by the dramatist in order to break them from their routine reactions, to render every particle of experience new and astonishing, so that it is observed with joy or terror, amusement or fear, pity or detestation. The dislocation of routine reactions is a perennial aim of great art, and Fry pursues it with surprising felicity. He gives back to his spectators the eyes of children. There is something charmingly and disarmingly naïve

---

[13] Taylor tells the story in *The Rule and Exercises of Holy Dying*, 1651, 326, in order to moralize on the fluctuations of violent passions from one extreme to the other.

about his plays in spite of their verbal complications. The achievement of this second *naïveté* of the artist is rare in our period.

Another important aspect of Fry's plots is their open-air quality. *BC* and *TA* have their setting in the open air. *FB* has its terrace scene, *VO* its acts in the park, and even when Fry takes us into rooms he has much to say of the sights through the windows. The room in which *LB* takes place is a good instance of this. But our sense of the sun, of meadows and trees does not spring from the setting of the scenes alone. It permeates the whole fabric of the plays, their descriptions, similes and metaphors. The atmosphere of April belongs as inevitably to *LB* as that of autumn to *VO*. The latter may properly be described as an autumn play; its hero is forced in it to face the autumn of his life, and autumnal imagery abounds in it. This is the most striking example of how plot and setting, characters and ideas, mood and imagery all spring from one and the same creative impulse in Fry's best work. The pervasive open-air quality points to the fact that man and the universe is Fry's great theme and not man in his man-made surroundings.

The same fact accounts for his love of motifs that are far away in time. He is afraid of the obtrusive modern setting because it can hide the essential things. All this means a breaking away from the traditions of realism and also from the insistence on the modern *façade* in Eliot's later plays, but it does not lead Fry to any form of escapism. His thought and his language are modern, and his present-day experience informs every line he writes, and lives in his imagery.

We are tempted to turn from this account of Fry's plots directly to his imagery, which seems to be the core of his art, but a few observations must be made concerning his ideas, characters and dramatic technique. Though there is plenty of thought in his plays,[14] they do not discuss problems, express views or doctrines. It seems that the philosophical climate in which he writes is rather

---

[14] A recurrent idea is the Christian one according to which our responsibility towards our fellows cannot possibly include a part of mankind only; it seems meaningless if it does not embrace the whole race. Cf. *FB*, 18, *VO*, 23 and also the conclusion of Fry's "Letters to an Actor Playing Hamlet", *Shakespeare Survey*, V, 1952, 58—61.

favourable for the dramatist, trying to cut loose from the problem play. Fry's passion for the facts of experience, his conviction that these facts are irrational, paradoxical, grotesque and even terrifying, link him with what we may roughly call the contemporary existentialist attitude. Fry also goes in fear of abstractions, rationalizations, systems of thought: an attitude eminently suitable for artistic creation. He has thrown off the yoke that the problem mongers and social critics have carried so patiently and even proudly. Nor does he adhere to any existentialist doctrine. Although he has felt horror, despair and helplessness in living through the forty-five years of his life in our century, and wants to express them in his art, he is not overwhelmed by them so as to know nothing else and to keep whining about the human condition. For him, as for Eliot, the horror, though very real, is partial only, and it is irrationally and strangely accompanied, not compensated, by partial ecstasy. And among the facts of his experience that go into his plays, there is God, not a comprehensible God, in spite of His revelation, but the mystery of mysteries. The mysteries of God and his creation hold him spell-bound. He can approach them in many different ways and formulate his vision of them accordingly, but he never attempts to solve them. He loves what he sees or he hates it, he triumphs with the glories of the creation, and he suffers its torments. He speaks with tragic intensity in *FB*, in *TA* and in *SP*; he sees with the eyes of unbroken faith in *BC*; but what is probably his most characteristic attitude is revealed in the comedies, an attitude of amusement, bitter sometimes and sometimes tender, rendering smiles and even laughter possible in the face of incongruity and paradox. An occasional note of strain in his laughter reminds us how closely related the comic and the tragic vision of human existence are, but more often we sit fascinated by Fry's bravado and sense of fun. These are the dramatist's own remarks on tragedy and comedy: "The difference between tragedy and comedy is the difference between experience and intuition. In the experience we strive against every condition of our animal life: against death, against the frustration of ambition, against the instability of human love. In the intuition we trust the arduous eccentricities we're born to, and see the oddness of a creature who has never got acclimatised to being created.

Laughter inclines me to know that man is essential spirit; his body, with its functions and accidents and frustrations, is endlessly quaint and remarkable to him; and though comedy accepts our position in time, it barely accepts our posture in space."[15]

The fact that Fry is interested above all in the metaphysics of the human condition has its influence on the way his characters are drawn. They are never psychological case studies, as he explores precisely what is not reducible to logic in our psyche, and loves people who behave as unusually and madly as to defy all psychological systems. His legendary, his biblical and his fairy-tale figures are real as creatures of the imagination; certain spiritual attitudes come to life in them, but they are not made palatable to a modern audience by being interpreted in terms of current psychology. Fry does not use the trick of Bridie and Giraudoux and many another translator of mythological stories into a modern dramatic idiom. On the other hand he knows as much about the processes in our minds as all the considerable dramatists have known. He can give convincing psychological versions of the way how the widow of Ephesus turns from her late husband to her new lover or how the Duke of Altair comes to terms with the fact that the splendid girl Perpetua, whom he has hoped to win in his old cavalier fashion, prefers his son Edgar. Psychology is this dramatist's handmaid, not his mistress.

Turning to Fry's dramatic technique we are once more surprised by the simplicity of his methods. He does not strive after originality or experiment for the sake of experiment in this sphere. In BC the traditional legends concerning Cuthman are strung together rather artlessy. Eliot's early methods appear in the use of "The People of South England" as a Chorus, in the mixing of prose and verse scenes and in the quality of the choral verse, which borrows some of its effects from Middle-English alliterative poetry. The verse used in the dialogues is very free, mixing iambic and anapaestic feet and permitting a variable number of stresses on each line. And yet it is here, as in the later plays, more than a way of helping the actor with his stresses and pauses. It is a very free blank

<hr>

[15] Cf. Fry's essay on "Comedy", *The Adelphi*, XXVII, No. 1, November 1950, 27—29.

verse that is quite natural to the author, who never permits it to interfere with the normal rhythms of the spoken language. In "Poetry and the Theatre" Fry defends this metre after saying that he wondered at one time whether the loose alexandrines of Robert Bridges' *Testament of Beauty* would not meet his requirements: "But I didn't wonder for long. It seemed to me then, as it seems to me now, that the five-foot line was as likely a basis for common speech as any other; was, is, and ever shall be; and it has the advantage of being there already, it is in our blood; and, though we have seen that this can also be a disadvantage and if not properly captured can make us talk like lines of print, it sets us free at least of contrivance. We do not have to be so aware of our form, and, as I have said, the less self-conscious we are when writing for the theatre the better."[16]

Fry is another modern dramatist who has been helped by the possibility of writing short plays. What an advantage for him that he was not obliged to expand the story of the widow of Ephesus into a full-length play! *PF* is a compact one-act play, containing a simple and shapely sequence of scenes. It profits from Fry's art of rousing expectation, of preparing events by hints and pointers that are highly effective, even if only half understood at a first hearing of the play. A good example of this is Dynamene's way of speaking of her late husband, whom she is about to follow into death. The irony in the following speech is the author's, not Dynamene's, who speaks quite seriously and admiringly. It makes the spectator suspect that Dynamene's marriage did not exhaust all the delights of companionship and that another man could have a chance with her after all:

He was one of the coming men.
He was certain to have become the most well-organized
provost
The town has known, once they had made him provost.
He was so punctual, you could regulate
The sun by him. He made the world succumb
To his daily revolution of habit. But who,
In the world he has gone to, will appreciate that?

[16] *Adam, International Review*, XIX, Nos. 214–215, 1951, 7.

O poor Virilius! To be a coming man
Already gone — it must be distraction.
Why did you leave me walking about our ambitions
Like a cat in the ruins of a house? Promising husband,
Why did you insult me by dying? Virilius,
Now I keep no flower, except in the vase
Of the tomb.[17]

Fry's latest play, *SP*, is his first experiment with a kind of expressionistic technique. The atmosphere of the empty church, where four prisoners of war spend a restless night, is powerfully evoked. The plan of making the four men re-enact in their dreams the murder of Cain, the stories of David and Absolom, of the sacrifice of Isaac and that of Shadrac, Meshac and Abednego and of distributing the dream-roles among them so as to give their natural peculiarities a metaphysical meaning is ambitious, and its execution, except in the all too difficult last part of the play, highly successful. The eternal struggle between passion and control, violence and love, the necessity of patience, suffering and sacrifice are the dream themes of the play, which leads to an acceptance of existence in a time of crisis. In his other post-war plays Fry has freed himself from the direct influence of Eliot, but in *SP* it is stronger again. Its language is unusually severe and subdued for Fry, and some of its rhythms are clearly Eliotian. A passage from the end of the play will illustrate this:

The human heart can go to the lengths of God.
Dark and cold we may be, but this
Is no winter now. The frozen misery
Of centuries breaks, cracks, begins to move;
The thunder is the thunder of the floes,
The thaw, the flood, the upstart Spring.
Thank God our time is now when wrong
Comes up to face us everywhere,
Never to leave us till we take
The longest stride of soul men ever took.
Affairs are now soul size.

[17] *PF*, 3.

> The enterprise
> Is exploration into God.[18]

This leads us to our remarks on Fry's most striking gifts: his power over language. It is the main source of the vitality of his art. It is true, some have suspected him of being a mere juggler of words, a punster, who strives to beat the Elizabethans, the metaphysicals and the great talkers in the plays of Synge and O'Casey at their own game of inventing surprising, grotesque and outrageous similes and metaphors. We can readily admit that he is a punster and that he is acquainted with those authors. But he knows how to control his punning, and his image-making faculty has created too many delightful things to be denied the quality of originality. Before I try to prove this I wish to point out that it is no small achievement to use imagery spontaneously and without too much self-consciousness in an age when so much theorizing by poets and critics concerning the nature and function of similes and metaphors is going on. Fry certainly knows the theories of the symbolists and imagists, the pronouncements of T. S. Eliot on the objective correlative, the excellent things written by John Middleton Murry and C. Day Lewis on metaphor and on the poetic image, but for his own part, he does the thing itself, thus excelling in the poetic accomplishment most highly valued by the critics of our age. He indulges in theorizing on comparatively rare occasions only. On one such occasion he reminded his critics that the idea of his being a fast-writing author, who produces his linguistic fireworks, intoxicated by the sound of flowing sentences and by the high colours and strange shapes of his imagery, is quite wrong. He represents himself as a slow and painstaking writer, and insists that, even in his comedies, there ought to be few decorative words that are not also "an essential part of the meaning".[19] This cannot invalidate our impression that Fry's delight in language is unbounded. He likes to toy with words. There is even a sort of James Joyce hidden away in him, who would like to break them up and put them together again in the queerest of ways, so as to produce

---

[18] *SP*, 49. For further traces of Eliot cf. *FB*, 41 & 79, *SP*, 16.
[19] *An Experience of Critics*, London 1952, 24.

new shapes, amusing and almost nonsensical. Usually the hard and scientific terms fall victims to this tendency, as in Perpetua's:

> What made you supercherify with chousery
> The Duke?[20]

and in her:

> he would have eased the path
> To Reedbequity without the bother of iniquity.[21]

It also appears in those passages of abandoned and picturesque abuse which Fry cultivates with evident pleasure and success, as, for instance, in Reedbeck's outburst against his son:

> You're a vain, vexing, incomprehensible,
> Crimping, constipated duffer. What's your heart?
> All plum duff! Why do I have to be
> So inarticulate? God give me a few
> Lithontriptical words! You grovelling little
> Gobemouche!
> ... ...
> You spigoted, bigoted, operculated prig![22]

Fry's experimental passion appears no less clearly in his many puns, which play an important part in his strategy of giving his hearers frequent delightful shocks and surprises. They are sometimes merely clever and amusing:

> Where in this small-talking world can I find
> A longitude with no platitude?[23]

sometimes rather strained and artificial, as when the Duke alludes to the beginning of the eclipse of the sun:

> The sun has mooned
> Away half its light already.[24]

But quite frequently their functions are more essential: the different meanings of a word, which are called up in the pun, are emphasized and clarified by their juxtaposition, and they can

[20] *VO*, 36.
[21] *VO*, 37.
[22] *VO*, 42.   [23] *LB*, 64.   [24] *VO*, 14.

become representative of the difference between appearance and reality and of the paradoxical nature of our experience. Seti's words on the homecoming of Moses may be quoted here:

> I am tempted to call this a visitation and not
> A visit.[25]

Or Mayor Tyson's praise of the "standard soul", whose ideal is:

> One God, one point of view.
> A general acquiescence to the mean.

And Thomas Mendip's commentary on it:

> And God knows when you say the mean, you mean
> The mean. You'd be surprised to see the number
> Of cloven hoof-marks in the yellow snow of your soul.[26]

And finally the Duke of Altair's paradox of

> The unrevealing revelation of love.[27]

The interest in puns springs, in part, from the poet's acute sense for the past and all but lost energies of words, for the dead and dormant metaphors in the language. In *FB* the Pharaoh asks his sister reproachfully:

> Is this
>
> Your influence?

and receives the answer:

> Am I a planet, to be
> So influential?[28]

Another example is Tappercoom's answer to the question:

> And how
> Does that strike you?
> With a dull thud, Tyson,
>
> If I may say so.[29]

We may also consider here the Duke of Altair's remark:

> I've behaved according to my lights of love

---

[25] *FB*, 12. Omitted in the second edition, the cuts and revisions of which were mostly suggested by the performance of the play.

[26] *LB*, 71.

[27] *VO*, 89.

[28] *FB*, 38.

[29] *LB*, 47.

> Which were excellent and bright and much to be
> Remembered.[30]

Fry's linguistic exuberance appears also in his delight in witty circumlocutions. This is how the Duke of Altair speaks of the three ladies among whom his son Edgar is to choose his new mother:

> Here they will be, three handsome women,
> All of them at some time implicated
> In the joyous routine of my life.[31]

The same tendency appears in a less refined form when he translates the following speeches in Anouilh's *Invitation au Château:*

LADY INDIA: S'il s'en tient à ces signes, Romuald lui, est bien incapable d'en pénétrer jamais le sens! C'est un bénêt.

PATRICE BOMBELLES: *a un geste:* C'est un tigre! Et vous ne devez pas oublier que si vous êtes sa maîtresse, moi, je suis son secrétaire intime.

His rendering runs:

LADY INDIA: Little jokes and chuckles will pass right over Messerschmann's head. He suffers from terribly poor reception.

PATRICE: It's we who would have a poor reception if once he knew. Don't forget, you're his mistress and I'm his private secretary.[32]

A definitely popular metaphorical circumlocution, followed by a pun, replaces here the terribly short words "bénêt" and "tigre". Fry's enjoyment of the fine-sounding and highly coloured phrase has led him at other places of his resourceful translation to add a touch or two to Anouilh's text, as a comparison of the following lines will show:

HORACE: Pas un mot mon cher. Je me suis levé tôt ce matin, parce que je suis décidé à agir. Le jour qui vient nous réserve d'étranges surprises. Cette aube nous promet du nouveau. Quelle heure est-il?

---

[30] *VO*, 22   [31] *VO*, 1.

[32] Jean Anouilh, *Pièces Brillantes*, Paris 1951, 13. *Ring Round the Moon*. A Charade with Music. Translated by Christopher Fry, London 1950, 16.

JOSUÉ: Midi, Monsieur Horace.

HORACE: Nous serons fixés à midi trente.

HUGO: I got up early this morning because I've decided to take action. This dawn is the dawn of the unexpected. What's the time?

JOSHUA: Twelve o'clock, Mr. Hugo.

HUGO: By twelve-thirty, Joshua, I shall begin to loom big on the horizon.[33]

Fry supports and modifies the fun of the passage by introducing two flourishes of inflated poetic language into his prose. This is not to create the impression that he has generally sacrificed Anouilh's rapidity. Compare:

HORACE: Qui vous croira?

ROMAINVILLE: Tout le monde, puisque c'est la vérité.

HORACE: Quelle importance cela peut-il avoir que ce soit la vérité, mon bon Romainville, puisque cela n'en n'a pas l'air.

HUGO: Who's going to believe you?

ROMAINVILLE: Everybody — because it's true.

HUGO: That's no help. It doesn't seem likely.[34]

Our quotation indicates the range of Fry's language, which reaches from the great metaphorical flourish to the most economical colloquial directness. This range is one of the differences between the translation and the original, the language of which is keyed to a very lively, but more even tone.

In Fry's own plays the great flourish has its functions as well. It is sometimes expanded into long and elaborate speeches, and made a characteristic of the leading figures in the comedies, who are all of them fluent talkers. Thomas Mendip is given a speech of this type, when he describes the incongruities of the physical frame of man in comic disgust, and Jennet Jourdemayne another when she admits that women can be fatally attracted by that frame, however miserable, and even glories in her admission.[35] And the Duke of Altair is another master of this kind of speech, which

---

[33] *Pièces Brillantes*, 7. *Ring Round the Moon*, 12.
[34] *Pièces Brillantes*, 20. *Ring Round the Moon*, 21.
[35] *LB*, 58 f.

may be beautifully illustrated by the way how he explains his decision to marry again:

> Because I see no end
> To the parcelling out of heaven in small beauties,
> Year after year, flocks of girls, who look
> So lately kissed by God
> They come out on the world with lips shining,
> Flocks and generations, until time
> Seems like nothing so much
> As a blinding snowstorm of virginity,
> And a man, lost in the perpetual scurry of white,
> Can only close his eyes
> In a resignation of monogamy.[36]

Such speeches must be set against examples of a poetic rapidity that is no less characteristic of the plays than of Fry's translation. When Tegeus has fallen in love with Dynamene, he cries out:

> Beauty's bit is between my teeth.[37]

And when the Duke of Altair introduces Hilda to the company in his observatory, the dialogues runs:

REEDBECK: You see before you
> A creaking bough on which, at any moment,
> A dear young daughter may alight.
DUKE: My extension in time: Edgar.
EDGAR: Five feet ten
> Of my unlimited father.
HILDA: I have often
> Expected to meet you.
EDGAR: I suppose so;
> But until he's dead I'm really a redundancy.
> I make him feel bifurcated.[38]

In the long set speeches as well as in the quick give and take of such a conversation we find the dramatist rely upon imagery as his most effective instrument of expression. The abundant and quite

---

[36] *VO*, 2.
[37] *PF*, 15.
[38] *VO*, 14.

unashamed use of similes and of all the possible metaphorical combinations of sense impressions, ideas and images is the first most striking characteristic of the plays. It is the source from which they derive the power of making "a glory in the theatre".[39] In spite of his theatrical training Fry sees no harm in dramatic speeches that render their full meaning only after repeated hearings, supported by careful reading. He agrees with T. S. Eliot that dramatic speech must be based on the living conversation, but he does not take normal society talk for his point of departure. He turns to the language of the common people instead, when it is most lively, emphatic and colourful. He feels that Eliot, in *The Cocktail Party*, has gone rather far in his endeavour to surprise people into poetry without their really noticing it. At the end of a careful discussion of Eliot's method, he states: "To cope with all the moods and temperaments which are necessary to the stage, bombast, rhetoric, rage, passion, we cannot afford to be afraid of words. The great poetic simplicities do not come by fear, but by the life of poetry suddenly distilled."[40]

In his own works we find the great simplicities and the great complexities as well as the minor simplicities and the minor complexities. In all of them there is a wealth of nature imagery, a fact that must be related to the open-air quality we have noticed above. These are two simple specimens from *BC*. The grumbling Demiwulf, after having felt Cuthman's miraculous powers, says, as he is becoming his own self again:

> I feel like a toad crawling out from under a stone.

And the People of South England begin their final chorus:

> The candle of our story has burnt down
> And Cuthman's life is puffed like a dandelion
> Into uncertain places.[41]

The toad simile expresses a mood, and characterizes the speaker at the same time. The candle metaphor is mainly decorative, but

[39] E. Martin Browne, "From T. S. Eliot to Christopher Fry", *Adam, International Review*, XIX, Nos. 214—215, 1951, 16.
[40] In "Poetry and the Theatre", *Adam, International Review*, XIX, Nos. 214—215, 1951, 9.
[41] *BC*, 36 & 39.

the hint in it that we have heard a light-giving story must not be overlooked. The dandelion metaphor calls up a homely, yet striking image, which we take in easily enough and from which various allusive meanings radiate. A sharp and cutting effect is produced by a simile in an exhortation of Moses in *FB*, where he tries to teach the Pharaoh to recognize his own image in his twelve hundred thousand tortured Israelite prisoners:

> and you
> Are there, staring back at yourself from that mortal
> Mirror, twelve hundred thousand times yourself,
> Which, like a dog its own reflection,
> You don't recognize.[42]

In the comedies this simple nature imagery appears often enough touched with humour: When Margaret Devize chides her two sons and wants them to be impressed by the Mayor's anger, she has the following happy simile:

> Your uncle sent me
> To find you. I can tell he's put out; he's as vexed
> As a hen's hind feathers in a wind.[43]

Here the idea is first expressed by a traditional verb-adverb combination, the colloquial raciness of which is derived from the fact that two short and common functional words — relics of a dead metaphor — suggest a complicated and special meaning. Secondly, an abstract verb of Romance origin repeats the idea and, thirdly, a charming simile, based on fresh observation, gives it new colours and a new vigour. The combination "put out" is recharged with linguistic vitality by the following definition and simile.

In the next quotation we find something more complex. A simple nature simile brings, through its grotesque nature, an element of humour into a passionate speech, rendering its bitterness the more cutting: Rosabel accuses the Duke of being an egoist, incapable of true sympathy:

> Your moments of revelation! I only wonder
> What we revealed. Certainly not
> What goes on in other hearts than your own.

[42] *FB*, 16. Omitted in the second edition.
[43] *LB*, 66.

> That's as remote to you as a seaside lodging-house
> To a passing whale.[44]

In the Duke's defence we find a good representative of a fairly
frequent type of nature metaphor. A mood or state of mind is
aimed at, and is expressed with a new vividness and precision:

> Old men, young men, virgins,
> Viragoes, all walk hand in hand with me
> In the green enclosure of insensibility.[45]

We may compare this with one of the cool welcomes extended
by Thomas Mendip to the exquisite Jennet Jourdemayne:

> You've come too late.
> Romulus, Remus and I have just buried the world
> Under a heavy snowfall of disinterest.[46]

This conceit is effective enough. It is not serious like the preceding one. There is a touch of irony in it: the speaker seems to
be smiling at his own magniloquence. Many of the dazzling conceits in the comedies show this characteristic. The speakers indulge
in them with their tongues in their cheeks.

The theme of *PF* combines mockery, passion and tenderness in
a unique fashion, and this strange combination of conflicting
attitudes is present again in dozens of the play's images: a proof
that Fry does not cultivate his verbal skill as an end in itself. When
he is at his best, he knows how to integrate his imagery to perfection in the particular scene where it occurs. In fact, it may be
simultaneously related to an idea, a situation, an emotion, a mood
and a character.[47] This does not seem to be the result of a conscious

---

[44] *VO*, 23. [45] *VO*, 23. [46] *LB*, 68.

[47] This is as it should be according to the organic conception of the
relationship between the parts and the whole of a work of art. Fry
endorses it whole-heartedly, as is shown by this statement: "The life
of poetry is the whole contained by the part." The following sentences are no less important for an understanding of his aims: "every
moment in the action of a play should tell us that what is true of the
moment is not necessarily true of eternity, but what is true of
eternity pervades the moment." And: "Who understands the poetry
understands the construction, who understands the construction
understands the poetry, for the poetry is the action, and the action
— even apart from the words — is the figure of the poetry." ("Poetry
and the Theatre", *loc. cit.*, 10.)

arrangement but of a spontaneous grasp of unexpected parallels, similarities and relationships. His imagery often helps him to combine conflicting meanings and emotions in order to create fascinating new units of experience. To prove this we may return to a passage already quoted from *PF*, which contains the pun of

> To be a coming man already gone

and the lines

> Why did you leave me walking about our ambitions
> Like a cat in the ruins of a house?

The pity of Dynamene's loss is in the passage, tenderness also, a little bit of fun, and there is a wealth of associations in the figure of the disconsolate cat. In spite of their complications, these lines are not yet disturbed by passion. The same is true of the following speech of Doto, the maid, who has made up her mind to starve with her mistress. It is her reaction when she is tempted to eat by the Roman corporal Tegeus:

> You sex of wicked beards!
> It's no wonder you have to shave off your black souls
> Every day as they push through your chins.[48]

Dynamene indulges in decidedly mock-heroic imagery, too, before she is love-struck.

> Oafish, non-commissioned
> Young man! The boots of your conscience will pinch for ever
> If life's dignity has any self-protection.[49]

When she is tempted to live and love again, however, her imagery undergoes a change. At times it is tense and tragic, but never for long:

> When the thoughts would die, the instincts will set sail
> For life. And when the thoughts are alert for life
> The instincts will rage to be destroyed on the rocks.
> To Virilius it was not so; his brain was an ironing-board
> For all crumpled indecision: and I follow him,
> The hawser of my world.[50]

[48] *PF*, 9.
[49] *PF*, 15.
[50] *PF*, 18.

The two types of imagery have a dramatic function here; they express the difference between Dynamene's attitudes towards her new lover and her late husband, who is, at the same time, characterized again by the homely ironing-board conceit. Furthermore, the passage is a good instance of Fry's comedy manner. He is quite capable of expressing strong emotion, but he does not often permit it to grow to an absolute and overwhelming intensity or, at least, to remain so for any length of time. He likes to break it by wit, irony or humour, and, as a result of this, we experience emotion directly and intimately by identifying ourselves with the speaker, and, simultaneously, look at it from a distance as part and parcel of the human tragicomedy. This appears also in the following speech, which occurs in the love-scene between Tegeus and Dynamene. It shows at the same time how Fry introduces diminutive, but lively and colourful playlets into the play, where emotions and ideas come to life, go through their own actions and fight out conflicts of their own. Tegeus is frightened by the widow's wish to look more beautiful for his sake:

> If this is less than your best, then never, in my presence,
> Be more than your less: never! If you should bring
> More to your mouth or to your eyes, a moisture
> Or a flake of light, anything, anything fatally
> More, perfection would fetch her unsparing rod
> Out of pickle to flay me, and what would have been love
> Will be the end of me.[51]

We may note here that, although Fry loses no opportunity of renewing language and of adapting it to his own requirements through simile and metaphor, he sometimes remembers that abundance of imagery can cloy the most eager appetite, and then he introduces quite sober aphorisms, which are the more telling for the colourful context in which they find themselves. Dynamene, in the middle of the love-scene, says:

> What appears
> Is so unlike what is. And what is madness

[51] PF, 30.

To those who only observe, is often wisdom
To those to whom it happens.[52]

In turning to *VO* we find a comedy the strength of which is
largely derived from the varied interaction of the dominant motif
— the Duke's struggle against and acceptance of the fact of his
age — with the subsidiary motifs of the coming of autumn, of evening and night, of the mock-evening and mock-night produced by
the eclipse of the sun, and of the mock-morning produced by the
nocturnal conflagration. These motifs do not meet anywhere more
frequently than in the Duke's own speeches, and those meetings
usually take place in the spirit of comedy. He distrusts the power
of nature to create overwhelming emotions in the human mind,
and he resists it. His nature imagery is often worried and the
lyrical moods broken by his metaphysical wit. It reveals his
intention to play with those aspects of life which he refuses as yet
to face in seriousness.

When the easy-going and silly Jessie glibly compliments him
on account of his everlasting youthfulness, he answers:

> Flattery, Jessie; for years the frost has lain
> On my stubble beard. The swallows and other such
> Migratory birds have left me months ago.[53]

He has a very detached way of interpreting the eclipse of the sun
to his guests:

> Daylight, you see, is shamming twilight. Nature
> Is being made a fool of. Three or four stars, there,
> You can see them wince, where only a moment earlier
> Morning was all serene. The crows, with much
> Misgiving, talk themselves into their trees. Even
> The usually phlegmatic owls
> Care a hoot or two. The bats from the barn
> Make one flickering flight, and return to hang
> Their heads. All of them tricked and fuddled
> By the passing of a small cadaverous planet.[54]

[52] *PF*, 31.
[53] *VO*, 11.
[54] *VO*, 18.

When Rosabel begins to force a more serious attitude on him, he tries to divert her:

> Come now, think of it
> As the usual dipping of day's flag.[55]

But when he is hard pressed by her, he finds an answer in which the emotions of autumn and old age are merged without his habitual precaution of wit:

> So Rosabel believes when the cold spell comes
> And we're compelled to enter this draughty time
> And shuffle about in the slipshod leaves,
> Leaves disbanded, leaves at a loose end,
> And we know we're in for the drifting of the fall,
> We should merely shiver and be silent: never speak
> Of the climate of Eden, or the really magnificent
> Foliage of the tree of knowledge,
> Or the unforgettable hushed emerald
> Of the coiling and fettering serpent:
> Pretend we never knew it, because love
> Quite naturally condescended
> To the passing of time. But why should we, Rosabel?[56]

The imagery of autumn enters into another highly metaphorical passage, too, which is astir with the Duke's hope of winning Perpetua's love. He is teaching the girl how to handle bow and arrow:

> Take notice
> Of the excellent marksmanship of the year, whose arrow
> Singing from the April bow crossed over the width
> Of summer straight for the gold, where now, if you look,
> You will see it quivering.[57]

These lines are strangely ambivalent. They are meant to speak for the Duke, but, at the same time, they treacherously foretell his ultimate discomfiture, for the unswerving arrow of the year will surely reach the "bare ruin'd choirs, where late the sweet birds sang", not long after it has hit the gold of autumn. The play, how-

[55] VO, 20.
[56] VO, 22.
[57] VO, 39.

ever, does not end with the Duke's disappointment, but with his acceptance of his new condition. This finds expression in a new way of using autumn imagery. A prolonged and unbroken lyrical note prepares the harmonious close of the whole:

> Shall I be sorry for myself? In mortality's name
> I'll be sorry for myself. Branches and boughs,
> Brown hills, the valleys faint with brume,
> A burnish on the lake; mile by mile
> It's all a unison of ageing,
> The landscape's all in tune, in a falling cadence,
> All decaying. And nowhere does it have to hear
> The quips of spring, or, when so nearing its end,
> Have to bear the merry mirth of May.
> How fortunate to grow in the crow-footed woods,
> Eh, Reedbeck? But I see your're anxious to sleep.[58]

This growing quiet in the presence of nature is a rare thing in Fry, and it is, for that reason, particularly effective.

We must not look for it in *LB* with its delightfully tumultuous spring emotions, toying with the impressions of nature and forcing them into the most amusing and grotesque combinations and shapes. This is Thomas Mendip's description of night:

> Out here is a sky so gentle
> Five stars are ventured on it. I can see
> The sky's pale belly glowing and growing big,
> Soon to deliver the moon. And I can see
> A glittering smear, the snail-trail of the sun
> Where it crawled with its golden shell into the hills.
> A darkening land sunken into prayer
> Lucidly in dewdrops of one syllable,
> Nunc dimittis.[59]

The great thing about this youthful reaction to a night in spring is that it communicates, through its wilful and irreverent imagery, an intense sense of beauty, freshly and spontaneously perceived. In other passages of *LB* beauty is outrun by fun, e. g. in Thomas Mendip's accound of the moon:

[58] *VO*, 97.
[59] *LB*, 49.

>   Surely she knows,
> If she is true to herself, the moon is nothing
> But a circumambulating aphrodisiac
> Divinely subsidized to provoke the world
> Into a rising birth-rate — a veneer
> Of sheerest Venus on the planks of Time
> Which may fool the ocean but which fools not me.[60]

Here, and not only here, Fry is an intrepid acrobat, soaring from one trapeze to another over the heads of a breathless crowd. The learned and complicated words he uses give an air of precious rarity to his lines, modified by the outrageous pun "a veneer of sheerest Venus", in which the play on the sounds is rather more seductive than the image.

At the end of this survey we inspect a few individual examples of Fry's way with metaphors. The first illustrates once more his gift of avoiding abstractions and of apprehending the intellectual as well as the emotional aspects of an experience in terms of drama. Reedbeck, that inveterate snob and *laudator temporis acti*, complains of the disappearance of much of the comeliness of the old world:

> Dignity has dropped upon all fours.[61]

The following metaphor takes us to the frontier of language, that true fighting-ground of the poet, where new expressions are coined for which it is impossible to find a reasonable, satisfactory circumlocution in conventional language. Rosabel warns the Duke:

>   It's a thing I have no love for,
> To have to go groping along the corridors
> Of someone else's mind, so that I shan't
> Be hurt.[62]

Fry's inveterate image-making habit prepares stimulating shocks of surprise for us, even when he is composing his critical letters, lectures or essays. In his exposition of the view that Hamlet has

---

[60] *LB*, 68 f.
[61] *VO*, 37.
[62] *VO*, 13.

suffered the inner death before Shakespeare's tragedy begins, we come across the sentence:

> With his mother and Ophelia his affection is the thrashing of a harpooned whale.[63]

And when the dramatist complains of what he considers the contrary of "creative criticism", he says:

> The newly sprouting acorn is dug up several times a week, and solemnly told that, whatever it may think to the contrary, it is not an oak-tree.[64]

An image, once conceived in Fry's mind, often shows an irresistible tendency to sprout and grow into a whole *catena* of related expressions. Here we remember Moses' remark that certain hard facts cannot be removed by talk:

> Do you think
> If we swung the rattle of conversation
> Those centuries would fly off like so many crows?
> They would wheel above us and come to feed again.[65]

Merlin's speech on the fate of the Britons at the time of the coming of the Jutes is another example:

> When, years ago,
> The Romans fell away from our branching roads
> Like brazen leaves, answering
> The hopeless windy trumpets from their home,
> Your tribes waged winter upon us, till our limbs
> Ached with the carving cold.[66]

If we try to retrace the train of associations out of which these lines grew, suggesting in the most concentrated form what happened as well has how it happened and what it meant to the Britons, we find its probable germ in the simple verb-adverb combination "to fall away" with its traditional meanings "to desert, to vanish". Behind it the poet discovered the image of the falling

---

[63] *Letters to an Actor Playing Hamlet, loc. cit.*, 58.
[64] *An Experience of Critics*, 14.
[65] *FB*, 26.
[66] *TA*, 32.

leaves, which he combined with his comparison of the picture of the Roman roads on a map, branching out in all directions from a centre like London, and a tree, only to be led on to the two related ideas of the trumpet, calling the Roman troops to their useless retreat, and of the autumn wind, shaking the leaves from the trees. The final step is the perception of the disastrous war against the invading Jutes, which followed upon the Roman retreat, as of a cold winter, and of the wounds, suffered by the Kentish Britons, as of the biting of a winter's cold. Fry's way of giving a new turn to accepted idioms appears again in the striking metaphor "to wage winter".

A similar method has produced the following lines in the more chastened style of *SP:*

> Here we are, we lean on our lives
> Expecting purpose to keep her date,
> Get cold waiting, watch the overworlds
> Come and go, question the need to stay
> But do, in an obstinate anticipation of love.[67]

Here, the governing idea is supported by the figure of Everyman, presented without face and costume and thus making it easy for every spectator to identify himself with it. We see it leaning on a stick, waiting, getting cold, watching, questioning, waiting. The author makes use of a lean kind of imagery in his latest play, having learnt to give it strength through omissions also, instead of through additions only. We contrast it with a speech in his comedy manner, where a humorous image is relentlessly elaborated; the resulting series of images is clearly a creation of wit rather than of the imagination. Dynamene is reporting a dream, in which her late husband, always connected with useful things in her mind, appeared in the figure of a ship:

> He was the ship. He had such a deck, Doto,
> Such a white, scrubbed deck. Such a stern prow,
> Such a proud stern, so slim from port to starboard.
> If ever you meet a man with such fine masts
> Give your life to him, Doto. The figurehead

[67] *SP*, 13.

Bore his own features, so serene in the brow
And hung with a little seaweed. O Virilius,
My husband, you have left a wake in my soul.
You cut the glassy water with a diamond keel.
I must cry again.[68]

Such dangerous elaboration can also be found occasionally in Fry's prose. We quote a rather successful passage, where our author's daring manner of presentation renders interesting again an idea that is almost too well known to us from T. S. Eliot's dramatic criticism. He is discussing the fate of the verse drama between the days of Shakespeare and our own:

Let us think for a moment of the three hundred years of prose that have followed, and take a look at the prodigal's frequent backward look towards home. What seems most constant is a paralysing memory of Shakespeare, a kind of Oedipus complex with Shakespeare as mother, which made even the mature poets curl up as though in a womb as soon as they wrote for the stage. And what is most odd, it is a pre-Shakespearian womb they curl up in. Ignoring one of the greatest gifts that Shakespeare gave, the development of blank verse into a flexible speech rhythm, they go the rounds of their iambic pentameters as though the Master had written nothing after *A Comedy of Errors*. John Dryden escaped in his own way. Shelley, in *The Cenci*, was curled up but with such an air as might mean he would lie like that anyway, womb or no womb. Beddoes fought a prolonged, if desultory, battle to uncurl (he said "We must not write like the Elizabethans") and in the effort got himself into a baroque plait, from which he could only extricate himself by cutting his throat. It was a pathetic end to an odd, unhappy battle, in which he gave many fair kicks towards the straight, but died a contortionist still.[69]

Our sketch of Fry's imagery has been less rapid than that of other aspects of his art because we have thought it essential to show that it is not merely a varied and cleverly manipulated arti-

[68] *PF*, 2.
[69] "Poetry and the Theatre", *loc. cit.*, 3.

fice, but often springs from an original gift of apprehending new relations between the facts of experience and from that loving participation in the past and the present life of the language which has characterized many of its masters. Another important point we hope to have proved is the essentially dramatic quality of Fry's image-making.   (1954)

INDEX